Squid Proxy Server 3.1
Beginner's Guide

Improve the performance of your network using the caching and access control capabilities of Squid

Kulbir Saini

PUBLISHING

BIRMINGHAM - MUMBAI

Squid Proxy Server 3.1
Beginner's Guide

First published: February 2011

Production Reference: 1160211

Published by Packt Publishing Ltd.
32 Lincoln Road
Olton
Birmingham, B27 6PA, UK.

ISBN 978-1-849513-90-6

www.packtpub.com

Cover Image by Faiz Fattohi (faizfattohi@gmail.com)

Credits

Author

Kulbir Saini

Reviewers

Mihai Dobos

Siju Oommen George

Amos Y. Jeffries

Rajkumar Seenivasan

Acquisition Editor

Sarah Cullington

Development Editor

Susmita Panda

Technical Editor

Sakina Kaydawala

Copy Editor

Leonard D'Silva

Indexer

Hemangini Bari

Editorial Team Leader

Mithun Sehgal

Project Team Leader

Ashwin Shetty

Project Coordinator

Michelle Quadros

Proofreader

Lindsey Thomas

Graphics

Nilesh Mohite

Production Coordinators

Aparna Bhagat

Kruthika Bangera

Cover Work

Aparna Bhagat

About the Author

Kulbir Saini is an entrepreneur based in Hyderabad, India. He has had extensive experience in managing systems and network infrastructure. Apart from his work as a freelance developer, he provides services to a number of startups. Through his blogs, he has been an active contributor of documentation for various open source projects, most notable being The Fedora Project and Squid. Besides computers, which his life practically revolves around, he loves travelling to remote places with his friends. For more details, please check http://saini.co.in/.

There are people who served as a source of inspiration, people who helped me throughout, and my friends who were always there for me. Without them, this book wouldn't have been possible.

I would like to thank Sunil Mohan Ranta, Nirnimesh, Suryakant Patidar, Shiben Bhattacharjee, Tarun Jain, Sanyam Sharma, Jayaram Kowta, Amal Raj, Sachin Rawat, Vidit Bansal, Upasana Tegta, Gopal Datt Joshi, Vardhman Jain, Sandeep Chandna, Anurag Singh Rana, Sandeep Kumar, Rishabh Mukherjee, Mahaveer Singh Deora, Sambhav Jain, Ajay Somani, Ankush Kalkote, Deepak Vig, Kapil Agrawal, Sachin Goyal, Pankaj Saini, Alok Kumar, Nitin Bansal, Nitin Gupta, Kapil Bajaj, Gaurav Kharkwal, Atul Dwivedi, Abhinav Parashar, Bhargava Chowdary, Maruti Borker, Abhilash I, Gopal Krishna Koduri, Sashidhar Guntury, Siva Reddy, Prashant Mathur, Vipul Mittal, Deepti G.P., Shikha Aggarwal, Gaganpreet Singh Arora, Sanrag Sood, Anshuman Singh, Himanshu Singh, Himanshu Sharma, Dinesh Yadav, Tushar Mahajan, Sankalp Khare, Mayank Juneja, Ankur Goel, Anuraj Pandey, Rohit Nigam, Romit Pandey, Ankit Rai, Vishwajeet Singh, Suyesh Tiwari, Sanidhya Kashap, and Kunal Jain.

I would also like to thank Michelle Quadros, Sarah Cullington, Susmita Panda, Priya Mukherji, and Snehman K Kohli from Packt who have been extremely helpful and encouraging during the writing of the book.

Special thanks go out to my parents and sister, for their love and support.

About the Reviewers

Mihai Dobos has a strong background in networking and security technologies, with hands on project experience in open source, Cisco, Juniper, Symantec, and many other vendors.

He started as a Cisco trainer right after finishing high school, then moved on to real-life implementations of network and security solutions. Mihai is now studying for his Masters degree in Information Security in the Military Technical Academy.

Siju Oommen George works as the Senior Systems Administrator at HiFX Learning Services, which is part of Virtual Training Company. He also over sees network, security, and systems-related aspects at HiFX IT & Media Services, Fingent, and Quantlogic.

He completed his BTech course in Production Engineering from the University of Calicut in 2000 and has many years of System Administration experience on BSD, OS X, Linux, and Microsoft Windows Platforms, involving both open source and proprietary software. He is also a contributor to the DragonFlyBSD Handbook. He actively advocates the use of BSDs among Computer Professionals and encourages Computer students to do the same. He is an active participant in many of the BSD, Linux, and open source software mailing lists and enjoys helping others who are new to a particular technology. He also reviews computer-related books in his spare time. He is married to Sophia Yesudas who works in the Airline Industry.

I would like to thank my Lord and Savior Jesus Christ who gave me the grace to continue working on reviewing this book during my busy schedule and sickness, my wife Sophia for allowing me to steal time from her and spend it in front of the computer at home, my Father T O Oommen and my Late mother C I Maria who worked hard to pay for my education, my Pastor Rajesh Mathew Kottukapilly who was with me in all the ups and downs of life, and finally my employer Mohan Thomas who provided me with the encouragement and facilities to research, experiment, work, and learn almost everything I know in the computer field.

Amos Y. Jeffries' original background is in genetic engineering, physics, and astronomy. He was introduced to computing in 1994. By 1996, he was developing networked multiplayer games and accounting software on the Macintosh platform. In 2000, he joined the nanotechnology field working with members of the Foresight Institute and others spreading the foundations of the technology. In 2001, he graduated from the University of Waikato with a Bachelor of Science (Software Engineering) degree with additional topical background in software design, languages, compiler construction, data storage, encryption, and artificial intelligence. In 2002, as a post-graduate, Amos worked as a developer creating real-time software for multi-media I/O, networking, and recording on Large Interactive Display Surfaces [1]. Later in 2002, he began a career in HTTP web design and network administration, founding Treehouse Networks Ltd. in 2003 as a consultancy. This led him into the field of SMTP mail networking and as a result data forensics and the anti-spam/anti-virus industry. In 2004, he returned to formal study in the topics of low-level networking protocols and human-computer interaction. In 2007, he entered the Squid project as a developer integrating IPv6 support and soon stepped into the position of Squid-3 maintainer. In 2008, he began contract work for the Te Kotahitanga research project at the University of Waikato developing online tools for supporting teacher professional development [2,3].

Acknowledgements should go to Robert Collins, Henrik Nordstrom, Francesco Chemolli, and Alex Rousskov[4]. Without whom Squid-3 would have ceased to exist some years back.

[1]http://www.waikato.ac.nz/php/research.php?author=123575&mode=show

[2]http://edlinked.soe.waikato.ac.nz/departments/index.php?dept_id=20&page_id=2639

[3](Research publication due out next year).

[4] Non-English characters exist in the correct spelling of these names

www.PacktPub.com

Support files, eBooks, discount offers, and more

You might want to visit www.PacktPub.com for support files and downloads related to your book.

Did you know that Packt offers eBook versions of every book published, with PDF and ePub files available? You can upgrade to the eBook version at www.PacktPub.com and as a print book customer, you are entitled to a discount on the eBook copy. Get in touch with us at service@packtpub.com for more details.

At www.PacktPub.com, you can also read a collection of free technical articles. Sign up for a range of free newsletters and receive exclusive discounts and offers on Packt books and eBooks.

http://PacktLib.PacktPub.com

Do you need instant solutions to your IT questions? PacktLib is Packt's online digital book library. Here, you can access, read, and search across Packt's entire library of books.

Why Subscribe?

- Fully searchable across every book published by Packt
- Copy and paste, print and bookmark content
- On demand and accessible via web browser

Free Access for Packt account holders

If you have an account with Packt at www.PacktPub.com, you can use this to access PacktLib today and view nine entirely free books. Simply use your login credentials for immediate access.

Table of Contents

Preface

Squid proxy server enables you to cache your web content and return it quickly on subsequent requests. System administrators often struggle with delays and too much bandwidth being used, but Squid solves these problems by handling requests locally. By deploying Squid in accelerator mode, requests are handled faster than on normal web servers, thus making your site perform quicker than everyone else's!

The Squid Proxy Server 3.1 Beginner's Guide will help you to install and configure Squid so that it is optimized to enhance the performance of your network. Caching usually takes a lot of professional know-how, which can take time and be very confusing. The Squid proxy server reduces the amount of effort that you will have to spend and this book will show you how best to use Squid, saving your time and allowing you to get most out of your network.

Whether you only run one site, or are in charge of a whole network, Squid is an invaluable tool which improves performance immeasurably. Caching and performance optimization usually requires a lot of work on the developer's part, but Squid does all that for you. This book will show you how to get the most out of Squid by customizing it for your network. You will learn about the different configuration options available and the transparent and accelerated modes that enable you to focus on particular areas of your network.

Applying proxy servers to large networks can be a lot of work as you have to decide where to place restrictions and who to grant access. However, the straightforward examples in this book will guide you through step-by-step so that you will have a proxy server that covers all areas of your network by the time you finish reading.

What this book covers

Chapter 1, Getting Started with Squid, discusses the basics of proxy servers and web caching and how we can utilize them to save bandwidth and improve the end user's browsing experience. We will also learn to identify the correct Squid version for our environment. We will explore various configuration options available for enabling or disabling certain features while we compile Squid from the source code. We will explore steps to compile and install Squid.

Chapter 2, Configuring Squid, explores the syntax used in the Squid configuration file, which is used to control Squid's behavior. We will explore the important directives used in the configuration file and will see related examples to understand them better. We will have a brief overview of the powerful access control lists which we will learn in detail in later chapters. We will also learn to fine-tune our cache to achieve a better HIT ratio to save bandwidth and reduce the average page load time.

Chapter 3, Running Squid, talks about running Squid in different modes and various command line options available for debugging purposes. We will also learn about rotating Squid logs to reclaim disk space by deleting old/obsolete log files. We will learn to install the `init` script to automatically start Squid on system startup.

Chapter 4, Getting Started with Squid's Powerful ACLs and Access Rules, explores the Access Control Lists in detail with examples. We will learn about various ACL types and to construct ACLs to identify requests and responses based on different criteria. We will also learn about mixing ACLs of various types with access rules to achieve desired access control.

Chapter 5, Understanding Log Files and Log Formats, discusses configuring Squid to generate customized log messages. We will also learn to interpret the messages logged by Squid in various log files.

Chapter 6, Managing Squid and Monitoring Traffic, explores the Squid's **Cache Manager** web interface in this chapter using which we can monitor our Squid proxy server and get statistics about different components of Squid. We will also have a look at a few log file analyzers which make analyzing traffic simpler compared to manually interpreting the access log messages.

Chapter 7, Protecting your Squid with Authentication, teaches us to protect our Squid proxy server with authentication using the various authentication schemes available. We will also learn to write custom authentication helpers using which we can build our own authentication system for Squid.

Chapter 8, Building a Hierarchy of Squid Caches, explores cache hierarchies in detail. We will also learn to configure Squid to act as a parent or a sibling proxy server in a hierarchy, and to use other proxy servers as a parent or sibling cache.

Chapter 9, Squid in Reverse Proxy Mode, discusses how Squid can accept HTTP requests on behalf of one or more web servers in the background. We will learn to configure Squid in reverse proxy mode. We will also have a look at a few example scenarios.

Chapter 10, Squid in Intercept Mode, talks about the details of intercept mode and how to configure the network devices, and the host operating system to intercept the HTTP requests and forward them to Squid proxy server. We will also have a look at the pros and cons of Squid in intercept mode.

Chapter 11, *Writing URL Redirectors and Rewriters*. Squid's behavior can be further customized using the URL redirectors and rewriter helpers. In this chapter, we will learn about the internals of redirectors and rewriters and we will create our own custom helpers.

Chapter 12, *Troubleshooting Squid*, discusses some common problems or errors which you may come across while configuring or running Squid. We will also learn about getting online help to resolve issues with Squid and filing bug reports.

What you need for this book

A beginner level knowledge of Linux/Unix operating system and familiarity with basic commands is all what you need. Squid runs almost on all Linux/Unix operating systems and there is a great possibility that your favorite operating system repository already has Squid.

On a server, the availability of free main memory and speed of hard disk play a major role in determining the performance of the Squid proxy server. As most of the cached objects stay on the hard disks, faster disks will result in low disk latency and faster responses. But faster hard disks (SCSI) are often very expensive as compared to ATA hard disks and we have to analyze our requirements to strike a balance between the disk speed we need and the money we are going to spend on it.

The main memory is the most important factor for optimizing Squid's performance. Squid stores a little bit of information about each cached object in the main memory. On average, Squid consumes up to 32 MB of the main memory for every GB of disk caching. The actual memory utilization may vary depending on the average object size, CPU architecture, and the number of concurrent users, and so on. While memory is critical for good performance, a faster CPU also helps, but is not really critical.

Who this book is for

If you are a Linux or Unix system administrator and you want to enhance the performance of your network or you are a web developer and want to enhance the performance of your website, this book is for you. You will be expected to have some basic knowledge of networking concepts, but may not have used caching systems or proxy servers until now.

Conventions

In this book, you will find several headings appearing frequently. To give clear instructions of how to complete a procedure or task, we use:

Time for action - heading

1. Action 1

2. Action 2

3. Action 3

Instructions often need some extra explanation so that they make sense, so they are followed with:

What just happened?

This heading explains the working of tasks or instructions that you have just completed.

You will also find some other learning aids in the book, including:

Pop quiz

These are short multiple choice questions intended to help you test your own understanding.

Have a go hero - heading

These set practical challenges and give you ideas for experimenting with what you have learned.

You will also find a number of styles of text that distinguish between different kinds of information. Here are some examples of these styles, and an explanation of their meaning.

Code words in text are shown as follows: "The directive `visible_hostname` is used to set the hostname."

A block of code is set as follows:

```
acl special_network src 192.0.2.0/24
tcp_outgoing_address 198.51.100.25 special_network
tcp_outgoing_address 198.51.100.86
```

Any command-line input or output is written as follows:

```
$ mkdir /drive/squid_cache
```

New terms and **important words** are shown in bold. Words that you see on the screen, in menus or dialog boxes for example, appear in the text like this: "If we click on the **Internal DNS Statistics** link in the **Cache Manager menu**, we will be presented with various statistics about the requests performed by the internal DNS client".

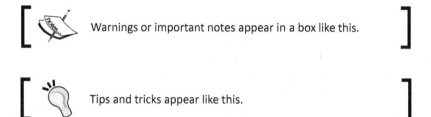

Warnings or important notes appear in a box like this.

Tips and tricks appear like this.

Reader feedback

Feedback from our readers is always welcome. Let us know what you think about this book—what you liked or may have disliked. Reader feedback is important for us to develop titles that you really get the most out of.

To send us general feedback, simply send an e-mail to feedback@packtpub.com, and mention the book title via the subject of your message.

If there is a book that you need and would like to see us publish, please send us a note in the **SUGGEST A TITLE** form on www.packtpub.com or e-mail suggest@packtpub.com.

If there is a topic that you have expertise in and you are interested in either writing or contributing to a book on, see our author guide on www.packtpub.com/authors.

Customer support

Now that you are the proud owner of a Packt book, we have a number of things to help you to get the most from your purchase.

> **Downloading the example code for the book**
>
> You can download the example code files for all Packt books you have purchased from your account at http://www.packtpub.com. If you purchased this book elsewhere, you can visit http://www.packtpub.com/support and register to have the files e-mailed directly to you.

Errata

Although we have taken every care to ensure the accuracy of our content, mistakes do happen. If you find a mistake in one of our books—maybe a mistake in the text or the code—we would be grateful if you would report this to us. By doing so, you can save other readers from frustration and help us improve subsequent versions of this book. If you find any errata, please report them by visiting http://www.packtpub.com/support, selecting your book, clicking on the **errata submission form** link, and entering the details of your errata. Once your errata are verified, your submission will be accepted and the errata will be uploaded on our website, or added to any list of existing errata, under the Errata section of that title. Any existing errata can be viewed by selecting your title from http://www.packtpub.com/support.

Piracy

Piracy of copyright material on the Internet is an ongoing problem across all media. At Packt, we take the protection of our copyright and licenses very seriously. If you come across any illegal copies of our works, in any form, on the Internet, please provide us with the location address or website name immediately, so that we can pursue a remedy.

Please contact us at copyright@packtpub.com with a link to the suspected pirated material.

We appreciate your help in protecting our authors, and our ability to bring you valuable content.

Questions

You can contact us at questions@packtpub.com if you are having a problem with any aspect of the book, and we will do our best to address it.

1
Getting Started with Squid

In this chapter, we will have a look at how proxy servers and web caching works in general. We will proceed to download the correct Squid package for our operating system, based on the system requirements that we learned about in the Preface. We will learn how to compile and build additional Squid features. We will also learn the advantages of compiling Squid manually from the source over using a pre-compiled binary package.

In the final section, we will learn how to install Squid from a compiled source binary package, using popular package managers. Installation is a crucial part in getting started with Squid. Sometimes, we need to compile Squid with custom flags, depending on the environment requirements.

So let's get started with the real stuff.

Proxy server

A proxy server is a computer system sitting between the client requesting a web document and the target server (another computer system) serving the document. In its simplest form, a proxy server facilitates communication between client and target server without modifying requests or replies. When we initiate a request for a resource from the target server, the proxy server hijacks our connection and represents itself as a client to the target server, requesting the resource on our behalf. If a reply is received, the proxy server returns it to us, giving a feel that we have communicated with the target server.

In advanced forms, a proxy server can filter requests based on various rules and may allow communication only when requests can be validated against the available rules. The rules are generally based on an IP address of a client or target server, protocol, content type of web documents, web content type, and so on.

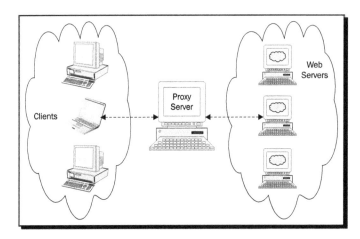

As seen in the preceding image, clients can't make direct requests to the web servers. To facilitate communication between clients and web servers, we have connected them using a proxy server which is acting as a medium of communication for clients and web servers.

Sometimes, a proxy server can modify requests or replies, or can even store the replies from the target server locally for fulfilling the same request from the same or other clients at a later stage. Storing the replies locally for use at a later time is known as **caching**. Caching is a popular technique used by proxy servers to save bandwidth, empowering web servers, and improving the end user's browsing experience.

Proxy servers are mostly deployed to perform the following:

- Reduce bandwidth usage
- Enhance the user's browsing experience by reducing page load time which, in turn, is achieved by caching web documents
- Enforce network access policies
- Monitoring user traffic or reporting Internet usage for individual users or groups
- Enhance user privacy by not exposing a user's machine directly to Internet
- Distribute load among different web servers to reduce load on a single server
- Empower a poorly performing web server
- Filter requests or replies using an integrated virus/malware detection system
- Load balance network traffic across multiple Internet connections
- Relay traffic around within a local area network

In simple terms, a proxy server is an agent between a client and target server that has a list of rules against which it validates every request or reply, and then allows or denies access accordingly.

Reverse proxy

Reverse proxying is a technique of storing the replies or resources from a web server locally so that the subsequent requests to the same resource can be satisfied from the local copy on the proxy server, sometimes without even actually contacting the web server. The proxy server or web cache checks if the locally stored copy of the web document is still valid before serving the cached copy.

The life of the locally stored web document is calculated from the additional HTTP headers received from the web server. Using HTTP headers, web servers can control whether a given document/response should be cached by a proxy server or not.

Web caching is mostly used:

- ◆ To reduce bandwidth usage. A large number of static web documents like CSS and JavaScript files, images, videos, and so on can be cached as they don't change frequently and constitutes the major part of a response from a web server.

- ◆ By ISPs to reduce average page load time to enhance browsing experience for their customers on Dial-Up or broadband.

- ◆ To take a load off a very busy web server by serving static pages/documents from a proxy server's cache.

Getting Squid

Squid is available in several forms (compressed source archives, source code from a version control system, binary packages such as RPM, DEB, and so on) from Squid's official website, various Squid mirrors worldwide, and software repositories of almost all the popular operating systems. Squid is also shipped with many Linux/Unix distributions.

There are various versions and releases of Squid available for download from Squid's official website. To get the most out of a Squid installation its best to check out the latest source code from a **Version Control System (VCS)** so that we get the latest features and fixes. But be warned, the latest source code from a VCS is generally leading edge and may not be stable or may not even work properly. Though code from a VCS is good for learning or testing Squid's new features, you are strongly advised not to use code from a VCS for production deployments.

If we want to play safe, we should probably download the latest stable version or stable version from the older releases. Stable versions are generally tested before they are released and are supposed to work out of the box. Stable versions can directly be used in production deployments.

Time for action – identifying the right version

A list of available versions of Squid is maintained at `http://www.squid-cache.org/Versions/`. For production environments, we should use versions listed under the **Stable Versions** section only. If we want to test new Squid features in our environment or if we intend to provide feedback to the Squid community about the new version, then we should be using one of the **Beta Versions**.

Stable Versions:

Current recommended versions meant for production use.

Version	First Production Release Date	Latest Release	Latest Release Date
3.1	29 Mar 2010	3.1.10	22 Dec 2010
2.7	27 May 2008	STABLE9	17 Mar 2010
langpack	18 Sep 2008	N/A (dated)	today

As we can see in the preceding screenshot, the website contains the **First Production Release Date** and **Latest Release Date** for the stable versions. If we click on any of the versions, we are directed to a page containing a list of all the releases in that particular version. Let's have a look at the page for version 3.1:

Squid version 3.1

Release	Date	diff	Download
Latest 3.1 series release			
squid-3.1.10	22 Dec 2010		tar.gz (sig) / tar.bz2 (sig) / rsync
See langpack for latest Language Package			
Daily auto-generated release. This is the most recent bug-fixed update to the formal release. see Change details for the fixes included in this bundle.			
squid-3.1.10-20110106	Jan 6 2011		tar.gz(md5) / tar.bz2(md5) / rsync
Squid-3.1 BZR			Launchpad Mirror
Older Releases			
squid-3.1.9	Oct 15, 2010	diff (sig)	tar.gz (sig) / tar.bz2 (sig)
squid-3.1.8	Sep 04, 2010	diff (sig)	tar.gz (sig) / tar.bz2 (sig)

For every release, along with a release date, there are links for downloading compressed source archives.

Different versions of Squid may have different features. For example, all the features available in Squid version 2.7 may or may not be available in newer versions such as Squid 3.x. Some features may have been deprecated or have become redundant over time and they are generally removed. On the other hand, Squid 3.x may have several new features or existing features in an improved and revised manner.

Therefore, we should always aim for the latest version, but depending on the environment, we may go for stable or beta version. Also, if we need specific features that are not available in the latest version, we may choose from the available releases in a different branch.

What just happened?

We had a brief look at the pages containing the different versions and releases of Squid, on Squid's official website. We also learned which versions and releases that we should download and use for different types of usage.

Methods of obtaining Squid

After identifying the version of Squid that we should be using for compiling and installation, let's have a look at the ways in which we can obtain Squid release 3.1.10.

Using source archives

Compressed source archives are the most popular way of getting Squid. To download the source archive, please visit Squid download page, `http://www.squid-cache.org/Download/`. This web page has links for downloading the different versions and releases of Squid, either from the official website or available mirrors worldwide. We can use either HTTP or FTP for getting the Squid source archive.

Time for action – downloading Squid

Now we are going to download Squid 3.1.10 from Squid's official website:

1. Let's go to the web page `http://www.squid-cache.org/Versions/`.
2. Now we need to click on the link to **Version 3.1**, as shown in the following screenshot:

Version	First Production Release Date	Latest Release	Latest Release Date
3.1	29 Mar 2010	3.1.10	22 Dec 2010

3. We'll be taken to a page displaying the various releases in version 3.1. The link with the display text **tar.gz** in the **Download** column is a link to the compressed source archive for Squid release 3.1.10, as shown in the following screenshot:

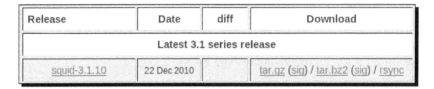

Release	Date	diff	Download
Latest 3.1 series release			
squid-3.1.10	22 Dec 2010		tar.gz (sig) / tar.bz2 (sig) / rsync

4. To download Squid 3.1.10 using the web browser, just click on the link.

5. Alternatively, we can use `wget` to download the source archive from the command line as follows:

```
wget http://www.squid-cache.org/Versions/v3/3.1/squid-3.1.10.tar.gz
```

What just happened?

We successfully retrieved Squid version 3.1.10 from Squid's official website. The process of retrieving other stable or beta versions is very similar.

Obtaining the latest source code from Bazaar VCS

Advanced users may be interested in getting the very latest source code from the Squid code repository, using Bazaar. We can safely skip this section if we are not familiar with VCS in general. Bazaar is a popular version control system used to track project history and facilitate collaboration. From version 3.x onwards, Squid source code has been migrated to Bazaar. Therefore, we should ensure that we have Bazaar installed on our system in order to checkout the source code from repository. To find out more about Bazaar or for Bazaar installation and configuration manuals, please visit Bazaar's official website at `http://bazaar.canonical.com/`.

Once we have setup Bazaar, we should head to the Squid code repository mirrored on Launchpad at `https://code.launchpad.net/squid/`. From here we can browse all the versions and branches of Squid. Let's get ourselves familiar with the page layout:

Name	Status
lp:squid **Series:** trunk	Development
lp:squid/3.1 **Series:** 3.1	Mature
lp:squid/3.0 **Series:** 3.0	Mature
lp:~yadi/squid/cleanup-comm	Development

In the previous screenshot, **Series: trunk** represents the development branch, which contains code that is still in development and is not ready for production use. The branches with the status **Mature** are stable and can be used right away in production environments.

Time for action – using Bazaar to obtain source code

Now that we are familiar with the various branches, versions, and releases. Let's proceed to checking out the source code with Bazaar. To download code from any branch, the syntax for the command is as follows:

```
bzr branch lp:squid[/branch[/version]]
```

`branch` and `version` are optional parameters in the previous code. So, if we want to get branch 3.1, then the command will be as follows:

```
bzr branch lp:squid/3.1
```

The previous command will fetch source code from Launchpad and may take a considerable amount of time, depending on the Internet connection. If we are willing to download source code for Squid version 3.1.10, then the command will be as follows:

```
bzr branch lp:squid/3.1/3.1.10
```

In the previous code, 3.1 is the branch name and 3.1.10 is the specific version of Squid that we want to checkout.

What just happened?

We learned to fetch the source code for any Squid branch or release using Bazaar from Squid's source code hosted on Launchpad.

Have a go hero – fetching the source code

Using the command syntax that we learned in the previous section, fetch the source code for Squid version 3.0.stable25 from Launchpad.

- ◆ Solution:

  ```
  bzr branch lp:squid/3.0/3.0.stable25
  ```

- ◆ Explanation: If we browse to the particular version on Launchpad, the version number used in the command becomes obvious.

Using binary packages

Squid binary packages are pre-compiled and ready to install software bundles. Binary packages are available in the software repositories of almost all Linux/Unix-based operating systems. Depending on the operating system, only stable and sometimes well tested beta versions make it to the software repositories, so they are ready for production use.

Installing Squid

Squid can be installed using the source code we obtained in the previous section, using a package manager which, in turn, uses the binary package available for our operating system. Let's have a detailed look at the ways in which we can install Squid.

Installing Squid from source code

Installing Squid from source code is a three step process:

1. Select the features and operating system-specific settings.
2. Compile the source code to generate the executables.
3. Place the generated executables and other required files in their designated locations for Squid to function properly.

We can perform some of the above steps using automated tools that make the compilation and installation process relatively easy.

Compiling Squid

Compiling Squid is a process of compiling several files containing C/C++ source code and generating executables. Compiling Squid is really easy and can be done in a few steps. For compiling Squid, we need an ANSI C/C++ compliant compiler. If we already have a GNU C/C++ Compiler (GNU Compiler Collection (GCC) and g++, which are available on almost every Linux/Unix-based operating system by default), we are ready to begin the actual compilation.

Why compile?

Compiling Squid is a bit of a painful task compared to installing Squid from the binary package. However, we recommend compiling Squid from the source instead of using pre-compiled binaries. Let's walk through a few advantages of compiling Squid from the source:

- While compiling we can enable extra features, which may not be enabled in the pre-compiled binary package.

- When compiling, we can also disable extra features that are not needed for a particular environment. For example, we may not need Authentication helpers or ICMP support.

- `configure` probes the system for several features and enables or disables them accordingly, while pre-compiled binary packages will have the features detected for the system the source was compiled on.

- Using `configure`, we can specify an alternate location for installing Squid. We can even install Squid without root or super user privileges, which may not be possible with pre-compiled binary package.

Though compiling Squid from source has a lot of advantages over installing from the binary package, the binary package has its own advantages. For example, when we are in damage control mode or a crisis situation and we need to get the proxy server up and running really quickly, using a binary package for installation will provide a quicker installation.

Uncompressing the source archive

If we obtained the Squid in a compressed archive format, we must extract it before we can proceed any further. If we obtained Squid from Launchpad using Bazaar, we don't need to perform this step.

```
tar -xvzf squid-3.1.10.tar.gz
```

`tar` is a popular command which is used to extract compressed archives of various types. On the other hand, it can also be used to compress many files into a single archive. The preceding command will extract the archive to a directory named `squid-3.1.10`.

Configure or system check

Configure or system check is the first step in the compilation process and is achieved by running `./configure` from the command line. This program probes the system, making sure that the required packages are installed. This also checks the system capabilities and collects information about the system architecture and default settings such as, available file descriptors and so on. After collecting all the information, this program generates the `makefiles`, which are used in the next step to actually compile the Squid source code.

Running `configure` without any parameters uses the preset defaults. If we are willing to change the default Squid settings or if we want to disable some optional features that are enabled by default, or if we want to install Squid in an alternate location in the file system, we need to pass options to `configure`. Use the following the command to see the available options along with a brief description.

Let's run `configure` with the `--help` option to have a look at the available configuration options.

```
./configure --help | less
```

This will display the page containing the options and their brief description for `configure`. Use up and down arrow keys to navigate through the information. Now let's discuss a few of the commonly used options with `configure`:

--prefix

The `--prefix` option is the most commonly used option. If we are testing a new version or if we wanted to test multiple Squid versions, we will have multiple Squid version installed on our system. To identify the different versions and to prevent interference or confusion between the versions, it's a good idea to install them in separate directories.

For example, for installing Squid version 3.1.10, we can use the directory `/opt/squid/3.1.10/` and the corresponding `configure` command will be run as:

```
./configure --prefix=/opt/squid/3.1.10/
```

Similarly, for installing Squid version 3.1, we can use the directory `/opt/squid/3.1/`.

 From now onwards, `${prefix}` will represent the location where we have installed Squid, that is, the directory name used with the `--prefix` option while running `configure`, as shown in the previous command.

Squid provides even more control over the location of different types of files such as executables and documentation files. Their placement can be controlled with options such as `--bindir`, `--sbindir`, and so on. Please check the `configure` help page for further details on these options.

Now, let's check the optional features and packages. To enable any optional feature, we pass an option in the format `--enable-FEATURE_NAME` and to disable a feature, the option format is either `--disable-FEATURE_NAME` or `--enable-FEATURE_NAME=no`. For example, `icmp` is a feature name.

```
./configure --enable-FEATURE # FEATURE will be enabled
./configure --disable-FEATURE # FEATURE will be disabled
./configure --enable-FEATURE=no # FEATURE will be disabled
```

Similarly, to compile Squid with an available package, we pass an option in the format `--with-PACKAGE_NAME` and to compile Squid without a package, we pass the option `--without-PACKAGE_NAME`. `openssl` is an example package name.

--enable-gnuregex

Regular expressions are used for constructing Access Control Lists in Squid. If we are running a modern Linux/Unix-based operating system, we don't need to worry about this option. But if our system doesn't have built-in support for regular expressions, we should enable support for regular expressions using `--enable-gnuregex`.

--disable-inline

Squid has a lot of code that can be inlined, which is good for production use. But inline code takes longer to compile and is useful when we need to compile a source only once for setting up Squid for production use. This option is intended to be used during development when we need to compile Squid time and again.

--disable-optimizations

Squid is, by default, compiled with compiler optimizations that result in better performance. Again this option should be used while debugging a problem or testing different versions as it'll reduce compilation time. The `--disable-inline` option is automatically used if we use this option.

--enable-storeio

Squid's performance depends heavily on disk I/O performance when disk caching is enabled. The quicker Squid can read/write files from cache, the lesser time it'll take to satisfy a request, which in turn will result in smaller delays. Different storage techniques may lead to optimized performance, depending on the traffic type and usage. We can use this option to build Squid with support for various store I/O modules. Please check the `src/fs/` directory in the Squid source code for available store I/O modules.

```
./configure --enable-storeio=ufs,aufs,coss,diskd,null
```

--enable-removal-policies

While using disk caching, we instruct Squid to use a specified disk space for caching web documents. Over a period of time, the space is consumed and Squid will still need more space to cache new documents. Squid then has to decide which old documents should be removed or purged from the cache to make space for storing the new ones. There are different policies for purging the documents to achieve maximum benefits from caching.

The policies are based on heap and list data structures. List data structure is enabled by default. Please check the `src/repl/` directory in the Squid source code for available removal policies.

```
./configure --enable-removal-policies=heap,lru
```

--enable-icmp

This option is helpful in determining the distance from other cache peers and remote servers to estimate approximate latency. This is useful only if we have other cache peers in the network.

--enable-delay-pools

Squid uses delay pools to limit or control bandwidth that can be used by a client or a group of clients. Delay pools are like leaky buckets which leak data (web traffic) to clients and are refilled at a controlled rate. These come in handy when we need to control the bandwidth used by a group of users.

--enable-esi

This option enables Squid to use Edge Side Includes (see `http://www.esi.org` for more information). If this is enabled, Squid completely ignores cache-control headers from clients. This option is only intended to be used when Squid is used in accelerator mode.

--enable-useragent-log

This provides the capability of logging user agent headers from HTTP requests by clients.

--enable-referer-log

If we enable this option, Squid will be able to write a referer header field from HTTP requests.

--disable-wccp

This option disables support for **Cisco's Web Cache Communication Protocol** (**WCCP**). WCCP enables communication between caches, which in turn helps in localizing the traffic. By default, WCCP-support is enabled.

--disable-wccpv2

Similar to the previous option, this disables support Cisco's WCCP version 2. WCCPv2 is an improved version of WCCP and has built-in support for load balancing, scaling, fault-tolerance, and service assurance mechanisms. By default, WCCPv2 support is enabled.

--disable-snmp

In Squid versions 3.x, SNMP (Simple Network Management Protocol) is enabled by default. SNMP is quite popular among system administrators for monitoring servers and network devices.

--enable-cachemgr-hostname

Cache Manager (`cachemgr.cgi`) is a CGI utility to manage Squid's cache and view cache statistics using a web interface. The host name for accessing cache manager can be set using this option. By default, we can access cache manager web interface using `localhost` or the IP address of the Squid server.

```
./configure --enable-cachemgr-hostname=squidproxy.example.com
```

--enable-arp-acl

Squid supports building Access Control Lists based on MAC (or Ethernet) addresses. This feature is disabled by default. If we want to control client access based on Ethernet addresses, we should enable this feature. Enabling this is a good idea while learning Squid.

 This option will be replaced by `--enable-eui` which is enabled by default.

--disable-htcp

Hypertext Caching Protocol (**HTCP**) can be used by Squid to send and receive cache digests to neighboring caches. This option disables HTCP support.

--enable-ssl

Squid can terminate SSL connections. When Squid is configured in reverse proxy mode, Squid can terminate the SSL connections initiated by clients and handle it on behalf of the web server in the backend. This essentially means that the backend web server will not have to do any SSL work, which means significant computation savings. In this case, the communication between Squid and the backend web server will be pure HTTP, but clients will still see it as a secure connection with the web server. This is useful only when Squid is configured to work in accelerator or reverse proxy mode.

--enable-cache-digests

Cache digests are Squid's way of sharing information with neighboring Squid servers about the cached web documents, in a compressed format.

--enable-default-err-language

Whenever Squid encounters an error (for example, a page not found, access denied, or network unreachable error) that should be conveyed to the client, Squid uses default pages for showing these errors. The error pages are available in local languages. This option can be used to specify the default language for all the error pages. The default language for error pages is English.

```
./configure --enable-default-err-language=Spanish
```

--enable-err-languages

By default, Squid builds support for all available languages. If we only want to build Squid with languages which we are familiar with, we can use this option. Please check the errors/ directory in the Squid source code for available languages.

```
./configure --enable-err-languages='English French German'
```

--disable-http-violations

Squid has configuration options, and by using them, we can force Squid to violate HTTP protocol standards by replacing header fields in HTTP requests or responses. Tinkering with HTTP headers is against standard HTTP norms. We can disable support for all sorts of HTTP violations by using this option.

--enable-ipfw-transparent

IPFIREWALL (IPFW) is a firewall application for the FreeBSD system maintained by FreeBSD staff and volunteers. This option is useful while setting up Transparent Proxy Server on systems with IPFW. If our system doesn't have IPFW, we should avoid using this option, because Squid will fail to compile. The default behavior is auto-detect, which does the job quite well.

--enable-ipf-transparent

IPFilter (IPF) is also a stateful firewall for many Unix-like operating systems. It is provided by NetBSD, Solaris, and so on. If our system has IPF, then we should enable this option to be able to configure Squid in Transparent mode. Enabling this option in the absence of IPF on the system will result in compile errors.

--enable-pf-transparent

Packet Filter (PF) is yet another stateful firewall application originally developed for OpenBSD. This option is useful on systems with PF installed to achieve Transparent Proxy mode. Do not enable this option if PF is not installed.

--enable-linux-netfliter

Netfilter is the packet filtering framework in Linux kernels in series 2.4.x and 2.6.x. This option is useful for enabling Transparent Proxy support on Linux-based operating systems.

--enable-follow-x-forwarded-for

When a HTTP request is forwarded by a proxy, the proxy writes essential information about itself and the client for which the request is being forwarded, in HTTP headers. This option enables Squid to try to lookup the IP address of the original client for which the request was forwarded through one or more proxy servers.

--disable-ident-lookups

This prevents Squid from performing ident lookups or identifying a username for every connection. Disabling this may prevent our system from a possible Denial of Service attack by a malicious client requesting a large number of connections.

--disable-internal-dns

Squid has its own implementation of DNS protocol and is capable of building DNS queries. If we want to use Squid's internal DNS, then we should not disable it. Otherwise, we can disable support for Squid's internal DNS feature by using this option and can use external DNS servers.

--enable-default-hostsfile

Using this option, we can select the default location of the hosts file. On most operating systems, it's located in the `/etc/hosts` directory.

```
./configure --enable-default-hostsfile=/some/other/location/hosts
```

--enable-auth

Squid supports various authentication mechanisms. This option enables support for authentication schemes. This configure option (and related enable `auth` options) are undergoing change.

Old Syntax

Previously, this option was used to enable authentication support and a list of authentication schemes was also passed. The authentication schemes from the list were then built during compilation.

```
./configure --enable-auth=basic,digest,ntlm
```

New Syntax

Now, this option is used only to enable global support for authentication and a list of authentication schemes is not passed along. The authentication scheme is enabled with the option `--enable-auth-AUTHENTICATION_SCHEME` where `AUTHENTICATION_SCHEME` is the name of the authentication scheme. By default, all the authentication schemes are enabled and the corresponding authentication helpers are built during compilation. Authentication helpers are external programs that can authenticate clients using various authentication mechanisms, against different user databases.

```
./configure --enable-auth
```

--enable-auth-basic

This option enables support for a Basic Authentication scheme and builds the list of helpers specified. If the list of helpers is not provided, this will enable all the possible helpers. A list of available helpers for this scheme can be found in the `helpers/basic_auth/` directory in the Squid source code. To disable this authentication scheme, we can use `--disable-auth-basic`.

```
./configure --enable-auth-basic=PAM,NCSA,LDAP
```

If we want to enable this option but don't want to build any helpers, we should use `"none"` in place of a list of helpers.

```
./configure --enable-auth-basic=none
```

Previously, this option was known as `--enable-basic-auth-helpers`. The list of helpers is passed in a similar way.

```
./configure --enable-basic-auth-helpers=PAM,NCSA,LDAP
```

 The old and new option syntax for all other authentication schemes are similar.

--enable-auth-ntlm

Squid support for the NTLM authentication scheme is enabled with this option. The available helpers for this scheme reside in the `helpers/ntlm_auth/` directory in the Squid source code. To disable NTLM authentication scheme support, use the `--disable-auth-ntlm` option.

```
./configure --enable-auth-ntlm=smb_lm,no_check
```

--enable-auth-negotiate

This option enables the Negotiate Authentication scheme. Details and syntax are similar to the above authentication scheme option.

```
./configure --enable-auth-negotiate=kerberos
```

--enable-auth-digest

This option enables support for Digest Authentication scheme. Other details are similar to the above option.

--enable-ntlm-fail-open

If this option is enabled and a helper fails while authenticating a user, it can still allow Squid to authenticate the user. This option should be used with care as it may lead to security loopholes.

--enable-external-acl-helpers

Squid supports external ACLs using helpers. If we are willing to use external ACLs, we should consider using this option. We can also use this option while learning. A list of external ACL helpers should be passed to build specific helpers. The default behavior is to build all the available helpers. A list of available external ACL helpers can be found in the `helpers/external_acl/` directory in the Squid source code.

```
./configure --enable-external-acl-helpers=unix_group,ldap_group
```

--disable-translation

By default, Squid tries to present error and manual pages in a local language. If we don't want this to happen, then we may use this option.

--disable-auto-locale

Based on a client's request headers, Squid tries to automatically provide localized error pages. We can use this option to disable the automatic localization. The `error_directory` tag in the Squid configuration file must be configured if we use this option.

--disable-unlinkd

`unlinkd` is an external process which is used to make `unlink` system calls. This option disables `unlinkd` support in Squid. Disabling `unlinkd` is not a good idea as the `unlink` system call can block a process for a considerable amount of time, which can cause a delay in responses.

--with-default-user

We normally don't want to run Squid as the root user to omit any security risks. By default, Squid runs as the user `nobody`. However, if we have installed Squid from a pre-compiled binary, Squid may run as a 'squid' or 'proxy' user depending on the operating system we are using. Using this option, we can set the default user for running Squid. See the following example of how to use this option:

```
./configure --with-default-user=squid
```

--with-logdir

By default, Squid writes all logs and error reports to designated files in `${prefix}/var/logs/`. This location is different from the location used by all other processes and daemons to write their logs. In order to get quick access to the Squid logs, we may want to place them in the default system log directory, which is `/var/log/` in most of the Linux-based operating systems. See the following example of the syntax to achieve this:

```
./configure --with-logdir=/var/log/squid/
```

--with-pidfile

The default location for storing the Squid PID file is `${prefix}/var/run/squid.pid`, which is not the standard system location for storing PID files. On most Linux-based operating systems, the PID files are stored in `/var/run/`. So, we may want to change the default PIDfile location using the following option:

```
./configure --with-pidfile=/var/run/squid.pid
```

--with-aufs-threads

Using this option, we can specify the number of threads to use when the `aufs` storage system is used for managing the cache directories. If this option is not used, Squid automatically calculates the number of threads that should be used:

```
./configure --with-aufs-threads=12
```

--without-pthreads

Older versions of Squid were built without POSIX threads support. Now, Squid is built with `pthreads` support by default, therefore, if we don't want to enable `pthreads` support, we'll have to explicitly disable it.

--with-openssl

If we want to build Squid with OpenSSL support, we can use this option to specify the OpenSSL installation path, if it's not installed in the default location:

```
./configure --with-openssl=/opt/openssl/
```

--with-large-files

Under heavy traffic, Squid's log files (especially the access log) grow quickly and in the long run the file size may become quite large. We can use this option to enable support for large log files.

 For better performance, it is good practice to rotate log files frequently instead of going with large files.

--with-filedescriptors

Operating systems use file descriptors (basically integers) to track the open files and sockets. By default, there is a limit on the number of file descriptors a user can use (normally 1024). Once Squid has accepted connections which have consumed all the available file descriptors to the Squid user, it can't accept more connections unless some of the file descriptors are released.

Under heavy load, Squid frequently runs out of file descriptors. We can use the following option to overcome the file descriptor shortage problem:

```
./configure --with-filedescriptors=8192
```

 We also need to increase the system-wide limit on the number of file descriptors available to a user.

Have a go hero – file descriptors

Find out the maximum number of available file descriptors for your user. Also, write down the commands that will set the maximum available file descriptors limit to 8192.

Solution: To check the available file-descriptors use the following command:

```
ulimit -n
```

To set the file descriptor limit to 8192, we need to append the following lines to /etc/security/limits.conf:

```
    username hard nofile 8192
    username soft nofile 8192
```

The preceding action can be performed only with root or super user privileges.

Time for action – running the configure command

Now that we have had a brief look at several of the available options, we can layout the options for the environment for which we are building Squid. Now, we are ready to run the configure command with the following options:

```
./configure --prefix=/opt/squid/ --with-logdir=/var/log/squid/ --with-
pidfile=/var/run/squid.pid --enable-storeio=ufs,aufs --enable-removal-
policies=lru,heap --enable-icmp --enable-useragent-log --enable-referer-
log --enable-cache-digests --with-large-files
```

The preceding command will run for a while, probing the system for various capabilities and making decisions on the basis of the available libraries and modules. The configure writes debugging output to the config.log file in the same directory. It is always wise to check the config.log for any errors which may have occurred while running the configure command.

If everything goes fine, configure will generate the makefiles in several directories which will be required for compiling the source code in the next step.

What just happened?

Running the `configure` program with the options mentioned in the previous code example, will generate the `makefiles` needed to compile the Squid source code and source code of the modules enabled. It will also generate the `config.log` and `config.status` files. All the messages which are generated during the running of the `configure` program are logged to the `config.log` file. The `config.status` file is an executable which can be run to recreate the `makefiles`.

Have a go hero – debugging configure errors

In the Squid source directory, run the `configure` command, as shown in the following code:

```
./configure --enable-storeio='aufs,disk'
```

Now try to check what went wrong and fix the errors.

Time for action – compiling the source

After specifying our environment and building the requirements, we need to do the actual compilation. Compiling source code is very easy and is a matter of just one command:

```
make
```

We do not need to be the root or super user to execute this command. This command may take a considerable amount of time to execute, depending on the system hardware. Running `make` will produce a lot of output in the terminal. It may also produce a lot of compiler warnings which can safely be ignored in most cases.

If `make` ends with errors, we should check Squid bugzilla for similar problems. We can update an existing bug with our error report or create a new bug report if there is no similar bug already. For details on troubleshooting and completing bug reports, please refer to *Chapter 12, Troubleshooting Squid*.

If `make` ends without any errors, we can quickly proceed to the installation phase. We can also run `make` again to verify that everything is compiled successfully. Running `make` again should produce a lot of lines similar to the following:

```
Making all in compat
make[1]: Entering directory '/home/user/squid-source/compat'
make[1]: Nothing to be done for 'all'.
make[1]: Leaving directory '/home/user/squid-source/compat'
```

What just happened?

We have just run the `make` command that will compile the source code of Squid and related modules, to generate executables, if it finishes without errors. The generated executables are ready to be installed now.

Time for action – installing Squid

The successful compilation of the source code in the previous section will generate the required programs depending on the features and packages we have enabled or disabled. However, they should be moved to their designated locations, so that they can be used. Let's perform the final steps of the installation.

1. Depending on the ${prefix}, we may need root or super user privileges for installing Squid. If root or super user privileges are needed, we should first switch to root or super user by using the following command:

   su

2. Now all we need to do is to run the make command with install as the argument:

   make install

   This will install or simply move programs to their designated locations, depending on the path used with the --prefix option while running the configure program.

What just happened?

We just learned how to perform the final step in installing Squid, which is to place the generated programs and other essential files in their designated locations.

Time for action – exploring Squid files

Let's have a look at the files and directories generated during installation. The easiest way to checkout the directories and files generated is to use the tree command. If the tree command is not available, we can list files using the ls command as well.

```
tree ${prefix} | less
```

${prefix} is the directory used with the --prefix option for configure. Now let's have a brief overview at the important files generated by Squid during installation. All of the following directories and files listed, reside in ${prefix}:

bin

This directory contains programs which can be executed or run by a user without root or super user privileges.

bin/squidclient

squidclient is a HTTP client with advanced capabilities, which allow it to tinker HTTP requests to test the Squid server. Run squidclient to checkout the available options:

```
${prefix}/bin/squidclient
```

etc

This is the place where for all the configuration files related to Squid are located.

 It's a good idea to use the `--sysconfdir=/etc/squid/` option with `configure`, so that you can share the configuration across different Squid installations while testing.

etc/squid.conf

This is the default location for the Squid configuration file. The `squid.conf` generated during installation is the bare minimum configuration required for Squid to be used. We always make changes to this file if we need to alter the Squid configuration.

etc/squid.conf.default

Squid generates this default configuration file so that we can copy and rename it to `squid.conf` and start afresh.

etc/squid.conf.documented

This is a fully documented version of `squid.conf`, containing thousands of lines of comments. We should always refer to this file for the available configuration tags for the version of Squid when we have installed.

libexec

This directory contains helper programs built during Squid compilation.

libexec/cachemgr.cgi

This CGI program provides a web interface for managing the Squid cache called Cache Manager.

sbin

This directory contains programs which can only be executed by a user with root or super user privileges.

sbin/squid

This is the actual Squid program, which is generally run as a daemon.

share

This is the location for error page templates, documentation, and other files used by Squid.

share/errors

This directory contains localized error page templates. The templates are HTML pages and we can customize the error messages displayed by Squid, by modifying these HTML templates.

share/icons

This directory contains a number of small images used for FTP or gopher directory listing.

share/man

This is the place where the man pages for `squid`, `squidclient`, and helpers are built during compilation. Man pages are manual or help pages which can be viewed using the command man (available on all Linux/Unix distributions). To view a man page located at `/opt/squid/share/man/man8/squid.8`, we can use the man command as follows:

```
man /opt/squid/share/man/man8/squid.8
```

For more details about man pages, please visit `http://en.wikipedia.org/wiki/Man_page`.

var

A place for files that change frequently while Squid is running.

var/cache

This is the default directory for storing the cached web documents on a hard disk.

var/logs

This is the default home for all the log files (such as `cache.log`, `access.log`, and so on) used by Squid.

What just happened?

We have just looked at the various files and directories generated during installation and a had brief overview of what each directory contains.

Installing Squid from binary packages

Squid binary packages are available in the software repositories of most operating systems and we can install them by using the package managers provided by the respective operating systems. Next, we'll see how to use a package manager on a few operating systems to install Squid.

 The latest or beta versions may not be available in software repositories of all the operating systems. In such cases, we should get the latest or beta versions from the Squid website, as explained earlier in this chapter.

Fedora, CentOS or Red Hat

Yum is a popular package manager on RPM-based operating systems. Squid RPM is available in the Fedora, CentOS, and Red Hat repositories. To install Squid, we can simply use the following command:

```
yum install squid
```

Debian or Ubuntu

We can use `apt-get` to install Squid on Debian or Ubuntu:

```
apt-get install squid3
```

FreeBSD

Squid is available in the FreeBSD ports collection. The following command can be used to install Squid on FreeBSD:

```
pkg_add -r squid31
```

For more information on package management in FreeBSD, please go to `http://www.freebsd.org/doc/handbook/packages-using.html`.

OpenBSD or NetBSD

Installing Squid on OpenBSD or NetBSD is similar to installing it on FreeBSD and can be performed using the following command:

```
pkd_add squid31
```

To learn more about the package management system in OpenBSD and NetBSD, please refer to `http://www.openbsd.org/ports.html#Get` and `http://www.netbsd.org/docs/pkgsrc/using.html#installing-binary-packages` respectively.

Dragonfly BSD

To install Squid on Dragonfly BSD, we can use the following command:

```
pkg_radd squid31
```

For more information on installing binary packages on Dragonfly BSD, please visit `http://www.dragonflybsd.org/docs/newhandbook/pkgsrc/`.

Gentoo

We can install Squid on Gentoo Linux using `emerge`, as shown next:

```
emerge =squid-3.1*
```

Arch Linux

To install Squid on Arch Linux, we can use the package manager `pacman`, as shown in the following command:

```
pacman -S squid
```

For more information on `pacman`, please visit
`https://wiki.archlinux.org/index.php/Pacman`.

Pop quiz

1. Which of the following web documents can't be cached by a proxy server?

   a. A HTML page

   b. A JPEG image

   c. A PHP script that produces output based on a client's IP Address

   d. A JavaScript file

2. In which of the following scenarios, should we worry about the
   `--enable-diskio` option?

   a. Caching in RAM (main memory) is enabled

   b. Caching on hard disk is enabled

   c. Caching is disabled

   d. None of the above

3. When does a removal policy selection affect the overall Squid performance?

   a. If caching is disabled

   b. If caching on the hard disk and RAM is enabled

   c. A removal policy selection is not related to caching

   d. A removal policy doesn't affect overall Squid performance

Summary

We learned about proxy servers and web caching in general and the ways in which they can be useful, especially for saving bandwidth and improving end user experience. Then we moved on to exploring Squid, which is a powerful caching proxy server. The following are the important things that we learned in this chapter:

- Various ways to grab Squid for production use or development
- Meaning of various configure options
- Compiling Squid source code
- Installing Squid from source and binary package
- Pros and cons of compiling Squid from source

We also discussed about the directory structure and files generated by Squid during installation.

Now that we know how to install Squid, we are ready to learn how to configure Squid according to requirements for a given network environment. We'll learn about this with a few examples in the next chapter.

2
Configuring Squid

We have learned about compiling Squid source code and installing Squid from a source and binary package. In this chapter, we are going to learn to configure Squid according to the requirements of a given network. We will learn about the general syntax used for a Squid configuration file and then we will move on to exploring the different options available to fine tune Squid. There will be a few options which we will only cover briefly but there will be chapters dedicated to them while we will explore other options in detail.

In this chapter, we will cover the following:

◆ Quick exposure to Squid

◆ Syntax of the configuration file

◆ HTTP port, the most important configuration directive

◆ Access Control Lists (ACLs)

◆ Controlling access to various components of Squid

◆ Cache peers or neighbors

◆ Caching the web documents in the main memory and hard disk

◆ Tuning Squid to enhance bandwidth savings and reduce latency

◆ Modifying the HTTP headers accompanied with requests and responses

◆ Configuring Squid to use DNS servers

◆ A few directives related to logging

◆ Other important or commonly used configuration directives

So let's get started.

Quick start

Before we explore a configuration file in detail, let's have a look at the minimal configuration that you will need to get started. Get ready with the configuration file located at /opt/squid/etc/squid.conf, as we are going to make the changes and additions necessary to quickly set up a minimal proxy server.

```
cache_dir ufs /opt/squid/var/cache/ 500 16 256
acl my_machine src 192.0.2.21 # Replace with your IP address
http_access allow my_machine
```

We should add the previous lines at the top of our current configuration file (ensuring that we change the IP address accordingly). Now, we need to create the cache directories. We can do that by using the following command:

```
$ /opt/squid/sbin/squid -z
```

We are now ready to run our proxy server, and this can be done by running the following command:

```
$ /opt/squid/sbin/squid
```

Squid will start listening on port 3128 (default) on all network interfaces on our machine. Now we can configure our browser to use Squid as an HTTP proxy server with the host as the IP address of our machine and port 3128.

Once the browser is configured, try browsing to http://www.example.com/. That's it! We have configured Squid as an HTTP proxy server! Now try to browse to http://www.example.com:897/ and observe the message you receive. The message shown is an access denied message sent to you by Squid.

Now, let's move on to understanding the configuration file in detail.

Syntax of the configuration file

Squid's configuration file can normally be found at /etc/squid/squid.conf, /usr/local/squid/etc/squid.conf, or ${prefix}/etc/squid.conf where ${prefix} is the value passed to the --prefix option, which is passed to the configure command before compiling Squid.

In the newer versions of Squid, a documented version of squid.conf, known as squid.conf.documented, can be found along side squid.conf. In this chapter, we'll cover some of the import directives available in the configuration file. For a detailed description of all the directives used in the configuration file, please check http://www.squid-cache.org/Doc/config/.

The syntax for Squid's documented configuration file is similar to many other programs for Linux/Unix. Generally, there are a few lines of comments containing useful related documentation before every directive used in the configuration file. This makes it easier to understand and configure directives, even for people who are not familiar with configuring applications using configuration files. Normally, we just need to read the comments and use the appropriate options available for a particular directive.

The lines beginning with the character # are treated as comments and are completely ignored by Squid while parsing the configuration file. Additionally, any blank lines are also ignored.

```
# Test comment. This and the above blank line will be ignored by
Squid.
```

Let's see a snippet from the documented configuration file (squid.conf.documented)

```
#   TAG: cache_effective_user
# If you start Squid as root, it will change its effective/real
# UID/GID to the user specified below.  The default is to change
# to UID of nobody.
# see also; cache_effective_group
#Default:
# cache_effective_user nobody
```

In the previous snippet, the first line mentions the name of the directive, that is in this case, cache_effective_user. The lines following the tag line provide brief information about the usage of a directive. The last line shows the default value for the directive, if none is specified.

Types of directives

Now, let's have a brief look at the different types of directives and the values that can be specified.

Single valued directives

These are directives which take only one value. These directives should not be used multiple times in the configuration file because the last occurrence of the directive will override all the previous declarations. For example, logfile_rotate should be specified only once.

```
logfile_rotate 10
# Few lines containing other configuration directives
logfile_rotate 5
```

In this case, five logfile rotations will be made when we trigger Squid to rotate logfiles.

Boolean-valued or toggle directives

These are also single valued directives, but these directives are generally used to toggle features on or off.

```
query_icmp on
log_icp_queries off
url_rewrite_bypass off
```

We use these directives when we need to change the default behavior.

Multi-valued directives

Directives of this type generally take one or more than one value. We can either specify all the values on a single line after the directive or we can write them on multiple lines with a directive repeated every time. All the values for a directive are aggregated from different lines:

```
hostname_aliases proxy.exmaple.com squid.example.com
```

Optionally, we can pass them on separate lines as follows:

```
dns_nameservers proxy.example.com
dns_nameservers squid.example.com
```

Both the previous code snippets will instruct Squid to use `proxy.example.com` and `squid.example.com` as aliases for the hostname of our proxy server.

Directives with time as a value

There are a few directives which take values with time as the unit. Squid understands the words `seconds`, `minutes`, `hours`, and so on, and these can be suffixed to numerical values to specify actual values. For example:

```
request_timeout 3 hours
persistent_request_timeout 2 minutes
```

Directives with file or memory size as values

The values passed to these directives are generally suffixed with file or memory size units like `bytes`, `KB`, `MB`, or `GB`. For example:

```
reply_body_max_size 10 MB
cache_mem 512 MB
maximum_object_in_memory 8192 KB
```

As we are familiar with the configuration file syntax now, let's open the `squid.conf` file and learn about the frequently used directives.

Have a go hero – categorize the directives

Open the documented Squid configuration file and find out at least three directives of each type that we discussed before. Don't use the directives already used in the examples.

HTTP port

This directive is used to specify the port where Squid will listen for client connections. The default behavior is to listen on port 3128 on all the available interfaces on a machine.

Time for action – setting the HTTP port

Now, we'll see the various ways to set the HTTP port in the `squid.conf` file:

◆ In its simplest form, we just specify the port on which we want Squid to listen:

```
http_port 8080
```

◆ We can also specify the IP address and port combination on which we want Squid to listen. We normally use this approach when we have multiple interfaces on our machine and we want Squid to listen only on the interface connected to local area network (LAN):

```
http_port 192.0.2.25:3128
```

This will instruct Squid to listen on port 3128 on the interface with the IP address as `192.0.2.25`.

◆ Another form in which we can specify `http_port` is by using hostname and port combination:

```
http_port myproxy.example.com:8080
```

The hostname will be translated to an IP address by Squid and then Squid will listen on port 8080 on that particular IP address.

◆ Another aspect of this directive is that, it can take multiple values on separate lines. Let's see what the following lines will do:

```
http_port 192.0.2.25:8080
http_port lan1.example.com:3128
http_port lan2.example.com:8081
```

These lines will trigger Squid to listen on three different IP addresses and port combinations. This is generally helpful when we have clients in different LANs, which are configured to use different ports for the proxy server.

◆ In the newer versions of Squid, we may also specify the mode of operation such as `intercept`, `tproxy`, `accel`, and so on.

Intercept mode will support the interception of requests without needing to configure the client machines. We'll learn more about interception proxy servers in *Chapter 10, Squid in Intercept Mode*.

```
http_port 3128 intercept
```

`tproxy` mode is used to enable Linux Transparent Proxy support for spoofing outgoing connections using the client's IP address.

```
http_port 8080 tproxy
```

 We should note that enabling `intercept` or `tproxy` mode disables any configured authentication mechanism. Also, IPv6 is supported for `tproxy` but requires very recent kernel versions. IPv6 is not supported in the `intercept` mode.

Accelerator mode is enabled using the mode `accel`. It's a good idea to listen on port 80, if we are configuring Squid in accelerator mode. This mode can't be used as it is. We must specify at least one website we want to accelerate. We'll learn more about the accelerator mode in *Chapter 9, Squid in Accelerator Mode*.

```
http_port 80 accel defaultsite=website.example.com
```

 We should set the HTTP port carefully as the standard ports like 3128 or 8080 can pose a security risk if we don't secure the port properly. If we don't want to spend time on securing the port, we can use any arbitrary port number above 10000.

What just happened?

In this section, we learned about the usage of one of the most important directives, namely, `http_port`. We have learned about the various ways in which we can specify HTTP port, depending on the requirement. We can force Squid to listen on multiple interfaces and on different ports, on different interfaces.

Access control lists

Access Control Lists (ACLs) are the base elements for access control and are normally used in combination with other directives such as `http_access`, `icp_access`, and so on, to control access to various Squid components and web resources. ACLs identify a web transaction and then directives such as `http_access`, `cache`, and then decides whether the transaction should be allowed or not. Also, we should note that the directives related to accessing resources generally end with `_access`.

Every access control list definition must have a name and type, followed by the values for that particular ACL type:

```
acl ACL_NAME ACL_TYPE value
acl ACL_NAME ACL_TYPE "/path/to/filename"
```

The values for any ACL name can either be specified directly after `ACL_TYPE` or Squid can read them from a separate file. Here we should note that the values in the file should be written as one value per line.

Time for action – constructing simple ACLs

Let's construct an access control list for the domain name `example.com`:

```
acl example_site dstdomain example.com
```

In this code, `example_site` is the name of the ACL with type `dstdomain`, which reflects that the value, `example.com`, is the domain name.

Now if we want to construct an access control list which can cover a lot of example websites, we have the following three possible ways of doing it:

1. Values on a single line: We can specify all the possible values on a single line:

    ```
    acl example_sites dstdomain example.com example.net example.org
    ```

    This works fine as long as there are only a few values.

2. Values on multiple lines: In case the list of values that we want to specify grows significantly, we can split the list and pass values on multiple lines:

    ```
    acl example_sites dstdomain example.com example.net
    acl example_sites dstdomain example.org
    ```

3. Values from a file: If case the number of values we want to specify is quite large, we can put them in a dedicated file and then instruct Squid to read the values from that particular file:

    ```
    acl example_sites dstdomain '/opt/squid/etc/example_sites.txt'
    ```

    We can place the example_sites.txt file in the same directory as `squid.conf` so that it's easy to locate. The contents of the example_sites.txt file should be as follows:

    ```
    # This file can also have comments
    # Write one value (domain name) per line
    example.net
    example.org # Temporarily remove example.org from example_sites
    acl
    example.com
    ```

ACL names are case-insensitive and are multi-valued. So we can use them, multiple times, and the values will aggregate:

```
acl NiCe_NaMe src 192.0.2.21
acl nIcE_nAmE src 192.0.2.23
```

This code doesn't represent two different access control lists. It's just one ACL with two addresses, namely, `192.0.2.21` and `192.0.2.23`, as values.

> We should carefully note that one ACL name can't be used with more than one ACL type.
>
> ```
> acl destination dstdomain example.com
> acl destination dst 192.0.2.24
> ```
>
> The above code is invalid as it uses ACL name `destination` across two different ACL types.

The previous examples of access lists are very basic and are simply to get us started. We'll explore access lists and controls in *Chapter 4, Getting Started with Squid's Powerful ACLs and Access Rules*.

What just happened?

We have just learned to create some simple ACLs of the ACL type `dstdomain`, which identifies the destination domain in a request.

Have a go hero – understanding the pre-defined ACLs

Jump to the ACL section in the Squid configuration file and try to understand the ACLs provided by Squid, by default.

Controlling access to the proxy server

While Squid is running on our server, it can be accessed in several ways for example, via normal web browsing by end users or as a parent or sibling proxy server by neighboring proxy servers. Squid provides various directives to control access to different resources. Next, we'll learn about granting or revoking access to different resources.

HTTP access control

ACLs help only in identifying requests based on different rules. ACLs are of no use by themselves, they should be combined with access control directives to allow or deny access to various resources. `http_access` is one such directive which is used to grant access to perform HTTP transactions through Squid.

Let's have a look at the syntax of `http_access`:

```
http_access allow|deny [!]ACL_NAME
```

Using `http_access`, we can either allow or deny access to the HTTP transactions through Squid. The `ACL_NAME` in the code signifies the requests for which the access must be granted or revoked. If a bang (`!`) is prefixed to the `ACL_NAME`, the access will be granted or revoked for all the requests that are not identified by `ACL_NAME`.

Time for action – combining ACLs and HTTP access

Let's have a look at a few cases for controlling HTTP access using example ACLs. When we have multiple access rules, Squid matches a particular request against them from top to bottom and keeps doing so until a definite action (`allow` or `deny`) is determined. Please note that if we have multiple ACLs within a single access rule, then a request is matched against all the ACLs from left to right, and Squid stops processing the rule as soon as it encounters an ACL that can't identify the request. An access rule with multiple ACLs results in a definite action, only if the request is identified by all the ACLs used in the rule.

```
acl my_home_machine src 192.0.2.21
acl my_lab_machine src 198.51.100.86
http_access allow my_home_machine
http_access allow my_lab_machine
```

The ACLs and access rules in the previous code will allow hosts `192.0.2.21` and `198.51.100.86` to access the proxy server. The aforementioned access rules may also be written as:

```
acl my_machines src 192.0.2.21 198.51.100.86
http_access allow my_machines
```

Default behavior is to allow access to all the clients in a local area network and deny access to all the other clients. If we want clients (who are not in our local area network) to be able to use our proxy server, we must add additional access rules to allow them.

 The default behavior of HTTP access control is a bit tricky if access for a client can't be identified by any of the access rules. In such cases, the default behavior is to do the opposite of the last access rule. If last access rule is `deny`, then the action will be to `allow` access and vice-versa. Therefore, to avoid any confusion or undesired behavior, it's a good practice to add a `deny all` line after the access rules.

```
http_access deny all
```

The parameter `all` is a special ACL element provided by Squid and it represents all the IP addresses. This line will deny access to everything. As this goes after all other access rules, requests from unknown clients will be denied.

What just happened?

We learned to combine ACLs with the `http_access` directive to allow or deny access to clients. We also learned how to group different ACLs of the same type and then use them to control access.

HTTP reply access

HTTP reply is the response received from the web server corresponding to a request initiated by a client. Using the `http_reply_access` directive, we can control the access to the replies received. The syntax of `http_reply_access` is similar to `http_access`.

```
http_reply_access allow|deny [!]ACL_NAME
```

This directive partially overrides the permissions granted by `http_access`. Let's see an example:

```
acl my_machine src 192.0.2.21
http_access allow my_machine
http_reply_access deny my_machine
```

We have allowed `http_access` to host `192.0.2.21` but still it will not be able to access the websites properly as it's not allowed to receive any replies. The host can only make requests to a proxy server for web documents but won't receive any reply.

This directive is normally used to deny access for content types such as audio, video, and so on, to prevent users from accessing media content.

> We should be really careful while using the `http_reply_access` directive. When a request is allowed by `http_access`, Squid will contact the original server, even if a rule with the `http_reply_access` directive denies the response. This may lead to serious security issues. For example, consider a client receiving a malicious URL, which can submit a client's critical private information using the HTTP POST method. If the client's request passes through `http_access` rules but the response is denied by an `http_reply_access` rule, then the client will be under the impression that nothing happened but a hacker will have cleverly stolen our client's private information.

ICP access

This directive is used to control the query access by our neighboring caches using the Internet Cache Protocol (ICP). It basically allows or denies access to the ICP port. The syntax is similar to http_access and the default behavior is to deny all ICP queries.

```
icp_access allow|deny [!]ACL_NAME
```

HTCP access

Using this directive, we can control whether Squid will respond to certain HTCP requests or not. The syntax is similar to http_access and the default behavior is to deny all queries.

HTCP CLR access

Neighboring caches can make requests to purge or remove cache objects in the form of HTCP CLR requests. The htcp_clr_access directive can be used to grant purge access to only trusted cache peers.

Miss access

This directive is used to specify which all cache peers or clients can use as their parent cache. When a cache peer or client tries to fetch content using our proxy server, the request may result in a MISS (not present in cache) or a HIT (can be satisfied from our cache). Generally, a MISS is fetched by our server on behalf of a client or peer. If we don't want our clients or peers to fetch content using our proxy, then we can use the miss_access directive, as shown:

```
acl bad_clients src 192.0.2.0/24
miss_access deny bad_clients
miss_access allow all
```

This code will not allow bad_clients to use our proxy server as a parent proxy. The default behavior is to allow all the clients who pass the http_access rule to use the proxy server as a parent.

Ident lookup access

This directive determines whether or not Squid should perform a username lookup for the client TCP requests.

```
acl ident_aware_hosts src 192.0.2.0/24
ident_lookup_access allow ident_aware_hosts
ident_lookup_access deny all
```

This code will allow Squid to perform ident lookups only for ident_aware_hosts. The default behavior is not to perform ident lookups for all queries.

Only TCP/IP-based ACLs are supported with this directive.

Cache peers or neighbors

Cache peers or neighbors are the other proxy servers with which our Squid proxy server can:

◆ Share its cache with to reduce bandwidth usage and access time

◆ Use it as a parent or sibling proxy server to satisfy its clients' requests

◆ Use it as a parent or sibling proxy server

We normally deploy more than one proxy server in the same network to share the load of a single server for better performance. The proxy servers can use each other's cache to retrieve the cached web documents locally to improve performance. Let's have a brief look at the directives provided by Squid for communication among different cache peers.

Declaring cache peers

The directive `cache_peer` is used to tell Squid about proxy servers in our neighborhood. Let's have a quick look at the syntax for this directive:

```
cache_peer HOSTNAME_OR_IP_ADDRESS TYPE PROXY_PORT ICP_PORT [OPTIONS]
```

In this code, `HOSTNAME_OR_IP_ADDRESS` is the hostname or IP address of the target proxy server or cache peer. `TYPE` specifies the type of the proxy server, which in turn, determines how that proxy server will be used by our proxy server. The other proxy servers can be used as a parent, sibling, or a member of a multicast group.

Time for action – adding a cache peer

Let's add a proxy server (`parent.example.com`) that will act as a parent proxy to our proxy server:

```
cache_peer parent.example.com parent 3128 3130 default proxy-only
```

`3130` is the standard ICP port. If the other proxy server is not using the standard ICP port, we should change the code accordingly. This code will direct Squid to use `parent.example.com` as a proxy server to satisfy client requests in case it's not able to do so itself.

The option `default` specifies that this cache peer should be used as a last resort in the scenario where other peers can't be contacted. The option `proxy-only` specifies that the content fetched using this peer should not be cached locally. This is helpful when we don't want to replicate cached web documents, especially when the two peers are connected with a high bandwidth backbone.

What just happened?

We added `parent.example.com` as a cache peer or parent proxy to our Squid proxy server. We also used the option `proxy-only`, which means the requests fetched using this cache peer will not be cached on our proxy server.

There are several other options in which you can add cache peers, for various purposes, such as, a hierarchy. We'll discuss cache peers in detail in *Chapter 8, Building a Hierarchy of Squid Caches*.

Quickly restricting access to domains using peers

If we have added a few proxy servers as cache peers to our Squid server, we may have the desire to have a little bit of control over the requests being forwarded to the peers. The directive `cache_peer_domain` is a quick way to achieve the desired control. The syntax of this directive is quite simple:

```
cache_peer_domain CACHE_PEER_HOSTNAME [!]DOMAIN1 [[!]DOMAIN2 ...]
```

In the code, `CACHE_PEER_HOSTNAME` is the hostname or IP address of the cache peer being used when declaring it as a cache peer, using the `cache_peer` directive. We can specify any number of domains which may be fetched through this cache peer. Adding a bang (`!`) as a prefix to the domain name will prevent the use of this cache peer for that particular domain.

Let's say we want to use the `videoproxy.example.com` cache peer for browsing video portals like Youtube, Netflix, Metacafe, and so on.

```
cache_peer_domain videoproxy.example.com .youtube.com .netflix.com
cache_peer_domain videoproxy.example.com .metacafe.com
```

These two lines will configure Squid to use the `videoproxy.example.com` cache peer for requests to the domains `youtube.com`, `netflix.com`, and `metacafe.com` only. Requests to other domains will not be forwarded using this peer.

Advanced control on access using peers

We just learned about `cache_peer_domain`, which provides a way to control access using cache peers. However, it's not really flexible in granting or revoking access. That's when `cache_peer_access` comes into the picture, which provides a very flexible way to control access using cache peers using ACLs. The syntax and implications are similar to other access directives such as `http_access`.

```
cache_peer_access CACHE_PEER_HOSTNAME allow|deny [!]ACL_NAME
```

Let's write the following configuration lines, which will allow only the clients on the network `192.0.2.0/24` to use the cache peer `acadproxy.example.com` for accessing Youtube, Netflix, and Metacafe.

```
acl my_network src 192.0.2.0/24
acl video_sites dstdomain .youtube.com .netflix.com .metacafe.com
cache_peer_access acadproxy.example.com allow my_network video_sites
cache_peer_access acadproxy.example.com deny all
```

In the same way, we can use other ACL types to achieve better control over access to various websites using cache peers.

Caching web documents

All this time, we have been talking about the caching of web documents and how it helps in saving bandwidth and improving the end user experience, now it's time to learn how and where Squid actually keeps these cached documents so that they can be served on demand. Squid uses main memory (RAM) and hard disks for storing or caching the web documents.

Caching is a complex process but Squid handles it beautifully and exposes the directives using `squid.conf`, so that we can control how much should be cached and what should be given the highest priority while caching. Let's have a brief look at the caching-related directives provided by Squid.

Using main memory (RAM) for caching

The web documents cached in the main memory or RAM can be served very quickly as data read/write speeds of RAM are very high compared to hard disks with mechanical parts. However, as the amount of space available in RAM for caching is very low compared to the cache space available on hard disks, only very popular objects or the documents with a very high probability of being requested again, are stored in cache space available in RAM.

As the cache space in memory is precious, the documents are stored on a priority basis. Let's have a look at the different types of objects which can be cached.

In-transit objects or current requests

These are the objects related to the current requests and they have the highest priority to be kept in the cache space in RAM. These objects must be kept in RAM and if there is a situation where the incoming request rate is quite high and we are about to overflow the cache space in RAM, Squid will try to keep the served part (the part which has already been sent to the client) on the disk to create free space in RAM.

Hot or popular objects

These objects or web documents are popular and are requested quite frequently compared to others. These are stored in the cache space left after storing the in-transit objects as these have a lower priority than in-transit objects. These objects are generally pushed to disk when there is a need to generate more in RAM cache space for storing the in-transit objects.

Negatively cached objects

Negatively cached objects are error messages which Squid has encountered while fetching a page or web document on behalf of a client. For example, if a request to a web page has resulted in a HTTP error 404 (page not found), and Squid receives a subsequent request for the same web page, then Squid will check if the response is still fresh and will return a reply from the cache itself. If there is a request for the same page after the negatively cached object corresponding to that page has expired, Squid will check again if the page is available.

Negatively cached objects have the same priority as hot or popular objects and they can be pushed to disk at any time in favor of in-transit objects.

Specifying cache space in RAM

So far we have learned about how the available cache space is utilized for storing or caching different types of objects with different priorities. Now, it's time to learn about specifying the amount of RAM space we want to dedicate for caching. While deciding the RAM space for caching, we should be neither greedy nor paranoid. If we specify a large percentage of RAM for caching, the overall system performance will suffer as the system will start swapping processes in case there is no free RAM left for other processes. If we use a very low percentage of RAM for caching, then we'll not be able to take full advantage of Squid's caching mechanism. The default size of the memory cache is 256 MB.

Time for action – specifying space for memory caching

We can use extra RAM space available on a running system after sparing a chunk of memory that can be utilized by the running process under heavy load. To find out the amount of free RAM available on our system, we can use either the `top` or `free` command. To find out the free RAM in Megabytes, we can use the `free` command as follows:

```
$ free -m
```

For more details, please check the `top(1)` and `free(1)` man pages.

Now, let's say we have 4 GB of total RAM on the server and all the processes are running comfortably in 1 GB of RAM space. After securing another 512 MB for emergency situations where running processes may take extra memory, we can safely allocate 2.5 GB of RAM for caching.

To specify the cache size in the main memory, we use the directive `cache_mem`. It has a very simple format. As we have learned before, we can specify the memory size in `bytes`, `KB`, `MB`, or `GB`. Let's specify the cache memory size for the previous example:

```
cache_mem 2500 MB
```

The previous value specified with `cache_mem` is in Megabytes.

What just happened?

We learned about calculating the approximate space in the main memory, which can be used to cache web documents and therefore enhance the performance of the Squid server by a significant margin.

Have a go hero – calculating cache_mem for your machine

Note down the total RAM on your machine and calculate the approximate space in megabytes that you can allocate for memory caching.

Maximum object size in memory

As we have limited space in memory available for caching objects, we need to use the space in an optimized way. We should plan to set this a bit low, as setting it to a too larger size will mean that there will be a lesser number of cached objects in the memory and the HIT (being found in cache) rate will suffer significantly. The default maximum size used by Squid is 512 KB, but we can change it depending on our value for `cache_mem`. So, if we want to set it to 1 MB, as we have a lot of RAM available for caching (as in the previous example), we can use the `maximum_object_size_in_memory` directive as follows:

```
maximum_object_size_in_memory 1 MB
```

This command will set the allowed maximum object size in memory cache to 1 MB.

Memory cache mode

With the newer versions of Squid, we can control which objects we want to keep in the memory cache for optimizing the performance. Squid offers the directive memory_cache_ mode to set the mode that Squid should use to utilize the space available in memory cache. There are three different modes available:

Mode	Description
always	The mode always is used to keep all the most recently fetched objects that can fit in the available space. This is the default mode used by Squid.
disk	When the disk mode is set, only the objects which are already cached on a hard disk and have received a HIT (meaning they were requested subsequently after being cached), will be stored in the memory cache.
network	Only the objects which have been fetched from the network (including neighbors) are kept in the memory cache, if the network mode is set.

Setting the mode is easy and can be set using the memory_cache_mode directive as shown:

```
memory_cache_mode always
```

This configuration line will set memory cache mode to always; this means that most recently fetched objects will be kept in the memory.

Using hard disks for caching

In the previous section, we learned about using the main memory for caching various types of objects or web documents to reduce bandwidth usage and enhance the end user experience. However, as the space available in RAM is small in size and we can't really invest a lot in the main memory as it's very expensive in terms of bytes per unit of money. As opposed to the mechanical disks, we prefer to deploy proxy servers with huge storage space which can be used for caching objects. Let's have a look at how to tell Squid about caching objects to disks.

Specifying the storage space

The directive cache_dir is used to declare the space on the hard disk where Squid will store or cache the web documents for use in future. Let's have a look at the syntax of cache_dir and try to understand the different arguments and options:

```
cache_dir STORAGE_TYPE DIRECTORY SIZE_IN_Mbytes L1 L2 [OPTIONS]
```

Storage types

Operating systems implement filesystems to store files and directories on the disk drives. In the Linux/Unix world, ext2, ext3, ext4, reiserfs, xfs, UFS (Unix File System), and so on, are the popular filesystems. Filesystems also expose a few system calls such as open(), close(), read(), and so on, so that other programs can read/write/remove files from the storage. Squid also uses these system calls to interact with the filesystems and manage the cached objects on the disk.

On top of the filesystems and with the help of the available system calls exposed by the filesystems, Squid implements storage schemes such as ufs, aufs, and diskd.

All the storage schemes supported by the operating system are built by default. The ufs is a very simple storage scheme and all the I/O transactions are done using the main Squid process. As some of the system calls are blocking (meaning the system call will not return until the I/O transaction is complete) in nature, they sometimes cause delays in processing requests, especially under heavy load, resulting in an overall bad performance. ufs is good for servers with less load and high speed disks, but is not really preferable for busy caches.

aufs is an improved version of ufs where a stands for asynchronous I/O. In other words, aufs is ufs with asynchronous I/O support, which is achieved by utilizing POSIX-threads (pthreads library). Asynchronous I/O prevents blocking of the main Squid process by some system calls, meaning that Squid can keep on serving requests while we are waiting for some I/O transaction to complete. So, if we have the pthreads library support on our operating system, we should always go for aufs instead of ufs, especially for heavily loaded proxy servers.

The Disk Daemon (diskd) storage scheme is similar to aufs. The only difference is that diskd uses an external process for I/O transactions instead of threads. Squid and diskd process for each cache_dir (of the diskd type) to communicate using message queues and shared memory. As diskd involves a queuing system, it may get overloaded over time in a busy proxy server. So, we can pass two additional options to cache_dir which determines how Squid will behave in case there are more messages in the queues than diskd is able to process. Let's have a look at the syntax of the cache_dir directive for diskd as STORAGE_TYPE

```
cache_dir diskd DIRECTORY SIZE_Mbytes L1 L2 [OPTIONS] [Q1=n] [Q2=n]
```

The value of Q1 signifies the number of pending messages in the queue beyond which Squid will not place new requests for I/O transactions. Though Squid will keep on entertaining requests normally, it'll not be able to cache new objects or check cache for any HITs. HIT performance will suffer in this period of time. The default value of Q1 is 64.

The value of Q2 signifies the number of pending messages in the queue beyond which Squid will cease to operate and will go in to block mode. No new requests will be served in this period until Squid receives a reply or the messages in the queue fall below this number. The default number of Q2 is 72.

As you can see from the explanation of Q1 and Q2, if the value of Q1 is more than Q2, Squid will go in to block mode first. If the queue is full it will result in higher latency but better HIT ratio. If the value of Q1 is less than Q2, Squid will keep on serving the requests from the network even if there is no I/O. This will result in lower latency, but the HIT ratio will suffer considerably.

Choosing a directory name or location

We can specify any location on the filesystem for the directory name. Squid will populate it with its own directory structure and will start storing or caching web documents in the space available. However, we must make sure that the directory already exists and is writable by the Squid process. Squid will not create the directory if it doesn't exist already.

Time for action – creating a cache directory

The cache directory location may not be on the same disk or partition. We can mount another disk drive and specify that as the directory for caching. For example, let's say we have another drive connected as /dev/sdb and one of the partitions is /dev/sdb1, we can mount it to the /drive/ and use it right away.

```
$ mkdir /drive/
$ mount /dev/sdb1 /drive/squid_cache/
$ mkdir /drive/squid_cache
$ chown squid:squid /drive/squid_cache/
```

In the previous code, we created a directory /drive/ and mounted /dev/sdb1, the partition from the other disk drive, to it. Then, we created a directory squid_cache in the directory /drive/ and changed the ownership of the directory to Squid, so that Squid can have write access to this directory. Now we can use /drive/squid_cache/ as one of the directories with the cache_dir directive.

What just happened?

We mounted a partition from a different hard disk and assigned the correct ownership to use it as a cache directory for disk caching.

Declaring the size of the cache

This is the easy part. We must keep in mind that we should not append MB or GB to the number while specifying the size in this directive. The size is always specified in Megabytes. So, if we want to use 100 GB of disk space for caching, we should set size to 102400 (102400 MB/1024 = 100 GB).

If we want to use the entire disk partition for caching, we should not set the cache size to be equal to the size of the partition because Squid may need some extra space for temporary files and the `swap.state` file. So, it's good practice to subtract 5-15 percent from the total disk space for temporary files and then set the cache size.

Configuring the number of sub directories

There are two arguments to `cache_dir` named as `L1` and `L2`. Squid stores the cacheable objects in a hierarchical fashion in directories named so that it'll be faster to lookup an object in the cache. The hierarchy is of two-levels, where `L1` determines the number of directories at the first level and `L2` determines the number of directories in each of the directories at the first level. We should set `L1` and `L2` high enough so that directories at the second level don't have a huge number of files.

Read-only cache

Sometimes we may want our cache to be in read-only mode so that Squid doesn't store or remove any cached objects from it but continues to serve the content from it. This is achieved by using an additional option named `no-store` with the `cache_dir` directive. Please note that Squid will not update any content in the read-only cache directory. This feature is used very rarely.

Time for action – adding a cache directory

So far we have learned the meaning of different parameters used with the `cache_dir` directive. Let's see an example of the cache directory `/squid_cache/` with 50GB of free space:

```
cache_dir aufs /squid_cache/ 51200 32 512
```

We have a cache directory `/squid_cache/` with 50 GB of free space with the values of `L1` and `L2` as 32 and 512 respectively. So, if we assume the average size of a cached object to be 16 KB, there will be *51200x1024÷(32x512x16) = 200* cached objects in each of the directories at the second level, which is quite good.

What just happened?

We added `/squid_cache/` with a 50 GB free disk space as a cache directory to cache web documents on the hard disk. Following the previous instructions, we can add as many cache directories as we want, depending on the availability of space.

Cache directory selection

If we have specified multiple caching directories, we may need a more efficient algorithm to ensure optimal performance. For example, when under a heavy load, Squid will perform a lot of I/O transactions. In such cases, if the load is split across the directories, this will obviously result in low latency.

Squid provides the directive `store_dir_select_algorithm`, which can be used to specify the way in which the cache directories should be used. It takes one of the values from `least-load` and `round-robin`.

```
store_dir_select_algorithm least-load|round-robin
```

If we want to distribute cached objects evenly across the caching directories, we should go for `round-robin`. If we want the best performance with least latency, we should certainly go for `least-load`, where Squid will try to pick the directory with the least I/O operations.

Cache object size limits

It is important to place limits on the size of the web documents which we are going to cache for achieving a better HIT ratio. Depending on the results we want to achieve, we may want to keep the maximum limit a bit higher than the default, which is 4 MB, which in turn depends on the size of the cache we have specified. For example, if we have a cache directory with a size of 10 GB and we set the maximum cacheable object size to 500 MB, there will be fewer objects in the cache and the HIT ratio will suffer significantly resulting in high latency. However, we shouldn't keep it really low either, as this will result in lots of I/O but fewer bandwidth savings.

Squid provides two directives known as `minimum_object_size` and `maximum_object_size` to set the object size limits. The minimum size is 0 KB, by default, meaning that there is no lower limit on the object size. If we have a huge amount of storage dedicated to caching, we can set the maximum limit to something around 100 MB, which will make sure that the popular software, audio/video content, and so on, are also cached, which may lead to significant bandwidth savings.

```
minimum_object_size 0 KB
maximum_object_size 96 MB
```

This configuration will set the minimum and maximum object size in the cache to 0 (zero) and 96 MB respectively, which means that objects with a size larger than 96 MB will not be cached.

Setting limits on object replacement

Over a period of time, the allocated space for the caching directories starts to fill up. Squid starts deleting cached objects from the cache once the occupied space by the objects crosses a certain threshold, which is determined by using the `cache_swap_low` and `cache_swap_high` directives. These directives take integral values between 0 and 100.

```
cache_swap_low 96
cache_swap_high 97
```

So, in accordance with these values, when the space occupied for a cache directory crosses 96 percent, Squid will start deleting objects from the cache and will try to maintain the utilization near 96 percent. However, if the incoming rate is high and the space utilization starts to touch the high limit (97 percent), the deletion becomes quite frequent until utilization moves towards the lower limit.

Squid's defaults for low and high limits are 90 percent and 95 percent respectively, which are good if the size of cache directory is low (like 10 GB). However, if we have a large amount of space for caching (such as a few hundreds GBs), we can push the limits a bit higher and closer because even 1 percent will mean a difference of more than a gigabyte.

Cache replacement policies

In the previous two sections, we learned about using the main memory and hard disks for caching web documents and how to configure Squid for optimal performance. As time passes, cache will start to fill and at some point in time, Squid will need to purge or delete old objects from the cache to make space for new ones. Removal of objects from the cache can be achieved in several ways. One of the simplest ways to do this is to start by removing the least recently used or least frequently used objects from the cache.

Squid builds different removal or replacement policies on top of the list and heap data structures. Let's have a look at the different policies provided by Squid.

Least recently used (LRU)

Least recently used (`lru`) is the simplest removal policy built by Squid by default. Squid starts by removing the cached objects that are oldest (since the last HIT). The LRU policy utilizes the list data structure, but there is also a heap-based implementation of LRU known as `heap lru`.

Greedy dual size frequency (GDSF)

GDSF (`heap GDSF`) is a heap-based removal policy. In this policy, Squid tries to keep popular objects with a smaller size in the cache. In other words, if there are two cached objects with the same popularity, the object with the larger size will be purged so that we can make space for more of the less popular objects, which will eventually lead to a better HIT ratio. While using this policy, the HIT ratio is better, but overall bandwidth savings are small.

Least frequently used with dynamic aging (LFUDA)

LFUDA (heap LFUDA) is also a heap-based replacement policy. Squid keeps the most popular objects in the cache, irrespective of their size. So, this policy compromises a bit of the HIT ratio, but may result in better bandwidth savings compared to GDSF. For example, if a cached object with a large size encounters a HIT, it'll be equal to HITs for several small sized popular objects. So, this policy tries to optimize bandwidth savings instead of the HIT ratio. We should keep the maximum object size in the cache high if we use this policy to further optimize the bandwidth savings.

Now we need to specify one of the policies which we have just learned, for cache replacement for the main memory caching as well as hard disk caching. Squid provides the directives memory_replacement_policy and cache_replacement_policy for specifying the removal policies.

```
memory_replacement_policy lru
cache_replacement_policy heap LFUDA
```

These configuration lines will set the memory replacement policy to lru and the on disk cache replacement policy to heap LFUDA.

Tuning Squid for enhanced caching

Although Squid performs quite well with default caching options, we can tune it to perform even better, by not caching the unwanted web objects and caching a few non-cacheable web documents. This will achieve higher bandwidth savings and reduced latency. Let's have a look at a few techniques that can be helpful.

Selective caching

There may be cases when we don't want to cache certain web documents or requests from clients. The directive cache is very helpful in such cases and is very easy to use.

Time for action – preventing the caching of local content

If we don't want to cache responses for certain requests or clients, we can deny it using this option. The default behavior is to allow all cacheable responses to be cached. As servers in our local area network are close enough that we may not want to waste cache space on our proxy server by caching responses from these servers, we can selectively deny caching for responses from local servers.

```
acl local_machines dst 192.0.2.0/24 198.51.100.0/24
cache deny local_machines
```

This code will prevent responses from the servers in the networks 192.0.2.0/24 and 198.51.100.0/24 from being cached by the proxy server.

What just happened?

To optimize the performance (especially the HIT ratio), we have configured Squid not to cache the objects that are available on the local area network. We have also learned how to selectively deny caching of such content.

Refresh patterns for cached objects

Squid provides the directive `refresh_pattern`, using which we can control the status of a cached object.

 Using `refresh_pattern` to cache the non-cacheable responses or to alter the lifetime of the cached objects, may lead to unexpected behavior or responses from the web servers. We should use this directive very carefully.

Refresh patterns can be used to achieve higher HIT ratios by keeping the recently expired objects fresh for a short period of time, or by overriding some of the HTTP headers sent by the web servers. While the `cache` directive can make use of ACLs, `refresh_pattern` uses regular expressions. The advantage of using the `refresh_pattern` directive is that we can alter the lifetime of the cached objects, while with the `cache` directive we can only control whether a request should be cached or not.

Let's have a look at the syntax of the `refresh_pattern` directive:

```
refresh_pattern [-i] regex min percent max [OPTIONS]
```

The parameter `regex` should be a regular expression describing the request URL. A refresh pattern line is applied to any URL matching the corresponding regular expression. There can be multiple lines of refresh patterns. The first line, whose regular expression matches the current URL, is used. By default, the regular expression is case-sensitive, but we can use `-i` to make it case-insensitive.

Some objects or responses from web servers may not carry an expiry time. Using the `min` parameter, we can specify the time (in minutes) for which the object or response should be considered fresh. The default and recommended value for this parameter is 0 because altering it may cause problems or unexpected behavior with dynamic web pages. We can use a higher value when we are absolutely sure that a website doesn't supply any dynamic content.

The parameter `percent` determines the life of a cached object in the absence of the `Expires` headers. An object's life time is considered to be the difference between the times extracted from the `Last-Modified` and `Date` headers. So, if we set the value of `percent` to 50 , and the difference between the times from `Last-Modified` and `Date` headers is one hour, then the object will be considered fresh for the next 30 minutes. The response age is simply the time that has passed since the response was generated by the web server or was validated by the proxy server for the freshness. The ratio of the response age to the object life time is termed as `lm-factor` in the Squid world.

Similarly the `min`, `max` parameters are the minimum and maximum times (in minutes) for which a cached object is considered fresh. If a cached object has spent more time in the cache than `max`, then it won't be considered fresh anymore.

 We should note that the `Expires` HTTP header overrides `min` and `max` values.

Let's have a look at the method used for determining the freshness or staleness of a cached object. A cached object is considered:

◆ Stale (or expired), if the expiry time that was mentioned in the HTTP response header is in the past.

◆ Fresh, if the expiry time mentioned in the HTTP response headers is in the future.

◆ Stale, if response age is more than the `max` value.

◆ Fresh, if `lm-factor` is less than the `percent` value.

◆ Fresh, if the response age is less than the `min` value.

◆ Stale, otherwise.

Time for action – calculating the freshness of cached objects

Let's see an example of a `refresh_pattern` and try to calculate the freshness of an object:

```
refresh_patten -i ^http://example.com/test.jpg$ 0 60% 1440
```

Let's say a client requested the image at `http://example.com/text.jpg` an hour ago, and the image was last modified (created) on the web server six hours ago. Let's assume that the web server didn't specify the expiry time. So, we have the following values for the different variables:

◆ At the time of the request, the object age was (6 - 1) = 5 hours.

◆ Currently, the response age is 1 hour.

◆ Currently, the `lm-factor` is 1÷5 = 20 percent

Let's check whether the object is still fresh or not:

◆ The response age is 60 minutes, which is not more than 1440 (`max` value), so this can't be the deciding factor.

◆ `lm-factor` is 20 percent, which is less than 60 percent, so the object is still fresh.

Now, let's calculate the time when the object will expire. The object age is 5 hours and percent value is 60 percent. So, object will expire in (5 x 60) ÷100 = 3 hours from the last request, that is, 2 hours from now.

What just happened?

We learned the formula for calculating the freshness or staleness of a cached object and also the time after which a cached object will expire. We also learned about specifying refresh patterns for the different content types to optimize performance.

Options for refresh pattern

Most of the time, the expiry time is specified by the web servers for all requests. But some web documents such as style sheets (CSS) or JavaScript (JS) files included on web page, change quite rarely and we can bump up their expiry time to a higher value to take full advantage of caching. As the web servers already specify the expiry time, the cached CSS/JS file will automatically expire. To forcibly ignore the Expires and a lot of other headers related to caching, we can pass options to the refresh_pattern directive.

Let's have a look at the options available for the refresh_pattern directive and how they can help us improve the HIT ratio.

 Please be warned that using the following options violates HTTP standards and may also cause unexpected browsing problems.

override-expire

The option override-expire, overrides or ignores the Expires header, which is the main player for determining the expiry time of a cached response. As the Expires header is ignored, the values of the min, max, and percent parameters will play an essential role in determining the freshness of a response.

override-lastmod

The option override-lastmod will force Squid to ignore the Last-Modified header, which will eventually enforce the use of min value to determine the freshness of an object. This option is of no use, if we have set the value of min to zero.

reload-into-ims

Using the reload-into-ims option will force Squid to convert the no-cache directives in the HTTP headers to the If-Modified-Since headers. The use of this option is useful only when the Last-Modified header is present.

ignore-reload

Using the option ignore-reload will simply ignore the no-cache or reload directives present in the HTTP headers.

ignore-no-cache

When the option `ignore-no-cache` is used, Squid simply ignores the `no-cache` directive in the HTTP headers.

ignore-no-store

The HTTP header `Cache-Control: no-store` is used to tell clients that they are not allowed to store the data being transmitted. If the option `ignore-no-store` is set, Squid will simply ignore this HTTP header and will cache the response if it's cacheable.

ignore-must-revalidate

The HTTP header `Cache-Control: must-revalidate` means that the response must be revalidated with the originating web server before it's used again. Setting the option `ignore-must-revalidate` will enforce Squid to ignore this header.

ignore-private

Private information or sensitive data generally carries an HTTP header known as `Cache-Control: private` so that intermediate servers don't cache the responses. However, the option `ignore-private` can be used to ignore this header.

ignore-auth

If the option `ignore-auth` is set, then Squid will be able to cache the authorization requests. Using this option may be really risky.

refresh-ims

This option can be pretty useful. The option `refresh-ims` forces Squid to validate the cached object with the original server whenever an `If-Modified-Since` request header is received from a client. Using this may increase the latency, but the clients will always get the latest data.

Let's see an example with these options:

```
refresh_pattern -i .jpg$ 0 60% 1440 ignore-no-cache ignore-no-store
reload-into-ims
```

This code will force all the JPEG images to be cached whether the original servers want us to cache them or not. They will be refreshed only:

◆ If the `Expires` HTTP header was present and the expiry time is in past.

◆ If the `Expires` HTTP header was missing and the response age has exceeded the `max` value.

Have a go hero – forcing the Google homepage to be cached for longer

Write a `refresh_pattern` configuration that forces the Google homepage to be cached for six hours.

Solution:

```
refresh_pattern -i ^http:\/\/www\.google\.com\/$ 0 20% 360 override-
expire override-lastmod ignore-reload ignore-no-cache ignore-no-store
reload-into-ims ignore-must-revalidate
```

Aborting the partial retrievals

When a client initiates a request for fetching some data and aborts it prematurely, Squid may continue to try and fetch the data. This may cause bandwidth and other resources such as processing power and memory to be wasted, however if we get subsequent requests for the same object, it'll result in a better HIT ratio. To counter act this problem, Squid provides three directives `quick_abort_min (KB)`, `quick_abort_max (KB)`, and `quick_abort_pct (percent)`.

For all the aborted requests, Squid will check the values for these directives and will take the appropriate action according to the following rules:

◆ If the remaining data that should be fetched is less than the value of `quick_abort_min`, Squid will continue to fetch it.

◆ If the remaining data to be transferred is more than the value of `quick_abort_max`, Squid will immediately abort the request.

◆ If the data that has already been transferred is more than `quick_abort_pct` percent of the total data, then Squid will keep retrieving the data.

Both the `quick_abort_min` and `quick_abort_max` values are in `KiloBytes (KB)` (or any allowed memory size unit) while `quick_abort_pct` is a percentage value. If we want to abort the requests in all cases, which may be required if we are short of bandwidth. We should set `quick_abort_min` and `quick_abort_max` to zero. If we have a lot of spare bandwidth, we can set a higher values for `quick_abort_min` and `quick_abort_max`, and a relatively low value for `quick_abort_pct`. Let's see an example for a high bandwidth case:

```
quick_abort_min 1024 KB
quick_abort_max 2048 KB
quick_abort_pct 90
```

Caching the failed requests

Requests for resources which doesn't exist (HTTP Error 404) or a client doesn't have permission to access the requested resource (HTTP Error 403) are common and requests to such resources make up a significant percentage of the total requests. These responses are cacheable by Squid. However, sometimes web servers don't send the Expires HTTP headers in responses, which prevents Squid from caching these responses. To solve this problem, Squid provides the directive negative_ttl that forces such responses to be cached for the time specified. The syntax of negative_ttl is as follows:

```
negative_ttl TIME_UNITS
```

Previously, this value was five minutes by default, but in the newer versions of Squid, it is set to zero seconds by default.

Playing around with HTTP headers

As all the requests and responses pass through Squid, it can add, modify, or delete the HTTP headers accompanied with requests and responses. These actions are usually performed to achieve anonymity or to hide the client-specific information. Squid has three directives, namely, request_header_access, reply_header_access, and header_replace to modify the HTTP headers in requests and responses. Let's have a brief look at them.

 Please be warned that using any of these directives violates HTTP standards and may cause problems.

Controlling HTTP headers in requests

The directive request_header_access is used in combination with ACLs to determine whether a particular HTTP header will be retained in a request or if it will be dropped before forwarding the request. The advantage of having ACLs here is that they provide a lot of flexibility. We can selectively drop some HTTP headers for a few clients.

Let's have a look at the syntax of request_header_access:

```
request_header_access HEADER_NAME allow|deny [!]ACL_NAME ...
```

So, if we are not willing to expose what browsers our clients are using, we can easily drop the User-Agent header from requests. The following code will drop this particular header for all the requests:

```
request_header_access User-Agent deny all
```

The parameter `all` is a special keyword here representing all the HTTP headers. Similarly, if we don't want web servers to know about the browsing habits of our clients, we can start by dropping the `Referer` header from all the requests.

```
request_header_access Referer deny all
```

Again, please be warned that dropping these headers may cause serious problems in browsing. By default, no headers are removed.

Controlling HTTP headers in responses

Similar to the directive `request_header_access`, we have the `reply_header_access` directive to drop the HTTP headers in responses. The syntax and usage is similar. For example, for dropping the `Server` HTTP header, the example configuration line will be:

```
reply_header_access Server deny all
```

By default, all headers are retained and are sent they are received.

Replacing the contents of HTTP headers

While the previous two directives can only be used to drop any unwanted HTTP headers, the directive `header_replace` can be used to send false information to replace the contents of the headers. Please note that this directive replaces contents of headers which have been denied using the `request_header_access` directive and is valid only for requests and not responses. We use this directive to replace the contents of the headers with a static fixed value. Let's have a look at the syntax of `header_replace`:

```
header_replace HEADER_NAME TEXT_VALUE
```

For example, we can send out the `User-Agent` header reflecting that all our clients use the Firefox web browser. Let's see the code for this example:

```
header_replace User-Agent Mozilla/5.0 (X11; U; Linux i686; en-US;
rv:0.9.3) Gecko/20010801
```

Again, we want to warn you that web servers generally validate or need the `User-Agent` and other HTTP headers to serve the right content for a client, and modifying these headers may cause unexpected problems.

DNS server configuration

For every request received from a client, Squid needs to resolve the domain name before it can contact the target web server. For this purpose, Squid can either use the built-in internal DNS client or, external DNS program to resolve the hostnames. The default behavior is to use the internal DNS client for resolving hostnames unless we have used the `--disable-internal-dns` option but it must be set with the `configure` program before compiling Squid, as shown:

```
$ ./configure --disable-internal-dns
```

Let's have a quick look at the DNS-related configuration directives provided by Squid.

Specifying the DNS program path

The directive `cache_dns_program` is used to specify the path of the external DNS program built with Squid. If we have not moved the Squid-related file after installing, this directive will have the correct value, by default. However, if the DNS program is located at a different location, we can specify the path using the following directive:

```
cache_dns_program /path/to/dnsprogram
```

Controlling the number of DNS client processes

The number of parallel instances of the DNS program specified by `cache_dns_program` can be controlled by using the directive `dns_children`. The syntax of the directive `dns_children` is as follows:

```
dns_children max startup=n idle=n
```

The parameter `max` determines the maximum number of DNS programs which can run at any one time. We should set it to a significantly high value as Squid has to wait for the response from the DNS program before it can proceed any further and setting this number to a lower value will keep Squid waiting for the response. The default value is set to 32.

The value of the parameter `startup` determines the number of DNS programs that will be started when Squid starts. This can be set to zero and Squid will not start any processes by default. The first ever request to Squid will result in the creation of the first child process.

The value of the parameter `idle` determines the number of processes that will be available at any one time. More requests will result in the creation of more processes, but keeping this many processes free (available) is subject to a total of `max` processes. A minimum acceptable value for this parameter is 1.

Setting the DNS name servers

By default, Squid picks up the name servers from the file `/etc/resolv.conf`. However, if we want to specify a list of different name servers, we can use the directive `dns_nameservers`.

Time for action – adding DNS name servers

A list of IP addresses can be passed to this directive or several IP addresses can be written on different lines like the following:

```
dns_nameservers 192.0.2.25 198.51.100.25
dns_nameservers 203.0.113.25
```

The previous configuration lines will set the name servers to `192.0.2.25`, `198.51.100.25`, and `203.0.113.25`.

What just happened?

We added three DNS name servers to the Squid configuration file which will be used by Squid to resolve the domain names corresponding to the requests received from the clients.

Setting the hosts file

Squid can read the hostname and IP address associations from the hosts file generally found at `/etc/hosts`. This file normally contains hostnames for the machines or servers in the local area network. We can specify the host's file location using the directive `hosts_file` as shown:

```
hosts_file /etc/hosts
```

If we don't want Squid to read the host's file, we can set the value to `none`.

Default domain name for requests

Using the directive `append_domain`, we can append a default domain name to the hostnames without any period (.) in them. This is generally useful for handling local domain names. The value of the `append_domain` must begin with a period (`.`). For example:

```
append_domain .example.com
```

Timeout for DNS queries

If the DNS servers do not respond to the query within the time specified by the directive `dns_timeout`, they are assumed to be unavailable. The default timeout value is two minutes. Considering the ever increasing network speeds, we can set this to a slightly lower value. For example, if there is no response within one minute, we can consider the DNS service to be unavailable.

Caching the DNS responses

The IP addresses of most domains change quite rarely, so it's safe to cache the positive responses from DNS servers for a few hours. This doesn't provide much of a saving in bandwidth, but caching DNS responses may reduce the latency quite significantly because a DNS query is done for every request. For caching DNS responses while using an external DNS program, Squid provides two directives known as `positive_dns_ttl` and `negative_dns_ttl` to tune the caching of DNS responses.

The directive `positive_dns_ttl` determines the maximum time for which a positive DNS response will be cached while `negative_dns_ttl` determines the time for which a negative DNS response will be cached. The directive `negative_dns_ttl` also serves as a minimum time for which the positive DNS responses can be cached.

Let's see the example values for both of the directives:

```
positive_dns_ttl 8 hours
negative_dns_ttl 30 seconds
```

We should keep the time to live (TTL) for negative responses to a lower value as the negative responses may be due to problems with the DNS servers.

Setting the size of the DNS cache

Squid performs domain name to address lookups for all the MISS requests and address to domain name lookups for requests involving ACLs such as `dstdomain`. These lookups are cached. To control the size of these cached lookups, Squid exposes four directives—`ipcache_size (number)`, `ipcache_low (percent)`, `ipcache_high (percent)`, and `fqdncache_size (number)`. Let's see what these directives mean.

The directive `ipcache_size` determines the maximum number of entries that can be cached for domain name to address lookups. As these entries take really small amounts of memory and the amount of available main memory is enormous these days, we can cache tens of thousands of these entries. The default value for this directive is 1024, but we can easily push it to 15,000 on busy caches.

The directives `ipcache_low` (let's say 95) and `ipcache_high` (let's say 97) are low and high water marks for the IP cache. So, Squid will try to keep the number of entries in the cache between 95 percent and 97 percent.

Using `fqdncache_size`, we can simply set the maximum number of address to domain name lookups that can be in the cache at any time. These entries also take really small amounts of memory, so we can cache a large number of these. The default value is 1024, but we can easily push it to 10,000 on busy caches.

Logging

Squid logs all the client requests and events to files. Squid provides various directives to control the location of log files, format of log messages, and to choose which requests to log. Let's have a brief look at some of the directives. We'll learn about logging in detail in *Chapter 5*, *Understanding Log Files and Log Formats*.

Log formats

We can define multiple log formats using the directive `logformat` as well as the pre-defined log formats supplied by Squid. Log formats are basically an arrangement of one or more pre-defined format codes. Various log formats such as `squid`, `common`, `combined`, and so on, are provided by Squid, by default. We'll have a detailed look at defining additional log formats in *Chapter 5*.

Log file rotation or log file backups

Over a period of time, the log files grow in size. The common practice is to move the older logs to separate files as a backup or for analysis, and then continue writing the logs to the original log file. The default Squid behavior is to keep 10 backups of log files. We can change this behavior with the directive `logfile_rotate` as follows:

```
logfile_rotate 20
```

Log access

By default, Squid logs requests from all the clients to the log file set by the directive `access_log`. If we want to prevent some client requests from being logged by Squid, we can use the `log_access` directive along with ACLs. An example may be that the CEO doesn't want his requests to be logged:

```
acl ceo_laptop src 192.0.2.21
log_access deny ceo_laptop
```

> We should note that the requests denied for logging using this directive will not count towards performance measurements.

Buffered logs

By default, all the log files are written without buffering any output. Buffering the logs enhances/improves performance under heavy usage or when debugging is enabled. This directive is rarely used.

Strip query terms

Query terms are key-value pairs passed using a URL in a HTTP request. Sometimes, this may contain sensitive or private information about the client requesting the web resource. By default, Squid strips all the query terms from a request URL before logging it. Another reason for stripping query terms is that the query terms are often very long and can make monitoring the access log very painful. However, we may want to disable it sometime, especially while debugging a problem, for example, a client is not able to access a website properly.

```
strip_query_terms off
```

This configuration will prevent query terms from being stripped before requests are logged. It's a good practice to set this directive to on for protecting clients' privacy.

URL rewriters and redirectors

URL rewriters and redirectors are third party, independent helper programs that we can use with Squid to modify or rewrite requests from clients. In most cases, we try to redirect a client to a different web page or resource from the one that was initially requested by the client.

The interesting part is that URL rewriters can be coded in any programming language. URL rewriters are run as independent processes and communicate with Squid using standard I/O.

URL rewriters provide a totally new area of opportunity as we can redirect clients to custom error pages for different scenarios, redirect users to local mirrors of websites or software repositories, block advertisements with small blank images, and so on.

Squid doesn't have any URL rewriters by default as we are supposed to write our own URL rewriters because the possibilities are enormous. It is also possible to download URL rewriters written by others and use them right away. We'll learn about how to use or write our own URL rewriters in detail in *Chapter 11, Writing URL Redirectors and Rewriters*.

Other configuration directives

Squid has hundreds of configuration directives to control it in various ways. It's not possible to discuss all of them here, we'll try to cover the important ones.

Setting the effective user for running Squid

Although we generally start the Squid server as root, it never runs with the privileges of the root user. Right after starting, Squid changes its real UID (User ID)/GID (Group ID) to the user determined by the directive `cache_effective_user`. By default, it is set to `nobody`. We can create a separate user for running Squid and set the value of this directive accordingly. For example, on some operating systems, Squid is run as `squid` user. The corresponding configuration line will be as follows:

```
cache_effective_user squid
```

Please make sure that the user specified as the value for `cache_effective_user` exists.

Configuring hostnames for the proxy server

Squid uses hostnames for the server for forwarding requests to other cache peers or for detecting the neighbor caches. There two different directives named `visible_hostname` and `unique_hostname` which are used to set the hostname of the proxy server for different purposes. Let's have a quick look at these directives.

Hostname visible to everyone

The directive `visible_hostname` is used to set the hostname, which will be visible on all the error or information pages used by Squid. We can set it as shown:

```
visible_hostname proxy.example.com
```

Unique hostname for the server

If we want to name all the proxy servers in our network as `proxy.example.com`, we can achieve it by setting `visible_hostname` for all of them to `proxy.example.com`. However, doing so will cause problems in forwarding requests among the caches and detecting forward loops. To solve this problem, Squid provides the directive `unique_hostname`. We should set this to a unique hostname value to get rid of forward loops.

```
unique_hostname proxy1.example.com
```

Controlling the request forwarding

If we have cache peers or neighbors in our network, Squid will try to contact them for HITs or for forwarding requests. We can control the manner in which the requests are forwarded to other caches using the directives `always_direct`, `never_direct`, `hierarchy_stoplist`, `prefer_direct`, and `cache_peer_access`. Next we'll have a look at a few of these directives with examples.

Always direct

Sometimes we may want Squid to fetch the content directly from origin servers instead of forwarding the queries to neighboring caches. This is achieved using the directive `always_direct`. The syntax is similar to `http_access`:

```
always_direct allow|deny [!]ACL_NAME
```

This directive is very useful in forwarding requests to servers in the local area network directly because contacting cache peers may introduce an unnecessary delay.

```
acl lan_servers dst 192.0.2.0/24
always_direct allow lan_servers
```

This code will instruct Squid to forward requests to destination servers identified by `lan_servers` directly to the origin servers and the requests will not be routed through other cache peers.

Never direct

This directive is opposite of `always_direct`, but we should understand it carefully before using it. If we want to enforce the use of a proxy server for all the client requests, then this directive comes handy.

```
never_direct allow all
```

This rule will enforce the usage of a proxy server for all the requests. However, generally, it's a good practice to allow clients to connect directly to local servers. So, we can use something similar to the following:

```
acl lan_servers dst 192.0.2.0/24
never_direct deny lan_servers
never_direct allow all
```

These rules will make sure that requests to all the servers, except those identified by `lan_servers`, go through another proxy server.

Hierarchy stoplist

This is a simple directive preventing the forwarding of client requests to neighbor caches. Let's have a look at the syntax:

```
hierarchy_stoplist word1 word2 word3 ...
```

If any of the words from the list of words is found in the request URL, the request will not be forwarded to the neighbor caches and the origin servers will be contacted directly. This directive is generally helpful for handling dynamic pages directly instead of routing them using cache peers.

```
hierarchy_stoplist cgi-bin jsp ?
```

This code will prevent the forwarding of URLs containing any of `cgi-bin`, `jsp`, or `?` to cache peers.

> Please note that the directive `never_direct` overrides `hierarchy_stoplist`.

Broken posts

Some web servers have broken implementations of the POST method (a method using which we can securely send data to the web server) and they expect a pair of CRLF (new-line) after the POST request data. Using the `broken_posts` directive, we can request Squid to send an extra CRLF pair after the POST request data.

```
acl bad_server dstdomain broken.example.com
broken_posts allow bad_server
```

The rules in this code will take care of the broken implementation of the POST method on the host `broken.example.com`. We should use this directive only if its absolutely necessary.

TCP outgoing address

This directive is useful for forwarding requests to different network interfaces, depending on the client's network. Let's have a look at the syntax for this directive:

```
tcp_outgoing_address ip_address [[!]ACL_NAME]
```

In this line, `ip_address` is the IP address of the outgoing interface which we want to use. The ACL name is totally optional. An example case may be when we want to route traffic for a specific network using a different network interface:

```
acl special_network src 192.0.2.0/24
tcp_outgoing_address 198.51.100.25 special_network
tcp_outgoing_address 198.51.100.86
```

The previous code will set the outgoing address for requests from clients in the network `192.0.2.0/24` to `198.51.100.25`, and for all other requests the outgoing address will be set to `198.51.100.86`.

PID filename

Just like several other programs for Unix/Linux, Squid writes the process ID of the current process in a PID file. This directive is used to control the location of a PID file.

```
pid_filename /var/run/squid.pid
```

If we don't want Squid to write its process ID to any file, we can use none instead of filename:

```
pid_filename none
```

 Setting the path of the PID file to none will prevent regular management operations like automatic log rotation or restarting Squid. The operating system will not be able to stop Squid at the time of a shutdown or restart.

Client netmask

By default Squid logs the complete IP address of the client for every request. To enhance the privacy of our clients, we can use this directive to hide the actual IP addresses of the clients. Let's see an example:

```
client_netmask 255.255.255.0
```

If a client with the IP address 192.0.2.21 accesses our proxy server, then his address will be logged as 192.0.2.0 instead of 192.0.2.21 because Squid will set the last 8 bits of the IP address to zero. Basically, a logical AND operation is performed between binary version of the netmask and the IP address to be logged. The same IP address will also be reflected in the cache manager's web interface.

Pop quiz

1. Consider the following snippet from the Squid configuration file:
    ```
    http_port 192.0.2.22:8080
    http_port 192.0.2.22:3128
    ```

    Which one of the following is true?

    a. Squid will listen on port 8080 on all interfaces.

    b. Squid will listen on port 3128 on all interfaces.

    c. Squid will listen on port 8080 and 3128 on all interfaces.

    d. Squid will listen on port 8080 and 3128 on interface with IP address 192.0.2.22.

2. Consider the following lines from the Squid configuration file:

   ```
   acl exapmile_sites dstdomain .example.com .example.net
   ```

   We want to deny access to the requests identified by the ACL `example_sites`. Which one of the following rules will not do it?

   a. `http_access deny example_sites`

   b. `http_access deny Example_sites`

   c. `http_access deny ExampleSites`

   d. `http_access deny Example_Sites`

3. Consider the following Squid configuration:

   ```
   acl blocked_clients src 192.0.2.0/24
   acl special_client src 192.0.2.21
   http_access deny blocked_clients
   http_access allow special_client
   ```

   What will happen when a client with an IP Address `192.0.2.21` tries to access the web through our Squid proxy server?

   a. They will be denied access.

   b. Sometimes because of the allow rule.

   c. The configuration is ambiguous and Squid will crash.

   d. Squid will not crash but it'll not be able to determine definite access permissions.

4. Which of the following is correct?

   a. Total memory used by Squid is determined by `cache_mem`.

   b. Total memory used by Squid is more than that specified using `cache_mem`.

   c. Total memory used by Squid is less than that specified using `cache_mem`.

   d. Total memory used by Squid is independent of the memory specified using `cache_mem`.

5. Let's say we have the following line in our configuration file:

   ```
   append_domain .google.com
   ```

   If a client tries to browse to the website `http://mail/`. What will the result be?

   a. The client will get an error saying domain not found.

   b. Nothing will happen.

   c. Squid will crash.

   d. Client will automatically be redirected to `http://mail.google.com/`.

Summary

We have learned a lot in this chapter about configuring Squid. After this chapter, we should feel more comfortable in dealing with the Squid configuration file. We should be able to apply the things we learnt in this chapter to fine tune Squid to achieve better performance.

Although we learned about a lot of configuration directives, we specifically covered:

♦ The syntax of the configuration file. We learned about various types of directives generally used in the configuration file and the possible types of values that they take.

♦ Caching in the main memory and hard disk in detail. We learned about using RAM and disks for caching in an optimized manner to achieve higher HIT ratio.

♦ Fine tuning the cache. We learned about achieving a better HIT ratio by tinkering with various HTTP headers.

♦ The required DNS configuration for Squid. We learned about specifying DNS servers and optimizing the DNS cache to reduce latency.

We also discussed restricting access to the Squid server, modifying HTTP headers, and had a brief overview of cache peers and the logging system.

Now that we have learned about configuring Squid, we are ready to proceed with running the Squid server, which is the topic of the next chapter.

3
Running Squid

In the previous chapters, we had learned about compiling, installing, and configuring the Squid proxy server. In this chapter, we are going to learn about the different ways of running Squid and the available options that can be passed to Squid from the command line. We will also learn about debugging the Squid configuration file.

In this chapter, we will learn the following:

- ◆ Various command line options for running Squid
- ◆ Parsing the squid configuration file for syntax errors
- ◆ Using an alternate squid configuration file for testing purposes
- ◆ Different ways of starting Squid
- ◆ Rotating log files generated by Squid

Let's get started and explore the previous points.

Command line options

Normally, all of the Squid configuration options reside with in the `squid.conf` file (the main Squid configuration file). To tweak the Squid functionality, the preferred method is to change the options in the `squid.conf` file. However there are some options which can also be controlled using additional command line options while running Squid.

These options are not very popular and are rarely used, but these are very useful for debugging problems without the Squid proxy server. Before exploring the command line options, let's see how Squid is run from the command line.

As we saw in the first chapter, the location of the Squid binary file depends on the `--prefix` option passed to the `configure` command before compiling. So, depending upon the value of the `--prefix` option, the location of the Squid executable may be one of `/usr/local/sbin/squid` or `${prefix}/sbin/squid`, where `${prefix}` is the value of the option `--prefix` passed to the `configure` command. Therefore, to run Squid, we need to run one of the following commands on the terminal:

- When the `--prefix` option was not used with the `configure` command, the default location of the Squid executable will be `/usr/local/sbin/squid`.
- When the `--prefix` option was used and was set to a directory, then the location of the Squid executable will be `${prefix}/sbin/squid`.

It's painful to type the absolute path for Squid to run. So, to avoid typing the absolute path, we can include the path to the Squid executable in our PATH shell variable, using the `export` command as shown in the following example:

```
$ export PATH=$PATH:/usr/local/sbin/
```

Alternatively, we can use the following command:

```
$ export PATH=$PATH:/opt/squid/sbin/
```

We can also add the preceding command to our `~/.bashrc` or `~/.bash_profile` file to avoid running the `export` command every time we enter a new shell.

After setting the PATH shell variable appropriately, we can run Squid by simply typing the following command on shell:

```
$ squid
```

This command will run Squid after loading the configuration options from the `squid.conf` file.

 We'll be using the `squid` command without an absolute path for running the Squid process. Please use the appropriate path according to the installation prefix which you have chosen.

Now that we know how to run Squid from the command line, let's have a look at the various command line options.

Getting a list of available options

Before actually moving forward, we should firstly check the available set of options for our Squid installation.

Time for action – listing the options

Like a lot of other Linux programs, Squid also provides the option -h which can be used
to retrieve a list of options:

`squid -h`

The previous command will result in the following output:

```
Usage: squid [-cdhvzCFNRVYX] [-s | -l facility] [-f config-file] [-[au]
port] [-k signal]
    -a port   Specify HTTP port number (default: 3128).
    -d level  Write debugging to stderr also.
    -f file   Use given config-file instead of
              /opt/squid/etc/squid.conf.
    -h   Print help message.
    -k   reconfigure|rotate|shutdown|interrupt|kill|debug|check|parse
             Parse configuration file, then send signal to
             running copy (except -k parse) and exit.
    -s | -l facility
             Enable logging to syslog.
    -u   port Specify ICP port number (default: 3130), disable with 0.
    -v   Print version.
    -z   Create swap directories.
    -C   Do not catch fatal signals.
    -F   Don't serve any requests until store is rebuilt.
    -N   No daemon mode.
    -R   Do not set REUSEADDR on port.
    -S   Double-check swap during rebuild.
. . .
```

We will now have a look at a few important options from the preceding list. We will also,
have a look at the squid(8) man page or http://linux.die.net/man/8/squid for
more details.

What just happened?

We have just used the squid command to list the available options which we can use on the
command line.

Getting information about our Squid installation

Various features may vary across different versions of Squid. Before proceeding any further, it's a good idea to know the version of Squid installed on our machine.

Time for action – finding out the Squid version

Just in case we want to check which version of Squid we are using or the options we used with the `configure` command before compiling, we can use the option `-v` on the command line. Let's run Squid with this option:

```
squid -v
```

If we try to run the preceding command in the terminal, it will produce an output similar to the following:

```
Squid Cache: Version 3.1.10
configure options:  '--config-cache' '--prefix=/opt/squid/' '--enable-
storeio=ufs,aufs' '--enable-removal-policies=lru,heap' '--enable-icmp'
'--enable-useragent-log' '--enable-referer-log' '--enable-cache-digests'
'--with-large-files' --enable-ltdl-convenience
```

What just happened?

We used the `squid` command with the `-v` option to find out the version of Squid installed on our machine, and the options used with the `configure` command before compiling Squid.

Creating cache or swap directories

As we learned in the previous chapter, the cache directories specified using the `cache_dir` directive in the `squid.conf` file, must already exist before Squid can actually use them.

Time for action – creating cache directories

Squid provides the `-z` command line option to create the swap directories. Let's see an example:

```
squid -z
```

If this option is used and the cache directories don't exist already, the output will look similar to the following:

```
2010/07/20 21:48:35| Creating Swap Directories
2010/07/20 21:48:35| Making directories in /squid_cache/00
```

```
2010/07/20 21:48:35| Making directories in /squid_cache/01
2010/07/20 21:48:35| Making directories in /squid_cache/02
2010/07/20 21:48:35| Making directories in /squid_cache/03
...
```

We should use this option whenever we add new cache directories in the Squid configuration file.

What just happened?

When the squid command is run with the option -z, Squid reads all the cache directories from the configuration file and checks if they already exist. It will then create the directory structure for all the cache directories that don't exist.

Have a go hero – adding cache directories

Add two or three test cache directories with different values of level 1 (8, 16, and 32) and level 2 (64, 256, and 512) to the configuration file. Then try creating them using the squid command. Now study the difference in the directory structure.

Using a different configuration file

The default location for Squid's main configuration file is ${prefix}/etc/squid/squid. conf. Whenever we run Squid, the main configuration is read from the default location. While testing or deploying a new configuration, we may want to use a different configuration file just to check whether it will work or not. We can achieve this by using the option -f, which allows us to specify a custom location for the configuration file. Let's see an example:

```
squid -f /etc/squid.minimal.conf
# OR
squid -f /etc/squid.alternate.conf
```

If Squid is run this way, Squid will try to load the configuration from /etc/squid.minimal. conf or /etc/squid.alternate.conf, and it will completely ignore the squid.conf from the default location.

Getting verbose output

When we run Squid from the terminal without any additional command line options, only warnings and errors are displayed on the terminal (or stderr). However, while testing, we would like to get a verbose output on the terminal, to see what is happening when Squid starts up.

Time for action – debugging output in the console

To get more information on the terminal, we can use the option -d. The following is an example:

```
squid -d 2
```

We must specify an integer with the option -d to indicate the verbosity level. Let's have a look at the meaning of the different levels:

- Only critical and fatal errors are logged when level 0 (zero) is used.

- Level 1 includes the logging of important problems.

- Level 2 and higher includes the logging of informative details and other actions.

Higher levels result in more output on the terminal. A sample output on the terminal with level 2 would look similar to the following:

```
2010/07/20 21:40:53| Starting Squid Cache version 3.1.10 for i686-pc-linux-gnu...

2010/07/20 21:40:53| Process ID 15861

2010/07/20 21:40:53| With 1024 file descriptors available

2010/07/20 21:40:53| Initializing IP Cache...

2010/07/20 21:40:53| DNS Socket created at [::], FD 7

2010/07/20 21:40:53| Adding nameserver 192.168.36.222 from /etc/resolv.conf

2010/07/20 21:40:53| User-Agent logging is disabled.

2010/07/20 21:40:53| Referer logging is disabled.

2010/07/20 21:40:53| Unlinkd pipe opened on FD 13

2010/07/20 21:40:53| Local cache digest enabled; rebuild/rewrite every 3600/3600 sec

2010/07/20 21:40:53| Store logging disabled

2010/07/20 21:40:53| Swap maxSize 0 + 262144 KB, estimated 20164 objects

2010/07/20 21:40:53| Target number of buckets: 1008

2010/07/20 21:40:53| Using 8192 Store buckets

2010/07/20 21:40:53| Max Mem  size: 262144 KB

2010/07/20 21:40:53| Max Swap size: 0 KB

2010/07/20 21:40:53| Using Least Load store dir selection

2010/07/20 21:40:53| Current Directory is /opt/squid/sbin

2010/07/20 21:40:53| Loaded Icons.
```

```
2010/07/20 21:40:53| Accepting  HTTP connections at [::]:3128, FD 14.
2010/07/20 21:40:53| HTCP Disabled.
2010/07/20 21:40:53| Squid modules loaded: 0
2010/07/20 21:40:53| Ready to serve requests.
2010/07/20 21:40:54| storeLateRelease: released 0 objects
...
```

As we can see, Squid is trying to dump a log of actions that it is performing. The messages shown are mostly startup messages and there will be fewer messages when Squid starts accepting connections.

 Starting Squid in debug mode is quite helpful when Squid is up and running and users complain about poor speeds or being unable to connect. We can have a look at the debugging output and the appropriate actions to take.

What just happened?

We started Squid in debugging mode and can now see Squid writing an output on the command line, which is basically a log of the actions which Squid is performing. If Squid is not working, we'll be able to see the reasons on the command line and we'll be able to take actions accordingly.

Full debugging output on the terminal

The option -d specifies the verbosity level of the output dumped by Squid on the terminal. If we require all of the debugging information on the terminal, we can use the option -X, which will force Squid to write debugging information at every single step. If the option -X is used, we'll see information about parsing the squid.conf file and the actions taken by Squid, based on the configuration directives encountered. Let's see a sample output produced when option -X is used:

```
...
2010/07/21 21:50:51.515| Processing: 'acl my_machines src 172.17.8.175
10.2.44.46 127.0.0.1 172.17.11.68 192.168.1.3'
2010/07/21 21:50:51.515| ACL::Prototype::Registered: invoked for type src
2010/07/21 21:50:51.515| ACL::Prototype::Registered:     yes
2010/07/21 21:50:51.515| ACL::FindByName 'my_machines'
2010/07/21 21:50:51.515| ACL::FindByName found no match
2010/07/21 21:50:51.515| aclParseAclLine: Creating ACL 'my_machines'
2010/07/21 21:50:51.515| ACL::Prototype::Factory: cloning an object for
type 'src'
```

```
2010/07/21 21:50:51.515|  aclParseIpData: 172.17.8.175
2010/07/21 21:50:51.515|  aclParseIpData: 10.2.44.46
2010/07/21 21:50:51.515|  aclParseIpData: 127.0.0.1
2010/07/21 21:50:51.515|  aclParseIpData: 172.17.11.68
2010/07/21 21:50:51.515|  aclParseIpData: 192.168.1.3
. . .
```

Let's see what this output means. In the first line, Squid encountered a line defining an ACL my_machines. The next few lines in the output describe Squid invoking different methods to parse, creating a new ACL, and then assigning values to it. This option can be very helpful while debugging ambiguous ACLs.

Running as a normal process

Sometime during testing, we may not want Squid to run as a daemon. Instead, we may want it to run as a normal process which we can interrupt easily by pressing CTRL-C. To achieve this, we can use the option -N. When this option is used, Squid will not run in the background it will run in the current shell instead.

Parsing the Squid configuration file for errors or warnings

It's a good idea to parse or check the configuration file (squid.conf) for any errors or warnings before we actually try to run Squid, or reload a Squid process which is already running in a production deployment. Squid provides an option -k with an argument parse, which, if supplied, will force Squid to parse the current Squid configuration file and report any errors and warnings. Squid -k is also used to check and report directive and option changes when we upgrade our Squid version.

Time for action – testing our configuration file

As we learned before, we can use the -k parse option to test our configuration file. Now, we are going to add a test line and see if Squid can catch the error.

1. For example, let's add the following line to our squid.conf file:
    unknown_directive 1234

2. Now we'll run Squid with the -k parse option as follows:
    ```
    squid -k parse
    ```

3. As `unknown_directive` is not a valid directive for the Squid configuration file, we should get an error similar to the following:

```
2010/07/21 22:28:40| cache_cf.cc(346) squid.conf:945 unrecognized:
'unknown_directive'
```

So, if we find an error within our configuration file, we can go back and fix the errors and then parse the configuration file again.

What just happened?

We first added an invalid line in to our configuration file and then tried to parse it using a `squid` command which resulted in an error. It is a good idea to always parse the configuration file before starting Squid.

Sending various signals to a running Squid process

Squid provides the `-k` option to send various signals to a Squid process which is already running. Using this option, we can send various management signals such as, reload the configuration file, rotate the log files, shut down the proxy server, switch to debug mode, and many more. Let's have a look at some of the important signals which are available.

 Please note that when the argument `parse` is used with the option `-k`, no signal is sent to the running Squid process.

Reloading a new configuration file in a running process

We may need to make changes to our Squid configuration file sometimes, even when it is deployed in production mode. In such cases, after making changes, we don't want to restart our proxy server because that will introduce a significant downtime and will also interrupt active connections between clients and remote servers. In these situations, we can use the option `-k` with `reconfigure` as an argument, to signal Squid to re-read the configuration file and apply the new settings:

```
squid -k reconfigure
```

The previous command will force Squid to re-read the configuration file, while serving the requests normally and not terminating any active connections.

 It's good practice to parse the configuration file for any errors or warning using the `-k parse` option before issuing the `reconfigure` signal.

Shutting down the Squid process

To shut down a Squid process which is already running, we can issue a shutdown signal with the help of the option -k as follows:

```
squid -k shutdown
```

Squid tries to terminate connections gracefully when it receives a shutdown signal. It will allow the active connection to finish before the process is completely shut down or terminated.

Interrupting or killing a running Squid process

If we have a lot of clients, Squid can take a significant amount of time before it completely terminates itself on receiving the -k shutdown signal. To get Squid to immediately stop serving requests, we can use the -k interrupt signal. The -k interrupt signal will not allow Squid to wait for active connections to finish and will stop the process immediately.

In some cases, the Squid process may not be stopped using -k shutdown or -k interrupt signals. If we want to terminate the process immediately, we can issue a -k kill signal, which will immediately kill the process. This signal should only be used when Squid can't be stopped with -k shutdown or -k interrupt. For example, to send a -k kill signal to Squid, we can use the following command:

```
squid -k kill
```

This command will kill the Squid process immediately.

 Please note that shutdown, interrupt, and kill are Squid signals and not the system kill signals which are emulated.

Checking the status of a running Squid process

To know whether a Squid process is already running or not, we can issue a check signal which will tell us the status of the Squid process. Squid will also validate the configuration file and report any fatal problems. If the Squid process is running fine, the following command will exit without printing anything:

```
squid -k check
```

Otherwise, if the process has exited, this command will give an error similar to the following error message:

```
squid: ERROR: Could not send signal 0 to process 25243: (3) No such
process
```

Have a go hero – check the return value

After running `squid -k check`, find out the return value or status in scenarios when:

- Squid was running
- Squid was not running

Solution: The return value or the status of a command can be found out by using the command `echo $?`. This will print the return status or value of the previous command that was executed in the same shell. Return values should be (1) -> 0, (2) -> 1.

Sending a running process in to debug mode

If we didn't start Squid in debug mode and for testing we don't want to stop an already running Squid process, we can issue a `debug` signal which will send the already running process into debug mode. The debugging output will then be written to Squid's `cache.log` file located at `${prefix}/var/logs/cache.log` or `/var/log/squid/cache.log`.

 The Squid process running in debug mode may write a log of debugging output to the `cache.log` file and may quickly consume a lot of disk space.

Rotating the log files

The log files used by Squid grow in size over a period of time and can consume a significant amount of disk space. To get rid of the older logs, Squid provides a `rotate` signal that can be issued when we want to rotate the existing log files. Upon receiving this signal, Squid will close the current log files, move them to other filenames, or delete them based on the configuration directive `logfile_rotate` (in `squid.conf`) then reopen the files to write the logs.

It's quite inconvenient to rotate log files manually. So, we can automate the process of log file rotation with the help of a cron job. Let's say we want to rotate the log files at midnight, the corresponding cron tab entry will be:

```
59 23 * * * /opt/squid/sbin/squid -k rotate
```

Please note that the path to Squid executable may differ depending on the installation prefix. We'll learn more about log files in *Chapter 5, Understanding Log Files and Log Formats*.

Forcing the storage metadata to rebuild

When Squid starts, it tries to load the storage metadata. If Squid fails to load the storage metadata, then it will try to rebuild it. If it receives any requests during that period, Squid will try to satisfy those requests in parallel, which results in slow rebuild. We can force Squid to rebuild the metadata before it starts processing any requests using the option -F on the command line. This may result in a quick rebuild of storage metadata but clients may have to wait for a significant time, if the cache is large. For large caches, we should try to avoid this option:

```
squid -F
```

Squid will now rebuild the cache metadata and will not serve any client requests until the metadata rebuild process is complete.

Double checking swap during rebuild

The option -F determines whether Squid should serve requests while the storage metadata is being rebuilt. We have another option, -S, which can be used to force Squid to double check the cache during rebuild. If we use the -S option along with the option -d as follows:

```
squid -S -d 1
```

This will produce a debugging output on the terminal which will look similar to the following:

```
2010/07/21 21:29:22| Beginning Validation Procedure

2010/07/21 21:29:22| UFSSwapDir::doubleCheck: SIZE MISMATCH

2010/07/21 21:29:22| UFSSwapDir::doubleCheck: ENTRY SIZE: 1332, FILE
SIZE: 114

2010/07/21 21:29:22| UFSSwapDir::dumpEntry: FILENO 00000092

2010/07/21 21:29:22| UFSSwapDir::dumpEntry: PATH /squid_
cache/00/00/00000092

2010/07/21 21:29:22| StoreEntry->key: 0060E9E547F3A1AAEEDE369C5573F8D9

2010/07/21 21:29:22| StoreEntry->next: 0

2010/07/21 21:29:22| StoreEntry->mem_obj: 0

2010/07/21 21:29:22| StoreEntry->timestamp: 1248375049

2010/07/21 21:29:22| StoreEntry->lastref: 1248375754

2010/07/21 21:29:22| StoreEntry->expires: 1279911049

2010/07/21 21:29:22| StoreEntry->lastmod: 1205097338

2010/07/21 21:29:22| StoreEntry->swap_file_sz: 1332

2010/07/21 21:29:22| StoreEntry->refcount: 1

2010/07/21 21:29:22| StoreEntry->flags: CACHABLE,DISPATCHED

2010/07/21 21:29:22| StoreEntry->swap_dirn: 0
```

```
2010/07/21 21:29:22| StoreEntry->swap_filen: 146
2010/07/21 21:29:22| StoreEntry->lock_count: 0
2010/07/21 21:29:22| StoreEntry->mem_status: 0
...
```

Squid is basically trying to validate each and every cached object on the disk.

Automatically starting Squid at system startup

Once we have a properly configured and running proxy server, we would like it to start whenever the system is started or rebooted. Next, we'll have a brief look at the most common ways of adding or modifying the boot scripts for popular operating systems. These methods will most probably work on your operating system. If they don't, please refer to the corresponding operating system manual for information on boot scripts.

Adding Squid command to /etc/rc.local file

Adding the full path of the Squid executable file is the easiest way to start Squid on system startup. The file /etc/rc.local is executed after the system boots as the super or root user. We can place the Squid command in this file and it will run every time the system boots up. Add the following line at the end of the /etc/rc.local file:

```
${prefix}/sbin/squid
```

Please replace ${prefix} with the installation prefix which you used before compiling Squid.

Adding init script

Alternatively, we can add a simple init script which will be a simple shell script to start the Squid process or send various signals to a running Squid process. Init scripts are supported by most operating systems and are generally located at /etc/init.d/, /etc/rc.d/, or /etc/rc.d/init.d/. Any shell script placed in any of these directories is executed at system startup with root privileges.

Time for action – adding the init script

We are going to use a simple shell script, as shown in the following example, which takes a single command line argument and acts accordingly:

```
#!/bin/bash
# init script to control Squid server
case "$1" in
```

```
start)

  /opt/squid/sbin/squid

  ;;


stop)

  /opt/squid/sbin/squid -k shutdown

  ;;


reload)

  /opt/squid/sbin/squid -k reconfigure

  ;;


restart)

  /opt/squid/sbin/squid -k shutdown

  sleep 2

  /opt/squid/sbin/squid

  ;;


*)

  echo $"Usage: $0 {start|stop|reload|restart}"

  exit 2

esac

exit $?
```

Please note the absolute path to the Squid executable here and change it accordingly. We can save this shell script to a file with the name squid and then move it to one of the directories we discussed earlier depending on our operating system.

 The Squid source carries an init script located at contrib/squid.
rc, but it's installed only on a few systems by default.

What just happened?

We added an init script to control the Squid proxy server. Using this script, we can start, stop, restart, or reload the process. It's important that the script is placed in the correct directory, otherwise the Squid proxy server will not start on system startup.

Pop quiz

1. What should be the first step undertaken after adding new cache directories to the configuration file?

    a.   Reboot the server.

    b.   Run the `squid` command with the `-z` option.

    c.   Do nothing, Squid will take care of everything by itself.

    d.   Run Squid with root privileges.

2. Where should we look for errors in case Squid is not running properly?

    a.   Access log file.

    b.   Cache log file.

    c.   Squid configuration file.

    d.   None of the above.

3. In which scenario should we avoid debug mode?

    a.   While testing the server.

    b.   While Squid is deployed in production mode.

    c.   When we have a lot of spare disk space.

    d.   When we have a lot of spare RAM.

Summary

In this chapter, we learned about the various command line options which can be used while running Squid, how to start the Squid process in a different mode, and how to send signals to a process which is already running. We also learned about creating new cache directories after adding them to the Squid configuration file.

We specifically covered the following:

◆   Parsing the Squid configuration file for errors and warnings.

◆   Using various options to get suitable debugging outputs while testing.

◆   Reloading a new configuration in a Squid process which is already running, without interrupting service.

◆   Automatic rotation of log files to recover disk space.

We also learned about configuring our system to start a Squid process whenever the system boots up.

Now that we have learned about running a Squid process, we're ready to explore access control lists in detail and test them on a live Squid server.

4
Getting Started with Squid's Powerful ACLs and Access Rules

In the previous chapters, we learned about installing, configuring, and running Squid in different modes. We also learned the basics of protecting our Squid proxy server from unauthorized access, and granting or revoking access based on different criteria. We previously had a brief overview of Access Control Lists in Chapter 2, Configuring Squid. However, in this chapter, we are going to explore Access Control Lists in detail. We'll also construct rules for a few example scenarios.

In this chapter, we will learn about:

- Various types of ACL lists
- Types of access rules
- Mixing ACL lists and access list rules to achieve complex access rules
- Testing access rules with `squidclient`

Once we have a Squid proxy server up and running, we can define rules for allowing or denying access to different people or to control the usage of resources. It is also possible to define lower and upper limits on the usage of different resources. Access list rules, which are basically combinations of allow or deny keyword and ACL elements, play a vital role in achieving this type of control. So let's get started.

Access control lists

Access Control Lists are the base elements in the Squid configuration file, which help in identifying web transactions, by various attributes of that transaction. We have already learned about the syntax for constructing ACLs in *Chapter 2*. So, let's write an ACL element that can identify all the requests from a group of clients in the IP range `192.0.2.1` to `192.0.2.127`.

```
acl clients src 192.0.2.0/25
```

That was quite easy, as `192.0.2.0/25` denotes that the first 25 bits of the available 32 bits in the IP address are fixed and only the last seven bits can vary, which will result in the range 0-127. In the configuration above, `192.0.2.0/25` denotes a subnet with 127 possible IP addresses. For more information on subnets, please check `http://en.wikipedia.org/wiki/Subnetwork#IPv4_subnetting`.

In the previous ACL element, we used the `src` ACL type to identify the IP address of the source of the request. There are various other ACL types available, which can be used to identify requests and specify actions that should be taken for the identified requests. So, let's have a look at a few important ACL types.

Fast and slow ACL types

All ACL types fall into two major categories known as fast and slow ACL types. The fast ACL types use information accompanied with a web transaction. These ACL types generally perform matching against the source IP address, destination domain name, URL, HTTP request header fields, and so on. The slow ACL types need to perform additional lookups, and this introduces a significant delay which is why they are known as the slow ACL types. The examples of slow ACL types are `dst` and `srcdomain`, as these will involve DNS and reverse DNS lookups respectively. For a list of the latest fast and slow ACL types, please check `http://wiki.squid-cache.org/SquidFaq/SquidAcl#Fast_and_Slow_ACLs`.

Source and destination IP address

Every request received by Squid from a client has several properties such as the source IP address, destination IP address, source domain, destination domain, source MAC address, and so on. So, when we define an ACL element, we basically try to pick up a request and match its properties with a pre-determined value.

Time for action – constructing ACL lists using IP addresses

1. The two ACL types, `src` and `dst`, are used to identify the source and destination IP addresses of a particular request. There are different ways to specify the IP addresses. The first one is to specify a single IP address per ACL element, as follows:

   `acl client src 192.0.2.25/32`

2. The previous ACL element will match all the requests being generated from the client `192.0.2.25`. We are supposed to specify a mask while specifying the IP address, but if we don't then, Squid will try to determine the mask automatically. To learn more about mask, and Classless Inter Domain Routing (CIDR) notation, please check `http://en.wikipedia.org/wiki/Classless_Inter-Domain_Routing` and `http://en.wikipedia.org/wiki/CIDR_notation`. For example, the ACL following element will also identify the requests from the client `192.0.2.25`:

   `acl client src 192.0.2.25`

3. Therefore, in the previous example, Squid will automatically set the mask to `32`. So we have covered the ways to specify a single IP address, now let's a have a look at the ways in which to specify multiple IP address.

In its simplest form, we can specify multiple addresses using subnets. If we want to specify clients in multiple continuous subnets which can't be represented as a single subnet, we can specify them using a range of subnets. Let's say we want to identify all the clients in a small research lab which has IP addresses ranging from `192.0.2.0` to `192.0.2.31`. Let's see the ACL for this case:

`acl research_lab src 192.0.2.0/27`

The above ACL element will identify the IP addresses in the range `192.0.2.0` to `192.0.2.31` as only the last five bits of the last octet in the IP address are variable.

Constructing an ACL element with the ACL type `dst` is similar. Let's say we want to write an ACL that will identify all requests destined to `198.51.100.86`. We can use the following `dst` ACL type:

`acl website dst 198.51.100.86`

The previous ACL element will identify all requests that are destined to the IP address `198.51.100.86`.

 The `src` and `dst` are fast and slow ACL types respectively.

What just happened?

We have just learned about two simple ways of specifying multiple IP addresses while constructing ACL lists which use source and destination IP addresses in a request. These are the most popular techniques of specifying IP addresses because they are simple to interpret and chances of confusion are very low.

Time for action – using a range of IP addresses to build ACL lists

Now, let's say in a company, the marketing department is spread over five floors. We have used a convention 10.1.FLOOR_NUM.MACHINE_NUM to assign IP addresses to each machine on every floor. The floor number starts from two and goes up to six. So, we basically have the following subnets.

```
10.1.2.0/24 # 2nd Floor
10.1.3.0/24 # 3rd Floor
10.1.4.0/24 # 4th Floor
10.1.5.0/24 # 5th Floor
10.1.6.0/24 # 6th Floor
```

A simple way to identify all these client computers is defined in the following ACL:

```
acl mkt_dept src 10.1.2.0/24 10.1.3.0/24 10.1.4.0/24 10.1.5.0/24
10.1.6.0/24
```

The previous methods are a bit cluttered and long winded. Squid provides a simple way to specify multiple addresses the following is an example of this:

```
acl mkt_dept src 10.1.2.0-10.1.6.0/24
```

The preceding ACL defining mkt_dept is simply a shortened version of the following:

```
acl mkt_dept src 10.1.2.0/24
acl mkt_dept src 10.1.3.0/24
acl mkt_dept src 10.1.4.0/24
acl mkt_dept src 10.1.5.0/24
acl mkt_dept src 10.1.6.0/24
```

So, we can use the shortened example for specifying continuous subnets. Another good use of this method is to specify continuous IP addresses in a subnet. For example, let's say we want to identify all the requests from client in the range of 10.2.44.25 to 10.2.44.35. The IP address range we are trying to identify can't be put under a subnet as that will include other IP addresses too. So, we can use the shortened version to identify this IP address range as follows:

```
acl bad_clients src 10.2.44.25-10.2.44.35/32
```

or

```
acl bad_clients src 10.2.44.25-10.2.44.35
```

The previous example also works, as Squid will try to establish a mask automatically.

So far in this section, we learned about the different ways in which to identify client requests on the basis of clients' IP addresses. The method to identify the requests on the basis of destination IP addresses is similar. We just need to use the dst ACL type instead of src.

 ACL elements configured with dst as a ACL type works slower compared to ACLs with the src ACL type, as Squid will have to resolve the destination domain name before evaluating the ACL, which will involve a DNS query.

What just happened?

We have just learned how to utilize the range feature to specify a range of IP addresses to minimize the number of IP addresses we have to specify while constructing ACL lists. We also learned that we should try not to use the ACL type dst, as it's slower compared to the src ACL type because Squid will have to resolve the destination domain before it can match ACL lists of the dst type.

Have a go hero – make a list of the client IP addresses in your network

Try to make an exhaustive list of clients' IP addresses on your network and then construct ACL lists of the ACL type src. Now try to adjust the predefined ACL localnet in the Squid configuration file and remove the ranges which are not present in your network.

Identifying local IP addresses

There is one more ACL type, myip, which falls in to this category. This can be used to identify the local IP address on which Squid is serving requests. This is useful only if the server running Squid has more than one network interface.

For example, if we have a proxy server with the IP addresses 192.0.2.25, 198.51.100.25, and a public IP address. Let's say our research centers use 198.51.100.25 to connect to the Squid proxy, and student labs use 192.0.2.25 to connect to Squid, then we can define the following two ACLs:

```
acl research_center_net myip 198.51.100.25
acl student_lab_ip myip 192.0.2.25
```

Now using these ACLs, we can easily provide different services to different subnets connecting to different interfaces on the proxy servers.

Although we use IP addresses to identify clients, in some rare cases, we can use a client's MAC address for identification. Let's have a look at this.

Client MAC addresses

We can identify client requests on the basis of a client's **MAC (Media Access Control** address) address. A MAC address is a unique identifier assigned to network interface cards usually by the manufacturer, for identification. Squid provides a special ACL type arp to identify requests. MAC addresses are generally represented as XX:XX:XX:XX:XX:XX, where X is a hexadecimal number. Let's construct an ACL using a client's MAC address

```
acl mac_acl arp 00:1D:7D:D4:F3:EE
```

So, the previous ACL mac_acl will match all requests originating from a client with the MAC address 00:1D:7D:D4:F3:EE.

 This ACL type is available only if Squid was compiled with the --enable-eui or --enable-arp-acl option, depending on the Squid version we have.

Please note that this ACL type is not supported on all operating systems and we should confirm it's availability on our operating system before using it.

 Squid can only detect MAC addresses of clients on the same broadcast domain. For more information on broadcast domains, please check http://en.wikipedia.org/wiki/Broadcast_domain.

Source and destination domain names

It's convenient to use IP addresses while identifying requests with respect to client IP addresses because we already know the network for which we are defining the ACLs. However, when we want to identify requests on the basis of destination addresses, it's not convenient or foolproof to use IP addresses because:

- The IP address of the remote host providing the blocked service may change
- Resolving the destination address is a slow process, which will introduce latency

Squid provides two ACL types namely, `srcdomain` and `dstdomain`, to construct ACLs based on source and destination domain names respectively. However, we prefer using domain names instead of IP addresses for identifying requests with respect to the destination , for the reason which we have explained previously. We should note that `srcdomain` and `dstdomain` are slow and fast ACL types respectively.

Time for action – constructing ACL lists using domain names

Let's construct an ACL to identify requests for pages on `www.example.com`.

```
acl example dstdomain www.example.com
```

The previous ACL element will be able to identify any request for any web page on the domain `www.example.com`. So, if we try to browse `http://www.example.com/` or `http://www.example.com/index.html`, the URLs will be identified by the ACL example.

However, the problem with this ACL is that it will not be able to identify requests to `example.com` or `some.example.com` and so on. So, if we browse to `http://example.com/` or `http://video.example.com/`, our requests will not be identified by the ACL `example`.

To overcome this problem, we can prefix the domain name with a period or dot (.). A dot is treated as a wildcard by Squid and an ACL will match that domain or any sub-domain of that particular domain. Let's see an example.

```
acl example dstdomain .example.com
```

The previous ACL element will match `example.com` or any of its sub-domains such as `video.example.com`, `news.example.com`, `www.exmaple.com` and so on.

Similarly, if we have an ACL defined as follows:

```
acl example_uk dstdomain .uk.example.com
```

We will be able to match requests to `uk.example.com` or any sub-domain of `uk.example.com` but not `example.com`, as it's not a sub-domain of `uk.example.com`.

So, now we know how to construct ACLs using destination domain names. Using source domain names to identify requests is similar, and the ACL type for that is `srcdomain`. Here is an example:

```
acl our_network srcdomain .company.example.com
```

The ACL `our_network` will match any requests originating from `company.example.com` or any of its sub-domains.

ACL elements with `srcdomain` as ACL types works slower, compared to ACLs with the `dstdomain` ACL type because Squid will have to perform a reverse DNS lookup before evaluating ACL. This will introduce significant latency. Moreover, the reverse DNS lookup may not work properly with local IP addresses.

What just happened?

In this section, we saw how we can specify domains or sub-domains of a domain while building ACL lists of the `srcdomain` or `dstdomain` type. We should also note here that ACL lists of the type `srcdomain` are slower than the ones of the type `dstdomain`, as Squid will try a reverse lookup on the source IP address before matching.

Have a go hero – make a list of domains hosted in your local network

Try to find out all the domains and their sub-domains which are hosted in your local area network and organize them into an ACL list `local_domains`.

Regular expressions for domain names

Squid provides two interesting ACL types, namely, `srcdom_regex` and `dstdom_regex`, which can be used to identify requests based on the source or destination domain names attached with each request. Let's say, we don't want to allow websites that have a torrent in their domain names, we would therefore need to construct the following ACL:

```
acl torrent_sites dstdom_regex -i torrent
http_access deny torrent_sites
```

This configuration will simply deny access to any website that has a torrent in its domain name. The ACL type `srcdom_regex` can be used in a similar way to control access from domains matching a specific regular expression.

Destination port

Whenever a client requests some web documents, Squid needs to connect to the remote server on a specific port number. For example, if a client requests `http://example.com/`, Squid will try to connect to a server at `example.com` on port 80, because that's the default port used for HTTP communication. Now, let's say a client requests `https://example.com/`, then Squid will try to connect to the server `example.com` on port 443 because 443 is the default port for secure HTTP (or HTTPS) communication.

Time for action – building ACL lists using destination ports

So, we can use network port numbers to identify requests and then combine them with an access rule to control access to resources. Squid provides an ACL type `port`, which can be used to declare one or more port numbers to construct an ACL. Let's see a simple example:

```
acl allowed_port port 80
```

The previous ACL will match any request for port 80 on the destination server requests. The ACL type `port` can take more than one port or a range of ports as an argument. So, if we want to assign multiple ports, we can list them as follows:

```
acl allowed_ports port 80 443 1025-65535
```

The ACL `allowed_ports` will match all the requests requesting a connection to ports 80, 443, or any within the range of 1025 to 65535.

Normally, the policy is to allow only needed ports and deny connection to all other ports to prevent any type of illegal or unauthorized access. Squid has a lot of pre-defined ports aggregated under the ACLs named `SSL_ports` and `Safe_ports`. The following lines are from the default configuration file:

```
acl SSL_ports port 443

acl Safe_ports port 80      # http
acl Safe_ports port 21      # ftp
acl Safe_ports port 443     # https
acl Safe_ports port 70      # gopher
acl Safe_ports port 210     # wais

acl Safe_ports port 280     # http-mgmt
acl Safe_ports port 488     # gss-http
acl Safe_ports port 591     # filemaker
acl Safe_ports port 777     # multiling http
acl Safe_ports port 1025-65535  # unregistered ports
```

The preceding example contains a list of ports for well-known services such as, HTTP, FTP, HTTPS, and so on and other ports over which HTTP is known to be safely transmitted. We should be careful while adding new ports to the safe ports lists. For example, if we add port 25 (Simple Mail Transfer Protocol or SMTP) to the safe ports list, clients will be able to relay mails through our proxy server due to the design similarities in HTTP and SMTP protocols. So, we should not add port 25 to safe ports list unless we are fully aware of the implications.

Also, the ports listed previously may not be an exhaustive list of allowed ports for our environment and we may need to allow more ports, depending upon the client requirements. For example, we don't have port 873 (rsync) listed above, which may be needed in some cases. So, we keep adding more ports to the safe ports list. Let's see an example:

```
acl SSL_ports port 443 563
acl SSL_ports port 444            # other SSL ports

acl Safe_ports port 80            # http
acl Safe_ports port 21            # ftp
acl Safe_ports port 443 563 444 # https
acl Safe_ports port 70            # gopher
acl Safe_ports port 119           # Usenet news group
acl Safe_ports port 210           # wais
acl Safe_ports port 280           # http-mgmt
acl Safe_ports port 488           # gss-http
acl Safe_ports port 591           # filemaker
acl Safe_ports port 777           # multiling http
acl Safe_ports port 873           # rsync
acl Safe_ports port 1025-65535    # unregistered ports
```

The general approach is to deny access to all the ports that are not in the allowed list. To deny all the unsafe ports, we'll write:

```
http_access deny !Safe_ports
```

Now, clients will not be able to connect to any port on the remote server, which is not listed in the `Safe_ports` list.

What just happened?

In this section, we learned to specify ports or a range of ports for constructing ACL lists of the type `port`. We also learned that we shouldn't allow all ports by default as that can lead to illegal or unauthorized access.

Local port name

Squid provides another ACL type `myportname`, to identify the network port name but it's different to `port`. The ACL type `myportname` identifies the port number on the Squid proxy server where clients connect to Squid. Just like the ACL type `myip`, `myportname` is also useful if we configure Squid to listen on more than one port using the `http_port` directive in the Squid configuration file.

Let's say we have Squid listening on port 3128 and 8080. Therefore, we can have the following ACLs:

```
http_port 192.0.2.21:3128 name=research_port
http_port 192.0.2.25:8080 name=student_port
acl research_lab_net myportname research_port
acl student_lab_net myportname student_port
```

Now, we can use these two ACLs to control access to different subnets.

HTTP methods

Every HTTP request is accompanied by a HTTP method. For example, when we type `http://example.com/` in our web browser's address bar, we make a GET request to the `example.com` server. Also, when we submit an online form, we make a POST request to the server. Similarly, PUT, DELETE, CONNECT, and so on, are other commonly used HTTP methods.

Squid provides the ACL type `method` to identify requests based on the HTTP method used for that particular request. Normally, all the methods are allowed by default, except the CONNECT method. The HTTP method CONNECT is a bit tricky and is used to tunnel requests through HTTP proxies. So, we should allow only trusted requests such as HTTPS through CONNECT.

Let's see an example of a method ACL from Squid's default configuration:

```
acl CONNECT method CONNECT
```

Don't confuse CONNECT the ACL name, with CONNECT the HTTP method. The, ACL CONNECT will identify all the requests with the HTTP method CONNECT. Now, let's see Squid's default configuration for using the CONNECT method:

```
acl SSL_ports port 443
http_access deny CONNECT !SSL_ports
```

By default, Squid will allow the CONNECT HTTP method only for SSL port 443, which is the standard port for HTTPS communication. Again, we should go with the default configuration and add more ports to the SSL_ports ACL as the need arises.

 We should note that the port numbers we add to the SSL ports list should be added to the safe ports list as well.

Identifying requests using the request protocol

Squid provides another ACL type, `proto`, which can be used to identify the communication protocol or URL scheme for a request. For example, when we access `http://example.com/`, the URL scheme used is `HTTP` and when we browse `ftp://example.com/`, the URL scheme being used is `FTP`. Other commonly used URL schemes are `gopher`, `urn`, `https`, and `whois`.

Time for action – using a request protocol to construct access rules

Let's say we want to deny all FTP requests from a particular subnet, known as, research labs. The configuration should look similar to the following:

```
acl ftp_requests proto FTP
acl research_labs src 192.0.2.0/24
http_access deny research_labs ftp_requests
```

The previous configuration lines will instruct Squid to deny all the FTP requests from the network `192.0.2.0/24`.

 Please note that some firewalls block active FTP by default. Please check `http://www.ncftp.com/ncftpd/doc/misc/ftp_and_firewalls.html` for more information.

Apart from the previously mentioned standard schemes, we have a Squid specific URL scheme called `cache_object`, which is used for the cache manager (`cachemgr`) interface. By default, the cache manager can only be accessed from the Squid proxy server itself because of the following code in `squid.conf`:

```
acl manager proto cache_object
acl localhost src 127.0.0.1/32
http_access allow manager localhost
http_access deny manager
```

Therefore the URL scheme `cache_object` can only be accessed from the `localhost` (the proxy server itself). If we want to access the `cache_object` URL scheme from other machines (for example, from the machines of all our administrators), we can add the following special access rules as follows:

```
acl manager proto cache_object
acl localhost src 127.0.0.1/32
acl admin_machines src 192.0.2.86 192.0.2.10
http_access allow manager localhost
http_access allow manager admin_machines
http_access deny manager
```

The previous configuration lines will ensure that only administrators can use Squid's cache manager interface.

What just happened?

We have just seen that it is possible to build ACL lists based on the protocol used by the client in the requests. By using this type of ACL we can completely deny requests to all other protocols than HTTP and HTTPS, in very restricted environments.

Time-based ACLs

Access control based on time is one of the most exciting features of Squid. Using the `time` ACL type, we can specify a time period in the form of day(s) or time range. Then the requests during that time period will be matched or identified by that ACL. The format of the `time` ACL type is as follows:

```
acl ACL_NAME time [day-abbreviation] [h1:m1-h2:m2]
```

Specifying days and time range are optional, but one of them must be specified. The following are the abbreviations used:

Day	Abbreviation
Sunday	S
Monday	M
Tuesday	T
Wednesday	W
Thursday	H
Friday	F
Saturday	A
All Weekdays	D

 We should note that time is taken only when the ACL is checked. Therefore, it may not affect the requests made during the allow period and performed during the deny period and vice-versa.

So, for identifying all the requests on Sunday, Monday, and Wednesday, we'll have the following ACL:

```
acl days time SMW
```

The day abbreviations should be written altogether. While specifying the time, `h1:m1` should be less than `h2:m2`. Moreover, time should be in a 24 hour format. Now, let's construct a few ACLs for the typical office hours:

```
acl morning_hrs time MTWHF 09:00-12:59
acl lunch_hrs time D 13:00-13:59
acl evening_hrs time MTWHF 14:00-18:00
```

Now, let's say we don't want our clients to access YouTube during office hours, but it's ok if they access it during lunch hours. Also, we will allow browsing only in office hours. So, we'll have the following lines in our configuration file:

```
acl youtube dstdomain .youtube.com
acl office dstdomain .office.example.com
http_access allow office
http_access allow youtube !morning_hours !evening_hours
http_access deny all
```

URL and URL path-based identification

Squid provides the ACL type `url_regex`, using which we can specify regular expressions which will be matched against the entire URL. URLs are generally of the form `http://example.com/path/directory/index.php?page=2&count=10` or `http://example.com/path2/index.html#example-section`. So, let's construct an ACL that will match all requests to JPG images on the `example.com` server.

```
acl example_com_jpg url_regex ^http://example.com/.*\.jpg$
```

By default, the regular expressions passed to any ACL type are treated as case-sensitive. Hence, the previous regular expression will not match if a JPG image on the server has a filename `linux.JPG`. To make the regular expressions case-insensitive, we can use the option `-i` while defining ACL. For example:

```
acl example_com_jpg url_regex -i ^http://example.com/.*\.jpg$
```

Now, the ACL `example_com_jpg` will match all the JPG images on the server `example.com`.

In the URL `http://example.com/path/directory/index.php?page=2&count=10`, the section `path/directory/index.php?page=2&count=10` is the URL path. So, the URL path is basically the URL minus the URL scheme and hostname.

Similar to `url_regex`, we have another ACL type called `urlpath_regex`. The only difference is that `url_regex` searches for the regular expression in the complete URL while `urlpath_regex` searches only in the URL path.

This ACL type is specifically helpful when we only want to search a string in the path and not in the hostname. Let's see an example:

```
acl torrent urlpath_regex -i torrent
```

In another example, let's try to block some video content:

```
acl videos urlpath_regex -i \.(avi|mp4|mov|m4v|mkv|flv)(\?.*)?$
```

The above ACL `videos` will match a few of the well known video formats.

> Please note that regular expression matching is slower than other ACL type matching. It is highly recommended to break the regular expression into `dstdomain` and `urlpath_regex` to enhance ACL matching performance.

Have a go hero – ACL list for audio content

Construct an ACL list which can be used to identify requests for at least three types of audio files.

Matching client usernames

Squid supports identifying clients using the `ident` protocol by providing the ACL type `ident`. Squid tries to connect to the `ident` server on the client machine and get the username corresponding to the current request, when the `ident` ACL type is used. The username that Squid will receive may not be the username of the logged in user. For example, when Squid tries to get the username of a down-stream proxy server, it may get the username `squid`, `proxy`, or `nobody`, depending on the value of the `cache_effective_user` directive.

> The `ident` protocol is not really secure and it's very easy to spoof an `ident` server. So, it should be used carefully.

If we have an exhaustive list of usernames for our network, we can construct an ACL as follows:

```
acl friends ident john sarah michelle priya
http_access allow friends
http_access deny all
```

If the previous configuration is used, only the users specified previously will be able to access our proxy server.

Please note that the ident lookups are blocking calls and Squid will wait for the reply before it can proceed with processing the request, and that may increase the delays by a significant margin.

Normally, it's not possible to specify all users especially if we have a large network. For such cases, Squid provides a special keyword, REQUIRED, which can be used to enforce a username for all the requests. If an ident lookup results in any username, the ACL is matched, otherwise the ACL will not be matched.

 To know more about the ident protocol, please visit http://en.wikipedia.org/wiki/Ident.

So, to enforce a username, we can have the following configuration in our Squid configuration file:

```
acl username ident REQUIRED
http_access allow username
http_access deny all
```

Regular expressions for client usernames

Similar to ident, we have another ACL type, ident_regex, which can be used to specify regular expressions instead of complete usernames. This is helpful in networks, where we have specific formats for usernames. For example, let's say we use the department name as a suffix to the usernames. Then we can construct the following ACLs:

```
acl mkt_dept ident_regex -i \.marketing$
acl cust_care_dept ident_regex -i \.cust_care$
```

Now, based on the above ACLs, we can have control over the way the resources are used by the two departments.

Proxy authentication

The best way to keep bad guys out of a proxy server is to use proxy authentication. In this case, a client will need to enter a username and password to be able to use our proxy server. If proxy authentication is enabled, the client will send an additional header with authentication credentials, which Squid will evaluate and check whether the client should be allowed to use our proxy server. The interesting part is that Squid can't validate credentials sent by the client on its own. Squid passes the credentials it receives from a client to a helper process, and the validity of credentials is determined by the external process.

So, we have the `proxy_auth` ACL type where we can specify a list of usernames for authentication. However, as we saw previously, Squid can't validate credentials itself; we must specify at least one authentication scheme for validating the username and password sent by the client. Authentication schemes are configured using the `auth_param` directives in our Squid configuration file.

Squid supports the Basic, Digest, NTLM, and Negotiate authentication schemes, and all of them are built by default.

Time for action – enforcing proxy authentication

If we want to enforce proxy authentication, we can add the following lines to our configuration file:

```
acl authenticated proxy_auth REQUIRED
http_access allow authenticated
http_access deny all
```

With the previous configuration, only authenticated users will be able to access the proxy server. If we want to specifically identify individual clients with usernames, we can pass a list of users as well. This may be needed if we want to give extra privileges to some users. For example:

```
acl authenticated proxy_auth REQUIRED
acl admins proxy_auth john sarah
acl special_website dstdomain admin.example.com
http_access allow admins special_website
http_access deny special_website
http_access allow authenticated
http_access deny all
```

Therefore, if we have the preceding lines in our configuration file, only the users `john` and `sarah` will be able to access `admin.example.com`, but other authenticated users will be able to access all websites except `admin.example.com`.

Regular expressions for usernames

Similar to `proxy_auth`, we have the `proxy_auth_regex` ACL type, which can be used to identify usernames using a regular expression. Let's say, we follow a nomenclature for allotting usernames to our employees and all employees in the accounts department will have the username of `accounts_username`, then we can construct an ACL matching the usernames of the employees from the accounts department as follows:

```
acl accounts_dept proxy_auth_regex ^accounts_
```

If we want employees in the accounts department to access only the accounts website, we can have the following configuration:

```
acl accounts_dept proxy_auth_regex ^accounts_
acl accounts_web dstdomain .account.example.com

http_access allow accounts_dept accounts_web
http_access deny all
```

In accordance with the previous configuration, employees in the accounts department will be able to access only the accounts website.

What just happened?

In the previous example, we saw how we can enforce proxy authentication for all the clients' or only a group of clients using different types of ACL lists. We'll learn more about proxy authentication in *Chapter 7*.

User limits

Squid provides different ACL types, using which we can construct ACL lists to limit the number of connections from a client and the number of logins per user. Let's have a look.

Maximum number of connections per client

Generally, we want to place a limit on the number of parallel connections a client can utilize to enforce a fair usage policy. Squid provides an ACL type maxconn, which will match if a client's IP address has more than the maximum specified active connections. An example of this could be if we want to enforce a maximum of 25 connections per client:

```
acl connections maxconn 25
http_access deny connections
```

According to the preceding configuration lines, a client will return an access denied error if it tries to open more than 25 parallel connections.

In a different scenario, we may want to enforce different parallel connection limits for different user groups. Let's see an example of such a configuration:

```
acl normal_users src 10.2.0.0/16
acl corporate_users src 10.1.0.0/16
acl norm_conn maxconn 15
acl corp_conn maxconn 30
http_access deny normal_users norm_conn
http_access deny corporate_users corp_conn
```

So, according to the preceding configuration lines, `normal_users` will have a maximum limit of 15 parallel connections, while `corporate_users` will enjoy a maximum limit of 30 parallel connections.

Maximum logins per user

Squid provides an ACL type `max_user_ip`, which is matched when a single username is used for authentication from more than a specified number of machines. A directive `authenticate_ip_ttl` is used to determine the timeout for the IP address entries. So, if we want our clients to log in from, no more than, three different machines, we can use the following configuration:

```
acl ip_limit max_user_ip 3
http_access deny ip_limit
```

The default behavior is to deny random requests once the limit is reached. We can deny complete access by specifying the option `-s` while constructing an ACL.

> At least one of the authentication schemes must be configured before we can use this feature.

Identification based on various HTTP headers

Requests or replies can be identified based on the information hidden in HTTP headers, which accompany every HTTP request or reply. Let's have a look at some of the important HTTP headers used for identifying requests.

User-agent or browser

Almost all the HTTP requests carry a `User-Agent` string in their headers, which is basically a string to identify the name and version of the HTTP client. For a certain version of Mozilla Firefox, it may look like:

```
Mozilla/5.0 (X11; U; Linux i686; en-US; rv:1.9.2.6) Gecko/20100625
Firefox/3.6.6 GTB7.1
```

The previous `User-Agent` string represents Mozilla Firefox 3.6.6 on a Linux-based 32 bit operating system.

Squid provides an ACL type `browser`, using which we can identify client requests based on the `User-Agent` header and combine that with an access rule to grant access to users with specific HTTP clients. The ACL type browser takes a regular expression as an argument. For example, if we want to restrict access to Mozilla Firefox and Internet Explorer, we can add following lines to our configuration files:

```
acl allowed_clients browser -i firefox msie
http_access allow allowed_clients
http_access deny all
```

It's very easy to spoof `User-Agent` header strings and we should not rely solely on User-Agent to control access.

Referer identification

HTTP requests generally carry a Referer header string, which represents the website from which the client was directed to the current request. An example Referer header string is `http://www.google.com/search?rlz=1C1GGLS_enIN345IN345&sourceid=chrome&ie=UTF-8&q=what+my+user+agent`. Squid has an ACL type `referer_regex`, which can be used to match requests on the basis of the Referer header string. It's useful when we don't want users to be directed to genuine websites from a malicious website. For example:

```
acl malicious_website dstdomain .malicious.example.com
acl malicious_referer referer_regex -i malicious.example.com
http_access deny malicious_website
http_access deny malicious_referer
```

The previous configuration will prevent our clients from visiting the malicious website and will also prevent them from being directed to genuine websites from the malicious website. This will in turn will prevent them from attacks like phishing.

Content type-based identification

Squid provides two ACL types, `req_mime_type` and `rep_mime_type`, which can be used to match the content type of requests and replies respectively. These are generally helpful in controlling the access to file uploads and downloads. Both these ACL types try to match the `Content-Type` HTTP header accompanied with requests and replies.

For uploads, the `req_mime_type` is used. For example, if we want to prevent the uploading of an MPEG video file, then we can have the following lines in our configuration file:

```
acl mpeg_upload req_mime_type -i video/mpeg
http_access deny mpeg_upload
```

Similarly, `rep_mime_type` is used for matching against the Content-Type header of replies from remote servers. To disable all video downloads, we can use the `http_reply_access` directive, which is used to control access to replies received from the remote servers. Therefore, we can have the following lines in our configuration file.

```
acl video_download rep_mime_type -i ^video/
http_reply_access deny video_download
```

These ACL types are only effective if the HTTP client and remote web servers set the `Content-Type` HTTP header properly.

Other HTTP headers

We have learned about the `browser`, `referer`, `req_mime_type`, and `rep_mime_type` ACL types, which identify requests or replies by matching a regular expression against different HTTP header fields. Squid provides two additional ACL types, namely, `req_header` and `rep_header`, which can be used to match any of the HTTP header fields in requests or replies.

The `req_header` ACL type is used to match HTTP headers in requests. Let's see an example:

```
acl user_agent req_header User-Agent -i ^Mozilla
http_access allow user_agent
http_access deny all
```

In the previous configuration, `User-Agent` is a HTTP header. Similarly, we can specify any of the known HTTP headers and Squid will try to match the regular expression against the value of that particular HTTP header.

In a similar manner, we can use `rep_header` for matching HTTP header fields in replies. However, it is worth noting that the `rep_header` ACL type is useful only when used with the `http_reply_access` directive as only replies can be matched.

HTTP reply status

When Squid tries to contact the remote server on the client's behalf, it'll receive a reply corresponding to every request. Depending upon the remote web server's ability to serve the current request, the reply will have a status code. For example, if the request can be served, a status code 200 will be returned.

> Please visit `http://en.wikipedia.org/wiki/List_of_HTTP_status_codes` for a complete list of HTTP status codes.

Squid has the ACL type `http_status` to identify replies on the basis of the HTTP status codes returned by a remote server. Let's say we want to identify all the server errors (5xx), our configuration would look similar to the following:

```
acl server_errors http_status 500-510
```

Similar to the `src` and `port` ACL types, we can pass a range as an argument to `http_status`. We can take the appropriate action based on the HTTP status or reply codes. The `https_status` ACL type can be helpful in bypassing adaptation rules.

Identifying random requests

The ACL type `random` can be used to identify random requests with a pre-defined probability. The following is the format for constructing ACLs of the type `random`:

```
acl ACL_NAME random probability
```

The parameter `probability` can be specified in the following three ways:

- Fraction: In the form of a fraction. For example, 2/3, 3/4, and so on.
- Decimal: In the form of a decimal number. For example, 0.67, 0.2, and so on.
- Ration: In the form of a matches:non-matches ratio. For example, 3:4, 2:3, and so on.

So, an example ACL matching 70 percent of requests can be written as:

```
acl random_req random 0.7
```

The ACL `random_req` will randomly match 70 percent of the total requests received by the Squid proxy server.

Access list rules

In the previous section, we learned about ACL lists in detail. However, as we saw, ACL lists can only be used to identify, and that is only of use if they are combined with some access rules to control access to various components of our proxy server. Squid provides a lot of access list rules, with `http_access` being the most widely used.

As we have learned in *Chapter 2*, when we have multiple access rules, Squid matches a particular request against them from top to bottom and keeps doing so until a definite action (allow or deny) is determined. We also learned that if we have multiple ACLs within a single access rule, then a request is matched against all the ACLs from left to right and Squid stops processing the rule as soon as it encounters an ACL that can't identify the request. An access rule with multiple ACLs results in a definite action only if the request is identified by all the ACLs used in the rule.

Now, let's have a brief look at the different access list rules provided by Squid.

Access to HTTP protocol

The `http_access` is the most important access list rule. Only the client allowed by this rule will be able to send HTTP requests and requests from all other clients will be denied. However, the behavior of this access list rule is a bit tricky.

The default behavior is to allow requests only from LAN clients. If no access rules are configured, then the default behavior is to deny all requests. Squid will stop at the first access rule with an ACL list matching the current request and will allow or deny the request depending on the rule. If the current request is not identified by any of the ACL lists in the access rules, the opposite action of the last access rule is performed. So, if the last access rule is to deny a request, the unmatched request will be allow and vice-versa.

Because of the above behavior, a deny all ACL rule is always recommended in the end, so that Squid can identify a definite action. The general rule is to allow known clients and deny the rest by default. So, our configuration file should look something like:

```
http_access allow employees
http_access allow customers
http_access allow guests
http_access allow vpn_users
http_access deny all
```

So, we allowed all of the possible genuine users and then at the end denied all the requests. If the need arises to add more users, we can simply add them to an existing or another ACL list and will add an allow access rule.

The line that denies all the requests at the end also prevents our proxy server from unauthorized access as a result of misconfiguration.

Adapted HTTP access

Squid provides the adapted_http_access rule, which is similar to http_acces but is checked after all the redirectors, URL rewriters, or ICAP/eCAP adaptations, which allows access control based on the output returned. This is only useful when we are using redirectors, URL rewriters, or ICAP/eCAP adaptation.

> For more information on ICAP/eCAP, please visit http://wiki.squid-cache.org/Features/ICAP and http://wiki.squid-cache.org/Features/eCAP.

It is not absolutely necessary to use this rule. The syntax and behavior is similar to http_access.

HTTP access for replies

We have seen that there are ACL types that can identify requests and replies. For example, src, dst, dstdomain, req_header, and so on are a few ACL types that identify clients on the basis of requests, while rep_header, http_status, rep_mime_type, and so on can identify replies. The ACL lists that identify replies should be used with the access rule http_reply_access to control access.

Squid fetches the replies from a remote server, even if the replies are denied using the `http_reply_access` rules, but they are not delivered to the clients. On the other hand, even when the replies are denied using the `http_reply_acess` rules, the clients will still receive replies in the form of access denied messages from Squid.

The usage and behavior of `http_reply_access` is similar to `http_access`.

 If a client is denied access by the `http_access` rule, it'll never match an `http_reply_access` rule. This is because, if a client's request is denied then Squid will not fetch a reply.

Access to other ports

Our neighbor proxy server can access a proxy server via ICP and HTCP ports. Also, our proxy server can be accessed via the SNMP port. Let's see how to control access to these ports.

ICP port

We have seen the `icp_port` directive in Squid, which is used to set the ICP port for communication with neighboring proxy servers. To limit access to the ICP port of our proxy server, we have an access list rule called `icp_access`. The default behavior is to deny all the requests to the ICP port. Generally, we prefer to enable ICP port access for all clients in our local area network, but it totally depends on our network policies.

The default Squid configuration file contains an ACL list, `localnet`, which identifies all the clients on our LAN. So, if we want to allow ICP access to all our local clients, we can use the following lines in the configuration file:

```
acl localnet src 10.0.0.0/8
acl localnet src 172.16.0.0/12
acl localnet src 192.168.0.0/16
acl localnet src fc00::/7
acl localnet src fe80::/10
icp_access allow localnet
icp_access deny all
```

HTCP port

HTCP (Hypertext Caching Protocol) is used for discovering HTTP caches and communication among the proxy servers. We set the HTCP port in the configuration file using the `htcp_port` directive. We can prevent access to the HTCP port on our proxy server by using the access list rule `htcp_access`, which has usage and behavior similar to `icp_access`. The default behavior is to deny all requests to the HTCP port.

Purge access via HTCP

A proxy server can send HTCP CLR or purge requests to other proxy servers using HTCP. We may want to allow access to only trusted clients to prevent a proxy server from unauthorized access. Squid provides the access rule `htcp_clr_access`, which can be used to determine the clients that will be able to issue HTCP CLR requests to purge content.

 We should note that HTCP CLR requests are relayed regardless of whether they are acted on locally.

SNMP port

We can restrict access to the SNMP port (specified by the `snmp_port` directive) on our proxy server using a combination of the access list rule `snmp_access`, the ACL list constructed from the ACL type `snmp_community` and any other ACL identifying the client requesting SNMP access. Let's see the following example:

```
acl admins src 127.0.0.1 192.0.2.21 192.0.2.86
acl snmppublic snmp_community public
snmp_access allow snmppublic admins
snmp_access deny all
```

So, now only `admins` will be able to access the SNMP port. The default behavior is to deny access to all clients.

Enforcing limited access to neighbors

When we have cache peers or neighbor proxy servers in our network, they can use our proxy server as a sibling or a parent proxy server. When they use our proxy server as a sibling proxy server, only HITS will be fetched from our proxy server and they will fetch all the MISS(s) on their own. However, if they are using our proxy server as a parent, then they'll be able to fetch MISS(s) via our proxy server. In some cases, this may not be a desirable behavior, as it will consume our upstream bandwidth.

Time for action – denying miss_access to neighbors

To force other proxy servers to use our proxy server as a sibling proxy server, we have an access rule `miss_access`. Let's say we have two neighbor proxy servers, namely, `192.0.2.25` and `198.51.100.25`, in our network. Now, we don't mind if `192.0.2.25` uses our proxy server as a parent proxy server, but we don't want to allow `198.51.100.25` to fetch MISS(s) via our proxy server. So, we can have the following configuration:

```
acl good_neighbour src 192.0.2.25
acl bad_neighbour src 198.51.100.25
```

```
miss_access allow good_neighbour # This line is not needed. Why?
miss_access deny bad_neighbour
miss_access allow all
```

The default behavior is to allow all proxy servers to fetch MISS(s) via our proxy server. In the previous configuration line, the first allow rule is not needed because we have the `allow all` rule at the end. The `allow` rule was just used to draw your attention towards the nature of `miss_access` directive.

What just happened?

We just learned the usage of the `miss_access` access list rule to prevent leakage of upstream bandwidth to unknown or misbehaving clients.

Requesting neighbor proxy servers

If there are neighbor proxy servers or cache peers in our network and we have added them to our Squid configuration file using the `cache_peer` directive, then our proxy server will try to contact those servers using HTTP, ICP, or HTCP protocols based on the options we used with `cache_peer` directive. By default, Squid will select the first or closest proxy server to contact for various communications. We can however control the selection with the access list rule `cache_peer_access`.

We can combine `cache_peer_access`, cache peer name, and the ACL lists to achieve control over a selection of the proxy servers for different domains, clients, or any other criterion. The following is the format for constructing a `cache_peer_access` rule:

```
cache_peer_access CACHE_HOST allow allow|deny [!]ACL_NAME ...
```

Let's have a look at the following example. We have two cache peers, namely, `cache1.example.com` and `cache2.example.com`, and we want all YouTube traffic to go through `cache1.example.com` and all Google traffic to go through `cache2.example.com`.

```
cache_peer cache1.example.com parent 8080 3130 proxy-only weight=1
cache_peer cache2.example.com parent 3128 3130 proxy-only weight=2
acl youtube dstdomain .youtube.com
acl google dstdomain .google.com
cache_peer_access cache1.example.com allow youtube
cache_peer_access cache1.example.com deny all
cache_peer_access cache2.example.com allow google
cache_peer_access cache2.example.com deny all
```

Have a go hero – make a list of proxy servers in your network

Make a list of the available proxy servers in your environment and add them as cache peers to your configuration file.

Forwarding requests to remote servers

When we have neighboring proxy servers or cache peers in our network and we have configured our Squid proxy server to use them via the `cache_peer` directive, then the requests from the clients will be forwarded through the peers depending on the options used with `cache_peer` while adding the peer hosts. However, Squid provides the following access list rules, namely, `always_direct` and `never_direct`, which can be used to determine whether a request should be forwarded through other peers or the remote servers should be contacted directly.

When we want to forward requests directly to remote servers without using any peers, we can use the `always_direct` access list rule. This is generally used to avoid contacting peers for serving content from websites on the local area network. For example, for forwarding requests to local web servers directly, we can use the following configuration:

```
acl local_domains dstdomain .local.example.com
acl local_ips dst 192.0.2.0/24
always_direct allow local_domains
always_direct allow local_ips
```

The previous configuration will successfully reduce the unnecessary latency introduced because of communication with peers while serving local content.

The access list rule `never_direct` is the opposite of `always_direct`. So, if we decided that all the requests must not be forwarded to remote servers directly, then we can have the following configuration:

```
never_direct allow all
```

Ident lookup access

We learned that we have the ACL type `ident`, using which we can force username identification before allowing any clients to access our proxy server. However by default, `ident` lookups are not performed even if we have ACL lists with the `ident` ACL type, unless the current requests are allowed by the access rule `ident_lookup_access`. The default behavior is not to perform any `ident` lookups at all.

It's actually a good idea to perform selective `ident` lookups because not all hosts support this feature. So, let's say we want to perform `ident` lookups for all the Unix/Linux hosts in our network `192.0.2.0/24`. We can add the following lines to our configuration file:

```
acl nix_hosts src 192.0.2.0/24
ident_lookup_access allow nix_hosts
ident_lookup_access deny all
```

Controlled caching of web documents

Squid tries to cache all the cacheable web documents for satisfying the subsequent requests for the same content. However, there may be times when we may not want to cache all of the replies. A good example is the content from websites on our local area network. We have an access list rule, `cache`, using which we can allow or deny caching of content with the help of ACL lists.

For example, for denying caching of any content on the local area network, we can add the following lines to our configuration file:

```
acl local_domain dstdomain .local.example.com
cache deny local_domain
cache allow all
```

 Don't use the `localnet` ACL list here because that identifies requests on the basis of source IP addresses and not on the basis of destination IP addresses.

URL rewrite access

When we have configured our Squid proxy server to use URL rewriters, Squid will send all the incoming requests to URL rewriters for further processing. Generally, URL rewriters are plugins designed for a specific purpose and will operate on selective websites. So, it's good practice to pass only selective URLs to a URL rewriter to save some CPU cycles, and Squid will not have to wait for the rewriter to process a URL that is not meant to be processed by the rewriter. We should also avoid rewriting CONNECT requests. Rewriting HTTP PUT and POST requests can also result in unexpected behavior.

We can pass only selective requests to URL rewriters using the access list rule `url_rewrite_access`. This access list rule is similar to `http_access` and `cache_peer_access` and only requests allowed by `url_rewrite_access` will be passed to the URL rewriter. Let's say we have defined a URL rewriter that acts only on the `videos.example.com` URLs; we would need the following configuration:

```
acl video_web dstdomain .videos.example.com
url_rewrite_access allow video_web
url_rewrite_access deny all
```

In accordance with the previous configuration, Squid will pass all the URLs to the URL rewriter program, which are matched by the `video_web` ACL.

HTTP header access

Another couple of access list rules which we have are `request_header_access` and `reply_header_access`. These can be combined with ACL lists to control access to different headers in HTTP requests and replies respectively. If we deny access to a certain HTTP header for some requests, then that particular HTTP header will be dropped from the headers while sending the request to remote servers. We should note that dropping HTTP headers from requests or replies is a violation of HTTP protocol standards.

Let's say we want to remove the User-Agent HTTP header from both requests and replies from the subnet `192.0.2.0/24`. We would need the following configuration for achieving this:

```
acl special_net src 192.0.2.0/24
request_header_access User-Agent deny special_net
reply_header_access Content-Type deny special_net
request_header_access User-Agent allow all
reply_header_access Content-Type allow all
```

Custom error pages

Whenever access is denied to a client for a particular request, Squid sends a standard access denied page to a client with instructions on contacting the system administrator. We can send custom error pages to the clients, redirect them to a different URL, or reset the TCP connection using the access list rule `deny_info`. There are three possible ways to do this by using `deny_info`; let's have a look at them. In the first form, we return a custom error page:

```
deny_info ERR_PAGE ACL_NAME
```

In this form, we write a HTML page and store it in the errors directory defined by the `error_directory` directive in `squid.conf`. Let's say we have a custom access denied error message in the `ERR_CUSTOM_ACCESS_DENIED` file in our errors directory. We would need the following configuration:

```
acl bad_guys src 192.0.2.0/24
deny_info ERR_CUSTOM_ACCESS_DENIED bad_guys
```

In the next form, we redirect clients to a custom URL:

```
acl bad_guys src 192.0.2.0/24
deny_info http://errors.example.com/access_denied.html bad_guys
```

In the last form, we simply reset the TCP connection:

```
acl bad_guys src 192.0.2.0/24
deny_info TCP_RESET bad_guys
```

Have a go hero – custom access denied page

Design a custom access denied page for your Squid proxy server, which explains the reason for revoking access.

Maximum size of the reply body

In some environments, where we don't have enough bandwidth, we may want to restrict people from downloading large files like movies, music, games, and so on. To achieve this goal, we can use the access list rule `reply_body_max_size` to put a limit on the maximum size of the reply body that a client can access. If the size of the reply body exceeds the maximum size, the client will be sent a proper denial message.

The syntax for using `reply_body_max_size` is as follows:

```
reply_body_max_size SIZE UNITS ACLNAME
```

So, let's say we want to limit the maximum reply body size to 10MB and 20MB for different subnets. We can have the following configuration:

```
acl max_size_10 src 192.0.2.0/24
acl max_size_20 src 198.51.100.0/24
reply_body_max_size 10 MB max_size_10
reply_body_max_size 20 MB max_size_20
reply_body_max_size none
```

The reply size is calculated on the basis of the CONTENT-LENGTH HTTP header received from the remote server. If the value is larger than the maximum allowed size for the current request, the client will get a 'reply too large' error. If there is no CONTENT-LENGTH HTTP header in the reply and the reply size is more than the maximum allowed, the connection is closed and client receives only a partial reply.

Logging requests selectively

By default, all the client requests are logged to Squid's access log file whose location is determined by the `access_log` directive in the configuration file. However, there may be requests which we may not want to log to the access log for privacy reasons.

For example, let's say we have a research lab in subnet `192.0.2.0/24` where people work on a secret project and we don't want their requests to be logged to the access log to prevent any collection of browsing patterns. We can use the access list rule `log_access` to prevent logging for certain requests as shown in the following example:

```
acl secret_req src 192.0.2.0/24
log_access deny secret_req
log_access allow all
```

The previous configuration will prevent logging of requests from the `192.0.2.0/24` subnet. We learn about gaining fine control over logging in *Chapter 5*.

Mixing ACL lists and rules – example scenarios

We have seen various ways in which to construct ACL lists to identify different requests from clients, and replies in some cases. We have also learned about the basic usage of access list rules. In this section, we'll be defining configurations for the different scenarios that a Squid administrator may face in day-to-day life.

Handling caching of local content

When we deploy a proxy server, normally all requests to external and internal websites flows through the proxy server. If we have caching enabled on our proxy server, then it's going to cache everything that is cacheable, which will result in caching of content from internal websites also. When we cache content from internal websites, we are unnecessarily wasting disk space on the proxy server because the advantage of caching the local content is almost none, as we generally have lots of free bandwidth on LAN.

Time for action – avoiding caching of local content

First of all, we'll need to identify the requests in which content on your local area network is being requested. So, let's say in our network, some clients have hosted FTP and HTTP servers on their machines to share content on the intranet. The client machines have IP addresses in the subnets `192.0.2.0/24` and `198.51.100.0/24`. So, we need to construct an ACL list that can identify all the requests directed to these machines. The following ACL list does exactly that:

```
acl client_servers dst 192.0.2.0/24 198.51.100.0/24
```

Also, we have `mail.internal.example.com` and `docs.internal.example.com` hosted in the local network. So, let's construct an ACL list to identify all the requests to these websites:

```
acl internal_websites dstdomain .internal.example.com
```

So, as we have identified the requests for local content, we just need to instruct Squid not to cache replies to any of these requests. Therefore, we will use the access list rule `cache` to deny caching, as shown in the following example:

```
cache deny client_servers
cache deny internal_websites
cache allow all
```

What just happened?

We just learned about optimizing our Squid proxy server to cache only the content that actually needs to be cached and will not waste the disk space on the proxy server unnecessarily. We can keep updating these ACL lists as we encounter the requests that do not need to be cached.

Denying access from external networks

When we deploy a proxy server, we normally want it to be available to users on our local area network and no other person should be able to use our proxy server to browse websites. In this case we will also have to identify all our clients on the local area network by using ACL lists. Generally, we assign IP addresses in the local network from the private address space. Squid already has ACL lists defined to identify the machines in the local network. If we go ahead with the default Squid configuration, requests from the local network will be allowed and all other requests will be denied. Let's have a look at the default configuration provided by Squid:

```
acl localhost src 127.0.0.1/32
acl localnet src 10.0.0.0/8
acl localnet src 172.16.0.0/12
acl localnet src 192.168.0.0/16
acl localnet src fc00::/7
acl localnet src fe80::/10
http_access allow localnet
http_access allow localhost
http_access deny all
```

If we want to allow any other clients from outside our network, we'll have to construct additional ACL lists and allow them by using `http_access`.

Denying access to selective clients

There may be several reasons for blocking a particular client but one of the most common reasons is a huge number of requests being sent from a single client to a particular website. This may be due to a virus infected computer or download managers with very low retry time in case access is denied.

For revoking access from such clients, first we'll need to construct an ACL list to identify such users and then we'll need to deny access using the `http_access` access list rule. We'll have to take care that the `deny` rule goes above all the `allow` rules, in case there are any.

```
acl bad_clients src 192.0.2.21 198.51.100.25
http_access deny bad_clients
http_access allow localnet
http_access allow localhost
http_access deny all
```

Blocking the download of video content

Most of the bandwidth is consumed by only a few clients for downloading video content such as movies, TV shows, and so on. So, we may want to deny access to all the video content so that we can provide quality bandwidth to the clients trying to browse other websites. This is generally required only when we have low bandwidth and a lot of clients.

Time for action – blocking video content

So, for blocking the video content, first we'll need to identify all the requests for video content. For this purpose, we can simply use the ACL type `url_regex` as follows:

```
acl video_content urlpath_regex -i \.(mpg|mpeg|avi|mov|flv|wmv|mkv|rm
vb)(\?.*)?$
```

The previous ACL list will match all the URLs ending with extensions of common video formats.

As a video can be served using dynamic URLs, the URL returning video content may not look like a URL to a video file at all. For achieving better control, we also need to use the ACL type `rep_mime_type` to detect the content type of the replies returned by webservers. So, we can construct another ACL list as follows:

```
acl video_in_reply rep_mime_type -i ^video\/
```

The previous ACL list will match all the replies with video as a part of their content type. So, now we need to deny access to these ACL lists, which we can do by using the following rules:

```
http_access deny video_content
http_reply_access deny video_in_reply
http_reply_access allow all
```

What just happened?

We have just seen a real life example of `http_reply_access`, in which we used it to control the download of video content. The previous list is not foolproof and it will not be able to match the replies containing video content if the remote web server doesn't send the `Content-Type` HTTP header.

Special access for certain clients

This is a common scenario when clients have restricted access. Generally, we need to provide special access to administrators. If this is the case, we need to identify all the requests by administrators either by their usernames or by the origin of the requests.

Time for action – writing rules for special access

Let's say `john`, `michelle`, and `sarah` are the usernames allotted to our administrators and `192.0.2.46`, `192.0.2.9`, and `192.0.2.182` are their respective IP addresses allotted to their laptops. In this case, we are allowing additional access when the requests are originating from the above IP addresses or if the requests are authenticated with the credentials of the aforementioned users. The required ACL lists should look similar to the following:

```
acl admin_laptops src 192.0.2.46 192.0.2.9 192.0.2.182
acl authenticated proxy_auth REQUIRED
acl admin_user proxy_auth john michelle sarah
acl work_related_websites dstdomain "/opt/squid/etc/work_websites"
```

Now, we need to allow everyone to access only work related websites, except administrators who should be able to access everything. Therefore, we should build the following access rules:

```
http_access allow admin_laptops
http_access allow admin_user
http_access allow localnet work_related_websites authenticated
http_access deny all
```

So, in accordance to the previous rules, requests identified by `admin_laptops` and `admin_user` are always allowed, but all other requests have to pass through three filters. First of all, the requests should be `authenticated`, then it should originate from an IP address in the local network, and then the requests should be to a website listed in the `/opt/squid/etc/work_websites` file. If all these criteria are matched, only then will a request be allowed; otherwise it's denied.

What just happened?

In the ACL lists we used a mixture of types (such as `src`, `dstdomain`, and `proxy_auth`) to achieve special access for a set of users. Similarly, we can use various other types of ACL lists to fine-tune our access control configuration.

Limited access during working hours

In some organizations, it's a part of the network usage policy to restrict access to only work related websites during working hours. This is mostly done either due to a lack of bandwidth or to enforce people to focus on work. In such cases, we will first need to construct an ACL list defining the working hours. This should look similar to the following:

```
acl working_hours time D 10:00-13:00
acl working_hours time D 14:00-18:00
```

In the previous code, we have kept 1300HRS - 1400HRS as lunch time, and we don't really mind what people browse in that period.

Now, we need to construct a list of allowed websites, which are allowed during working hours. Let's say we are going to load them from the file `work_related.txt`. So, we construct another ACL type as:

```
acl work_related dstdomain "/opt/squid/etc/work_related.txt"
```

As we have now identified the working hours and the websites which can be accessed during working hours, we can proceed with writing the following rules:

```
http_access allow working_hours localnet work_related
http_access allow !working_hours localnet
http_access deny all
```

If the previous configuration is applied, clients on the local network will be able to access only work related websites during working hours. However, they will be able to access all websites during non working hours.

Allowing some clients to connect to special ports

From time-to–time, there may be requests from various clients that need to connect to a website on a non-HTTP port. To handle such requests, we need to use the ACL type port to construct an ACL list of additional ports which are allowed for only a few clients.

For example, let's say we have requests for opening ports 119 (Usenet News Group), 2082, 3389, and 9418 (Git version control system). If we add these ports to the list of `Safe_ports`, which is a default ACL list provided by Squid, then everyone will be able to connect to these ports. However, we want only a few clients (who have requested to the special access) to connect to these ports. So, we'll need to construct another ACL list as follows:

```
acl special_ports port 119 2082 3389 9418
```

After identifying the ports, we need to identify the requests from the clients requesting special access. This can be achieved in two ways. The first, and most simple method is to identify the clients by their IP addresses. The other way is to identify the special clients by their usernames, but this method only works when we have authentication enforced. So, to identify the clients, we can use the following ACL lists:

```
acl special_clients src 192.0.2.9 192.0.2.46 192.0.2.182
acl authenticated proxy_auth REQUIRED
acl special_users proxy_auth sarah john michelle
```

Now we need to allow `special_clients` or `special_users` to connect to `special_ports`. However, we should remember that the rules we are going to construct for this scenario should go before the following line in `squid.conf`.

```
http_access deny !Safe_ports
```

The previous line will deny access to any port that doesn't exist in the `Safe_ports` ACL list.

So, the rules which we will need to construct will be as follows:

```
http_access allow special_ports special_clients
http_access allow special_ports special_user
http_access deny !Safe_ports
```

Testing access control with squidclient

We learned in *Chapter 3* that we should always test our configuration file for errors or warnings before deploying it on the production servers. Squid provides the command-line option `-k parse` using which the configuration file can be parsed quickly.

However, successful parsing of the configuration file doesn't guarantee that Squid will be able to allow or deny the requests or replies in the manner we are expecting. As the configuration files grows in size, the number ACL lists and corresponding rules keeps on increasing, which may sometimes lead to confusion. To test the access control in our new configuration file, we can use the `squidclient` program.

For this purpose, we'll either need a different test server or we'll need to compile Squid on the production server with a different `--prefix` option with the configure program. For example, we can compile Squid using the following commands:

```
configure --prefix=/opt/squidtest/
make
make install
```

The previous commands will install Squid in the `/opt/squidtest/` directory. We'll need to change the `http_port` option and set the port to 8080 or something other than the port which is used by the original installation.

After this, we need to copy the access control part from our new configuration file to the configuration file of our new test Squid installation in `/opt/squidtest/`. Once we have finished copying the access control configuration, we can start our test proxy server.

Options for squidclient

Squidclient executable or binary is generally located at ${prefix}/bin/squidclient. If we run squidclient without any arguments, it'll display a list of available options which we can specify on the command line. So, let's take a look at the available options for our version of the squidclient.

```
./squidclient
Version: 3.1.4
Usage: ./squidclient [options] url
```

The following table shows a brief overview of supported options:

Option	Usage
-a	Don't include the Accept HTTP header.
-g count	Ping mode. Performs count iterations (0 to count until interrupted).
-h host	Retrieve a URL from the proxy server on hostname. The default is localhost.
-H 'string'	Extra HTTP headers to send. We can use \n for new lines.
-i IMS	Specifies the If-Modified-Since time (in Epoch seconds).
-I interval	Ping interval in seconds. The default is 1 second.
-j hosthdr	Host HTTP header to send.
-k	Keep the connection active. The default is only one request.
-l host	Specify a local IP address to bind to. The default is none.
-m method	HTTP Request method to use. The default is GET.
-p port	Port number of the proxy server. The default is 3128.
-P filename	HTTP PUT request using the file named filename.
-r	Force proxy server to reload the URL.
-s	Operate in silent mode. Do not print data to the standard output (stdout).
-t count	Trace count proxy server hops.
-T timeout	Timeout value (in seconds) for read/write operations.
-u username	Provide username for proxy authentication.
-U username	Provide username for WWW authentication.
-v	Operate in verbose mode. Print outgoing messages to standard error (stderr).
-V version	HTTP Version to use. Use hyphen (-) for the HTTP/0.9 omitted case.
-w password	Provide password for proxy authentication.
-W password	Provide password for WWW authentication.

As you can see from the previous table, the options are pretty easy to understand. We don't really need to use all of them. We are most likely to need options such as `-i`, `-j`, `-l`, `-h`, `-p`, `-u`, `-w`, `-m`, and `-H`.

Using the squidclient

So, let's get started and begin testing our Squid server. Let's say we have blocked access to the website `malware.example.com` using the following access control in our configuration file:

```
acl malware dstdomain malware.example.com
http_access deny malware
```

Time for action – testing our access control example with squidclient

We now need to run the `squidclient` to fetch `http://malware.example.com/` to check if we get an access denied error or not. If we are running the `squidclient` on the production server, then we don't need to use the `-h` option to specify the hostname. In this scenario, we can run the `squidclient` with the `-p` option to specify the port.

```
./squidclient -p 8080 http://malware.example.com
```

However, if we are running the `squidclient` on a different machine, we will have to use the `-h` option to specify the hostname of the proxy server. In this scenario, we can run the `squidclient` with the following configuration:

```
./squidclient -h proxy.example.com -p 8080 http://malware.example.com
```

If our access control rules are working and they are rightly placed in the configuration file, we should get an output similar to the following:

```
HTTP/1.0 403 Forbidden
Server: squid/3.1.4
Date: Mon, 06 Sep 2010 09:28:38 GMT
Content-Type: text/html
Content-Length: 2408
Expires: Mon, 06 Sep 2010 09:28:38 GMT
X-Squid-Error: ERR_ACCESS_DENIED 0
X-Cache: MISS from proxy.example.com
X-Cache-Lookup: NONE from proxy.example.com:8080
Via: 1.0 proxy.example.com:8080 (squid/3.1.4)
Proxy-Connection: close

<!DOCTYPE html PUBLIC "-//W3C//DTD HTML 4.01//EN" "http://www.w3.org/
TR/html4/strict.dtd">
<html><head>
```

```
<meta http-equiv="Content-Type" content="text/html; charset=iso-8859-1">
<title>ERROR: The requested URL could not be retrieved</title>
...
```

In the previous output, the first line contains the HTTP status of the reply which denotes that the request was denied. So, we can say that the access rule which we have used in the configuration file is working fine.

What just happened?

We have seen an example of the basic usage of the `squidclient` to test the access control configuration before deploying a new configuration on the production server.

Time for action – testing a complex access control

An access control involving IP addresses from different subnets is a bit difficult to test but can be tested using the `squidclient`. This can be done by creating virtual or alias network interfaces on the machine. For example, the IP address of our proxy server is `192.168.36.204` and we have the following access control configuration in our `squid.conf`, which we want to test:

```
acl bad_guys src 10.1.33.9 10.1.33.182
http_access deny bad_guys
```

We can't test these rules directly as our IP address is different from the clients we have blocked and Squid will check for the source IP address in the requests. However, we can use option `-1`, which is available with the `squidclient`, which will bind it to a different IP address while sending requests to the Squid proxy server. To achieve this, we need to create an alias network interface on our server. In most Linux/Unix-based systems, this can be achieved by using the following command:

```
ifconfig eth0:0 10.1.33.9 up
```

Once the alias interface is up, we can use the following command to test our new configuration:

```
./squidclient -1 10.1.33.9 -p 8080 http://www.example.com/
```

We should get an output similar to the following:

```
HTTP/1.0 403 Forbidden
Server: squid/3.1.4
Mime-Version: 1.0
Date: Mon, 06 Sep 2010 09:40:22 GMT
Content-Type: text/html
Content-Length: 1361
```

```
Expires: Mon, 06 Sep 2010 09:40:22 GMT
X-Squid-Error: ERR_ACCESS_DENIED 0
X-Cache: MISS from proxy.example.com
X-Cache-Lookup: NONE from proxy.example.com:8080
Via: 1.0 proxy.bordeaux.com:8080 (squid/3.1.4)
Proxy-Connection: close

<!DOCTYPE html PUBLIC "-//W3C//DTD HTML 4.01//EN" "http://www.w3.org/
TR/html4/strict.dtd">
<html><head>
<meta http-equiv="Content-Type" content="text/html; charset=iso-8859-
1">
<title>ERROR: The requested URL could not be retrieved</title>
...
```

What just happened?

We created a virtual network interface or alias network interface and asked the `squidclient` to project us as a totally different client by sending out the IP address of the alias interface as the source IP address of the request. This helped us in testing our access control configuration in the reference frame of another client.

Similarly, we can use other options to test different access control configurations before deploying them on our production servers.

Pop quiz

1. Consider the following lines in the Squid configuration file:
   ```
   acl client1 src 10.1.33.9/255.255.255.255
   acl client2 src 10.1.33.9/32
   acl client3 src 10.1.33.0/24
   acl client4 src 10.1.33.0/30
   ```

   Which of the following ACL lists will not match a request from a client with the IP address `10.1.33.9`?

   a. client1

   b. client2

   c. client3

   d. client4

2. Consider the following line in the Squid configuration file:

   ```
   acl domain dstdomain amazon.com
   ```

   Which requests to of the following domain names will be matched by the ACL list domain?

   a. amazon.com

   b. www.amazon.com

   c. mail.amazon.com

   d. amazon.com.au

3. Consider the following configuration:

   ```
   acl manager proto cache_object
   acl localhost src 127.0.0.1
   acl admin1 src 10.2.44.46
   acl admin2 src 10.1.33.182
   http_access allow manager localhost
   http_access allow manager admin1 admin2
   http_access deny manager
   ```

   Which of the following clients will be able to access Squid's cache manager?

   a. localhost

   b. 10.1.33.9

   c. 10.1.33.182

   d. clients b and c

4. Consider the following configuration:

   ```
   acl client1 src 10.2.44.46
   acl client2 src 10.1.33.9
   http_access allow client1
   http_access allow client2
   http_reply_access deny all
   ```

   Which of the following clients will be able to view websites using our proxy server?

   a. 10.2.44.46

   b. 10.1.33.9

   c. a and b both

   d. None

Summary

We have learned a lot about access control lists and access list rules in this chapter. We had a detailed look at the various types of ACL and how to construct ACL lists for different scenarios. We took examples describing a general situation in which we needed to use a mixture of ACL types and rules to achieve the desired access control.

Specifically, we covered:

- Different types of ACL which can identify individual requests and replies.
- Different types of access list rules which can be used to control access to various components of the Squid proxy server.
- Achieving desired access control by mixing various ACL types with access rules.
- Testing our new Squid configuration with the `squidclient` before actually using it in a production environment.

We also discussed some example scenarios which can serve as the base configuration for various organizations.

Now that we have learned about compiling, installing, configuring, and running Squid, we can try to deploy Squid on some test machines and begin testing them. In the next chapter, we'll learn about logging in detail.

5
Understanding Log Files and Log Formats

Understanding Squid log files and log formats is pretty easy. In this chapter, we'll present a brief explanation of the log format and how we can customize it to fit our needs. We will cover the related Squid configuration options and look at how a client's privacy can be protected, by ensuring Squid is properly configured.

In this chapter, we will learn to interpret the different log files. We will also learn about configuring Squid to achieve different log messages, depending on requirements or network policies.

In this chapter, we shall learn about the following:

◆ Cache log

◆ Access log

◆ Customizing the access log

◆ Selective logging or protecting clients' privacy

◆ Referer log

◆ User agent log

◆ Emulating the HTTP server like logs

◆ Log file rotation

So let's get on with it.

Log messages

Log messages are a nice way for any application to convey messages about its current actions to human users. A log message is basically a computer-generated message that can be interpreted by a human being with prior knowledge of the location of the different fields in the message. Squid also tries to log every possible action in different log files at different stages. When Squid encounters any errors before starting, it logs them to the output log which generally goes to a file named `cache.log`. Similarly, when clients access our proxy server, a message is logged to the file named `access.log` whose location is determined by the `access_log` directive in the Squid configuration file.

Squid uses different formats for logging messages to these files. Log files are important and we can analyze resource consumption and the performance of our proxy server by reading through the log files, or by using various log file parsers available. In this chapter, we will learn to interpret the different log files.

Cache log or debug log

Squid logs all the errors and debugging messages to the `cache.log` file. This log file also contains messages about the integrity checks such as, availability and validity of cache directories, which are performed by Squid.

Time for action – understanding the cache log

Let's go through the log messages for a test Squid run and see what each line means:

```
2010/09/10 23:31:10| Starting Squid Cache version 3.1.10 for i686-pc-
linux-gnu...
2010/09/10 23:31:10| Process ID 14892
```

Looking at the preceding example, the first line represents the version of Squid we are currently running and provides some information about the platform. The next line contains the process ID for this instance of Squid.

```
2010/09/10 23:31:10| With 1024 file descriptors available
```

This line shows the number of file descriptors available for Squid in this run. We can check back similar lines in our cache log, if we increase or decrease the available number of file descriptors and restart the Squid process. Please refer to the section on *Configure or system check* in *Chapter 1, Getting Started with Squid*.

```
2010/09/10 23:31:10| Initializing IP Cache...
2010/09/10 23:31:10| DNS Socket created at [::], FD 7
2010/09/10 23:31:10| Adding nameserver 192.0.2.86 from /etc/resolv.
conf
```

When Squid is started, it'll initialize the DNS systems starting with IP cache, as shown in the first line. The second and third lines show information about the DNS configuration. Squid added `192.0.2.86` as a DNS server from the file `/etc/resolv.conf`, which is the default location for specifying DNS servers on Linux machines. If we have more than one DNS server in the `/etc/resolv.conf` file, there will be more lines similar to the last line.

```
2010/09/10 23:31:10| User-Agent logging is disabled.
2010/09/10 23:31:10| Referer logging is disabled.
```

In the aforementioned lines, Squid is trying to show the status of the optional modules which we have enabled while compiling Squid. It is clear to see in these lines, `User-Agent` and `Referer` logging is disabled for this run.

The following are the log messages related to logging:

```
2010/09/10 23:31:10| Logfile: opening log daemon:/opt/squid/var/logs/
access.log
2010/09/10 23:31:10| Unlinkd pipe opened on FD 13
2010/09/10 23:31:10| Local cache digest enabled; rebuild/rewrite every
3600/3600 sec
2010/09/10 23:31:10| Store logging disabled
```

In the preceding log message shown, the first line shows that Squid is going to use the file `/opt/squid/var/logs/access.log` as an access log file. It also shows that `unlinkd` is being used as the program to purge stale cache objects. Additionally, cache digest is enabled and will be rebuilt and rewritten every hour. The last line demonstrates that the logging of all storage-related activities has been disabled.

```
2010/09/10 23:31:10| Swap maxSize 1024000 + 262144 KB, estimated 98934
objects
2010/09/10 23:31:10| Target number of buckets: 4946
2010/09/10 23:31:10| Using 8192 Store buckets
2010/09/10 23:31:10| Max Mem  size: 262144 KB
2010/09/10 23:31:10| Max Swap size: 1024000 KB
2010/09/10 23:31:10| Version 1 of swap file with LFS support
detected...
2010/09/10 23:31:10| Rebuilding storage in /opt/squid/var/cache
(DIRTY)
2010/09/10 23:31:10| Using Least Load store dir selection
2010/09/10 23:31:10| Set Current Directory to /opt/squid/var/cache
```

The previous log message is referring to the cache directories and represents information about the various parameters involved in caching web documents onto the hard disks. The `Swap` in this log message refers to the Squid disk cache storage and should not be confused with the system swap memory.

```
2010/09/10 23:31:10| Loaded Icons.
2010/09/10 23:31:10| Accepting  HTTP connections at [::]:3128, FD 16.
2010/09/10 23:31:10| HTCP Disabled.
```

```
2010/09/10 23:31:10| Squid plugin modules loaded: 0
2010/09/10 23:31:10| Ready to serve requests.
```

From these lines, we can interpret that Squid has loaded the required modules and is now ready to accept connections from clients. We can also see that the HTCP module is disabled.

```
2010/09/10 23:31:10| Done reading /opt/squid/var/cache swaplog (0
entries)
2010/09/10 23:31:10| Finished rebuilding storage from disk.
2010/09/10 23:31:10|        0 Entries scanned
2010/09/10 23:31:10|        0 Invalid entries.
2010/09/10 23:31:10|        0 With invalid flags.
2010/09/10 23:31:10|        0 Objects loaded.
2010/09/10 23:31:10|        0 Objects expired.
2010/09/10 23:31:10|        0 Objects cancelled.
2010/09/10 23:31:10|        0 Duplicate URLs purged.
2010/09/10 23:31:10|        0 Swapfile clashes avoided.
2010/09/10 23:31:10|   Took 0.03 seconds (  0.00 objects/sec).
2010/09/10 23:31:10| Beginning Validation Procedure
2010/09/10 23:31:10|   Completed Validation Procedure
2010/09/10 23:31:10|   Validated 25 Entries
2010/09/10 23:31:10|   store_swap_size = 0
2010/09/10 23:31:11| storeLateRelease: released 0 objects
```

This log message contains information on the rebuilding of the cache from the hard disks.

The previous examples of log messages which we have looked at are for a successful startup of Squid. Let's see how the log messages look when Squid encounters some problems. For example, if Squid doesn't have write permissions on the cache directory, then the following log message will appear in the cache log:

```
2010/09/10 01:42:30| Max Mem  size: 262144 KB
2010/09/10 01:42:30| Max Swap size: 1024000 KB
2010/09/10 01:42:30| /opt/squid/var/cache/00: (13) Permission denied
FATAL:  Failed to verify one of the swap directories, Check cache.log
   for details.  Run 'squid -z' to create swap directories
   if needed, or if running Squid for the first time.
Squid Cache (Version 3.1.10): Terminated abnormally.
```

So, we can see that Squid is reporting 'Permission denied' on the cache directory. Whenever there is a problem, Squid will try to describe the possible cause and a resolution, or the most appropriate action that may fix the problem.

What just happened?

We learned the meaning of the various messages popping up in a cache log. Generally, if anything goes wrong with our proxy server, the first thing we should do is check the cache log for any error messages or warnings. If Squid is running out of resources such as memory, file descriptors, or disk space for example, then it will log appropriate messages in the cache log and will also try to log the possible fixes for the problems.

Have a go hero – exploring the cache log

Run the Squid proxy server and try to understand the messages being logged by Squid in the cache log file.

Access log

The `cache.log` file is important for debugging if Squid is misbehaving. But the most important log file is the `access.log` file, where Squid logs the live information about who is accessing our proxy server, and related information about the status of requests and replies. The location of the `access.log` file is determined by the directive `access_log`, in the Squid configuration file. By default it is set defaults to `${prefix}/var/logs/access.log`.

Understanding the access log

The log messages in the `access.log` file are not as readable as messages in the `cache.log` file, but once we understand what the different fields mean, it's very easy to interpret the log messages. There are multiple formats in which messages are logged in the `access.log` file. The messages that we are going to see next, are in the default log format called `squid`.

Time for action – understanding the access log messages

Let's look at a few lines from the `access.log` file before we actually explore the different fields in the log message:

```
1284565351.509    114 127.0.0.1 TCP_MISS/302 781 GET http://www.
google.com/ - FIRST_UP_PARENT/proxy.example.com text/html

1284565351.633    108 127.0.0.1 TCP_MISS/200 6526 GET http://www.
google.co.in/ - FIRST_UP_PARENT/proxy.example.com text/html

1284565352.610    517 127.0.0.1 TCP_MISS/200 29963 GET http://www.
google.co.in/images/srpr/nav_logo14.png - FIRST_UP_PARENT/proxy.
example.com image/png

1284565354.102    147 127.0.0.1 TCP_MISS/200 1786 GET http://www.
google.co.in/favicon.ico - FIRST_UP_PARENT/proxy.example.com image/x-
icon
```

In the previous example of a log message, the first column represents the seconds elapsed since a Unix epoch (for more information on the Unix epoch, refer to `http://en.wikipedia.org/wiki/Unix_epoch`), which can't really be interpreted by human users. To quickly convert the timestamps in access log messages, we can use Perl, as shown:

```
$ perl -p -e 's/^([0-9]*)/"[".localtime($1)."]"/e' < access.log > access.log.h
```

Now the access log messages should look similar to the following with timestamps converted to normal time:

```
[Wed Sep 15 21:12:31 2010].509    114 127.0.0.1 TCP_MISS/302 781 GET
http://www.google.com/ - FIRST_UP_PARENT/proxy.example.com text/html

[Wed Sep 15 21:12:31 2010].633    108 127.0.0.1 TCP_MISS/200 6526 GET
http://www.google.co.in/ - FIRST_UP_PARENT/proxy.example.com text/html

[Wed Sep 15 21:12:32 2010].610    517 127.0.0.1 TCP_MISS/200 29963 GET
http://www.google.co.in/images/srpr/nav_logo14.png - FIRST_UP_PARENT/
proxy.example.com image/png

[Wed Sep 15 21:12:34 2010].102    147 127.0.0.1 TCP_MISS/200 1786 GET
http://www.google.co.in/favicon.ico - FIRST_UP_PARENT/proxy.example.com
image/x-icon
```

The second column represents the response time in milliseconds. The third column represents the client's IP address. The fourth column is a combination of Squid's requests status and the HTTP status code. The fifth column represents the size of the reply including HTTP headers. The sixth column in the log message represents the HTTP request method which will be GET most of the time, but may also have values such as POST, PUT, DELETE, and so on.

The seventh column represents the request URL. The eighth column is the username, which is blank in this case because the request was not authenticated. The ninth column is a combination of the Squid hierarchy status and IP address or peer name of the cache peer. The last column represents the content type of the replies.

What just happened?

We had a look at a few log messages generated by Squid in the default log format. We also learned what the individual columns mean in the messages. We don't need to memorize this as the meaning of these columns will become obvious once we learn about the various format codes to construct the log formats.

Access log syntax

We can use different places for logging access log messages. We can use a combination of `access_log` and `logformat` directives to specify the location and format of the log messages. Next, we are going to explore them one by one.

Time for action – analyzing a syntax to specify access log

Let's have a look at the syntax of the `access_log` directive:

```
access_log <module>:<place> [<logformat name> [acl acl ...]]
```

The field `module` is one of the `none`, `stdio`, `daemon`, `syslog`, `tcp`, and `udp` methods, which determine how the messages will be logged to a `place`, and is the absolute path to the file or place where the messages should be logged. Let's take a brief look at the meaning of different modules:

- `none`—The log messages will not be logged at all.
- `stdio`—The log messages will be logged to a file immediately after the completion of each request.
- `daemon`—This module is similar to `stdio` module, however the log messages are not written to the disk and are passed to a daemon helper for asynchronous handling instead.
- `syslog`—This module is used to log each message using the `syslog` facility. The parameter `place` is specified in the form of the `syslog` facility and the priority level for the log entries. For example, `daemon.info` will use the `daemon syslog` facility and messages will be logged with the `info` priority.

  The valid values of the `syslog` facilities are `authpriv`, `daemon`, `local0`, `local1`, ..., `local7`, and `user`. The valid values of priority are `err`, `warning`, `notice`, `info`, and `debug`.
- `tcp`—When the `tcp` module is used, the log messages are sent to a TCP receiver. The format for specifying the place parameter is `\\host:port`.
- `udp`—When the `udp` module is used, the log messages are sent to a UDP receiver. The format for specifying a place parameter is `\\host:port`.

We can specify an optional `logformat name` and can control logging using ACL lists as well. The following is the default access log configuration used by Squid:

```
access_log daemon:/opt/squid/var/logs/access.log squid
```

In this configuration, `/opt/squid/` is the `${prefix}` and `squid` is the `logformat` being used.

What just happened?

We learned about specifying options for the `access_log` directive. We also had a brief look at the various modules available for writing logs. We also learned about optional controlling of log messages using ACL lists so that we can log the only requests that we are interested in.

Have a go hero – logging messages to the syslog module

Use the `access_log` directive to configure Squid to send log messages to the `syslog` module.

Log format

In the previous section, we had learned about sending log messages to different places. Now, we are going to learn about formatting the log messages according to our needs.

Time for action – learning log format and format codes

Log format can be defined using the `logformat` directive available in the Squid configuration file. The syntax for defining `logformat` is as follows:

```
logformat <name> <format specification>
```

`Format specification` is a series of format code, as described in the following information:

Format code	Format description
%	A literal % character.
sn	Unique sequence number per log line entry.
err_code	The ID of an error response served by Squid or a similar internal error identifier.
err_detail	Additional `err_code` dependent error information.
>a	Client's source IP address.
>A	Client's FQDN (Fully Qualified Domain Name).
>p	Client's source port.
<A	Server's IP address or peer name.
la	Local IP address of the Squid proxy server.
lp	Local port number on which Squid is listening.
<lp	Local port number of the last server or peer connection.
ts	Seconds since Unix epoch.
tu	Sub-second time (in milliseconds).
tl	Local time. Optional `strftime` format argument. The default is `%d/%b/%Y:%H:%M:%S %z`

Format code	Format description
tg	GMT time. Optional `strftime` format argument. The default is `%d/%b/%Y:%H:%M:%S %z`
tr	Response time (milliseconds).
dt	Total time spent making DNS lookups (milliseconds).
[http::]>h	Original request header. Optional header name argument on the format header `[:[separator]element]`.
[http::]>ha	The HTTP request headers after adaptation and redirection. Optional header name argument as for >h.
[http::]un	User name.
[http::]<h	Reply header. Optional header name argument as for >h.
[http::]ul	User name from authentication.
[http::]ui	User name from ident request.
[http::]>Hs	HTTP status code sent to the client.
[http::]<Hs	HTTP status code received from the next hop.
[http::]<bs	Number of HTTP-equivalent message body bytes received from the next hop, excluding chunked transfer encoding and control messages. Generated FTP/Gopher listings are treated as received bodies.
[http::]Ss	Squid request status (`TCP_MISS`, and so on).
[http::]Sh	Squid hierarchy status (`DEFAULT_PARENT`, and so on).
[http::]mt	MIME content type of the reply.
[http::]rm	HTTP request method (`GET/POST`, and so on).
[http::]ru	Request URL.
[http::]rp	Request URL path, excluding hostname.
[http::]rv	Request protocol version.
[http::]<st	Sent reply size including HTTP headers.
[http::]>st	Received request size including HTTP headers. In the case of chunked requests, the chunked encoding metadata is not included.
[http::]>sh	Received HTTP request headers' size.
[http::]<sh	Sent HTTP reply headers' size.
[http::]st	Request and reply size including HTTP headers.
[http::]<sH	Reply high offset sent.
[http::]<sS	Upstream object size.
[http::]<pt	Peer response time in milliseconds. The timer starts when the last request byte is sent to the next hop and stops when the last response byte is received.
[http::]<tt	Total server-side time in milliseconds. The timer starts with the first connect request (or write I/O) sent to the first selected peer. The timer stops with the last I/O with the last peer.

We can use any number of the aforementioned format codes to construct a log format according to our choice or requirement. While specifying a format code, we must prefix the format code with a % so that Squid can evaluate it.

What just happened?

We have just learned about the syntax for building new log formats that can be used with the `access_log` directive at a later stage, for custom logging. We also saw a list of format codes available for logging different information about a particular request from a client. Log formats are always a combination of these format codes.

Log formats provided by Squid

By default, Squid provides four log formats that can be used right away. Let's see the default log formats provided by Squid:

```
logformat squid %ts.%03tu %6tr %>a %Ss/%03>Hs %<st %rm %ru %un %Sh/%<A
%mt

logformat squidmime %ts.%03tu %6tr %>a %Ss/%03>Hs %<st %rm %ru %un
%Sh/%<A %mt [%>h] [%<h]

logformat common %>a %ui %un [%tl] "%rm %ru HTTP/%rv" %>Hs %<st
%Ss:%Sh

logformat combined %>a %ui %un [%tl] "%rm %ru HTTP/%rv" %>Hs %<st
"%{Referer}>h" "%{User-Agent}>h" %Ss:%Sh
```

As we saw, the default log format for access log is `squid`, therefore we can now interpret the log messages we saw earlier very easily. Let's see one of the lines from the log messages shown earlier:

```
1284565354.102    147 127.0.0.1 TCP_MISS/200 1786 GET http://www.
google.co.in/favicon.ico - FIRST_UP_PARENT/proxy.example.com image/x-
icon
```

If we refer to the table of format codes, we can observe that the seventh column (`%ru`) represents the request URL sent by the HTTP client.

Time for action – customizing the access log with a new log format

Squid has a lot of information about every client request and reply, however it writes only the requested information to the log file, which we can customize by defining several log formats.

Now, let's define a log format in which the time will appear in a human-readable format and use it with `access_log`:

```
logformat minimal %tl %>a %Ss/%03>Hs %rm %ru
access_log daemon:/opt/squid/var/logs/access.log minimal
```

So, we have constructed a new log format that will log the information we are most interested in. Let's see a few log messages in the preceding format:

```
11/Sep/2010:23:52:33 +0530 127.0.0.1 TCP_MISS/200 GET http://
en.wikipedia.org/wiki/Main_Page
```

```
11/Sep/2010:23:52:34 +0530 127.0.0.1 TCP_MISS/200 GET http://
en.wikipedia.org/images/wikimedia-button.png
```

Now the time in the log messages is human-readable and we can therefore tell when a particular URL was accessed.

We should note that if we are using custom formats for access log, then we may not be able to use several external programs that can parse and analyze Squid's access log. However, we can solve this problem by using multiple access log directives to log the messages in more than one format so that one log file is for analyzing, and the other file can be used for manual viewing.

What just happened?

We constructed a new log format and used it with the `access_log` directive. Now the time of requests in all the log messages will be in a human-readable format. Next, we can construct any number of log formats and use them with the `access_log` directive to achieve different types of log messages.

Selective logging of requests

Sometimes we may not want to log requests from certain clients. This could be because of several reasons. One reason may be that a team is working on a highly secret project and we don't want to leave any impressions of their browsing patterns anywhere.

Logging of requests can be controlled using two directives, namely, `log_access` and `access_log`. These directives may look confusing when used in the same sentence but we can interpret the meaning by the sequence in which the individual words appear in the directive name. The directive `access_log` is used for controlling the format of the log messages and the location where the messages will be logged. While the directive `log_access` is used to control whether a particular request should be logged or not.

We have already learned about the `log_access` directive in the *Log Access* section in *Chapter 2, Configuring Squid*. Now, we will learn about using the `access_log` directive to cache selective requests.

Time for action – using access_log to control logging of requests

As we have seen in a previous section of this chapter, the syntax of the `access_log` directive is as follows:

```
access_log <module>:<path> [<logformat name> [acl acl ...]]
```

So, here we have an option to specify ACL lists which we can use to control where the different requests will be logged, if at all. Let's consider a scenario where we don't want to log requests to Yahoo! servers and we do want to log requests to Google and Facebook servers to separate files, and all other requests go to the access log. This scenario can be realized with the following configuration:

```
acl yahoo dstdomain .yahoo.com
acl google dstdomain .google.com
acl facebook dstdomain .facebook.com
log_access deny yahoo
log_access allow all
access_log /opt/squid/var/logs/google.log squid google
access_log /opt/squid/var/logs/facebook.log squid facebook
access_log /opt/squid/var/logs/access.log
```

If we look at the configuration carefully, we are denying `log_access` for all the requests to Yahoo! servers. This means that clients will be able to browse Yahoo! websites, but the information will not be logged to any access log. Also, we are logging requests to Google websites in a file named `google.log` and requests to Facebook in a file named `facebook.log`. All requests will be logged to the `access.log` file, which is the default log file used by Squid.

What just happened?

We just learned about the control provided by Squid, using which we can log various requests to different log files for analysis at a later stage.

Referer log

When a client clicks a link to `other.example.com` on the website `example.com`, then the website `example.com` is a referrer and the client is referred to the website `other.example.com`. When a client is referred by a website, a HTTP header `referer` is sent by the HTTP clients. Squid has the ability to log `referer` HTTP headers, which can later be used for analyzing traffic patterns.

"Referer" is actually a misspelling of the word "Referrer", but it has been officially specified that way in HTTP RFCs.

Time for action – enabling the referer log

By default, there is no referer log. We can enable the referer log using the `access_log` directive in combination with a custom log format. To generate the referer log, first of all, we need to create a log format as shown:

```
logformat referer %ts.%03tu %>a %{Referer}>h %ru
```

This configuration defines a new log format called `referer`, which contains a request timestamp, IP address of the client, the referer URL, and the request URL. Now, we need to use the `access_log` directive with the aforementioned constructed log format as shown:

```
access_log /opt/squid/var/logs/referer.log referer
```

Now, let's look at a few lines from the referer log file:

```
1284576601.898 127.0.0.1 http://en.wikipedia.org/wiki/Main_Page
http://en.wikiquote.org/wiki/Main_Page

1284576607.732 127.0.0.1 http://en.wikiquote.org/wiki/Main_Page
http://upload.wikimedia.org/wikiquote/en/b/bc/Wiki.png
```

The referer log is a bit easier to understand. The first column is the time elapsed since epoch, which can't be customized to a human-readable time. The second column is the client's IP address. The third column is the referer link, and the fourth column is the link to which the client is referred.

What just happened?

We enabled the logging of referrers, which is not present by default. Now we can observe the web browsing patterns on our network. Referer logging is done mostly for analysis purposes.

Time for action – translating the referer logs to a human-readable format

We can translate a referer log to a human-readable format by using the command line utility `awk`. We can convert the entire `referer.log` file to a human-readable format by using the following command sequence:

```
$ cat referer.log | awk '{printf("%s ", strftime("%d/%b/
%Y:%H:%M:%S",$1)); print $2 " " $3 " " $4;}' > referer_human_readable.log
```

The log messages from `referer.log`, as shown, should look like the following messages after conversion:

```
12/Sep/2010:01:36:06 127.0.0.1 http://en.wikipedia.org/wiki/Main_Page
http://en.wikiquote.org/

12/Sep/2010:01:36:12 127.0.0.1 http://en.wikiquote.org/wiki/Main_Page
http://upload.wikimedia.org/wikiquote/en/b/bc/Wiki.png
```

The command we saw before works fine for the conversion of the entire log file, but is not useful if we want to see the live referer log with human-readable timestamps. For achieving this, we can use the following command:

```
$ tail -f referer.log | awk '{printf("%s ", strftime("%d/%b/
%Y:%H:%M:%S",$1)); print $2 " " $3 " " $4;}'
```

This will convert the timestamp to a human-readable time on the fly.

If we don't want to use the previous command combinations, we can modify our referer log format to log timestamps in a human-readable format, as shown:

```
logformat referer %tl %>a %{Referer}>h %ru
```

This log format contains the timestamp in a human-readable local time format.

What just happened?

We learned to use the command line utilities like `cat`, `tail`, and `awk` to print the timestamps in our proxy server's referer logs in a more user-friendly format.

Have a go hero – referer log

Enable referer logging on your proxy server. Now, using your proxy server, browse to any website and click a few links on that website. Now check your referer log file and observe the referer links.

User agent log

All requests from clients generally contain the `User-Agent` HTTP header, which is basically a formatted string describing the HTTP client being used for the current request. As Squid knows everything about the requests, it can log this HTTP header field to the log file defined by the `useragent_log` directive in the Squid configuration file.

Time for action – enabling user agent logging

By default, the user agent log is disabled and we can enable it by using the following line in our configuration file:

```
useragent_log /opt/squid/var/logs/useragent.log
```

Once we have the user agent log enabled, Squid will start logging the `User-Agent` HTTP header field from the requests, depending on the availability of the field. Let's see a few lines from an example user agent log:

```
127.0.0.1 [12/Sep/2010:01:55:33 +0530] "Mozilla/5.0 (X11; U; Linux
i686; en-US; rv:1.9.2.6) Gecko/20100625 Firefox/3.6.6 GTB7.1"
127.0.0.1 [12/Sep/2010:01:55:33 +0530] "Mozilla/5.0 (X11; U; Linux
i686; en-US; rv:1.9.2.6) Gecko/20100625 Firefox/3.6.6 GTB7.1
GoogleToolbarFF 7.1.20100830 GTBA"
```

The format of this file is quite simple and only the last column, representing the user agent, is of interest here. The user agent log can be used to analyze the popular web browsers on a network.

What just happened?

We learned to enable logging of the `User-Agent` HTTP header field from all client requests, which are subject to availability, and can be used for analyzing the popular HTTP clients at a later stage.

Emulating HTTP server-like logs

Squid has an optional feature that can help in generating log messages similar to messages generated for most HTTP servers. We can use the `access_log` directive to log messages with the log format `common`.

Time for action – enabling HTTP server log emulation

By default, Squid will generate a native log, which contains more information than the logs generated with the HTTP log emulation on. We can use the following line in our configuration line:

```
access_log daemon:/opt/squid/var/logs/access.log common
```

This configuration will log messages in a web server-like format. Let's have a look at a few log messages in the HTTP server-like log format:

```
127.0.0.1 - - [13/Sep/2010:17:38:57 +0530] "GET http://www.google.com/
HTTP/1.1" 200 6637 TCP_MISS:FIRSTUP_PARENT

127.0.0.1 - - [13/Sep/2010:17:40:11 +0530] "GET http://example.com/
HTTP/1.1" 200 1147 TCP_HIT:HIER_NONE

127.0.0.1 - - [13/Sep/2010:17:40:12 +0530] "GET http://example.com/
favicon.ico HTTP/1.1" 404 717 TCP_MISS:FIRSTUP_PARENT
```

These log messages are similar to log messages generated by the famous open source web server Apache and many others.

What just happened?

We learned to switch on the HTTP server-like log emulation of Squid access logs. Squid access logs can be easy to understand if we are already familiar with web server logs.

Log file rotation

As time passes, the size of the log files increases rapidly and starts occupying more and more disk space. To overcome this problem of the accumulation of logs over time, we generally keep the logs for the previous one or two weeks. To remove old log messages and retain the recent ones, Squid has a built-in feature of log file rotation, which can move older log messages to separate files. Moreover, Squid stores the incremental copy of the storage index in a file swap.state, which is also pruned down during log rotation.

To rotate logs, we have to use the squid command as follows:

```
$ squid -k rotate
```

This command will rotate logs depending on the value specified with the directive logfile_rotate in the configuration file. The default value of logfile_rotate is 10. This means that 10 older versions of all log files will be retained.

Have a go hero – rotate log files

Try to rotate log files on your proxy server and see how the log files are renamed.

Other log related features

We discussed important logging related directives in the previous sections. Squid has more directives related to logging, but they are less important and we should not have any problems in operating Squid normally, even if we are not aware of these features.

Cache store log

If we have disk caching enabled on our proxy server, Squid can log its entire disk caching related activities to a separate log file whose location is determined by the directive `cache_store_log`. This log file, contains information about the web objects being cached on the disk, stale objects being removed from the cache, and how long an object was in the cache. The information logged in this file is not particularly user-friendly. By default, logging of storage activity is disabled.

Pop quiz

1. Consider the following configuration line:

   ```
   access_log daemon:/opt/squid/var/logs/access.log
   ```

   Which log format will be used by Squid in accordance with the previous configuration?

   a. common

   b. squid

   c. combined

   d. squidmime

2. Which one of the following is a disadvantage of logging client requests?

   a. An administrator can figure out resource usage by several clients.

   b. A client's browsing behavior can be predicted by analyzing requests.

   c. It can help administrators in debugging anomalies.

   d. Logs can fill up hard disks.

3. Which of the following is a not valid reason for log rotation?

   a. Keeping old logs is a violation of client privacy.

   b. Old logs are generally not needed.

   c. Log rotation can help us in recovering disk space periodically.

   d. Generally, we analyze logs, store the results, and delete logs to save disk space.

Summary

In this chapter, we have learned to interpret several log files generated by Squid. We had a detailed look at the format codes that Squid uses to construct log messages and how we can construct custom log formats depending on the requirements.

Specifically, we understood cache log, debugged messages generated by Squid, and had a detailed overview of access log and format codes. We customized log messages using several log formats and selectively logged requests to various log files, and enabled the referer and user agent log messages.

We also discussed about rotating log files to prevent unnecessary wastage of disk space.

Now that we have learned about the various log files and log messages, we will go on to learn about using these messages to monitor our proxy server and analyze the performance of our cache, in the next chapter.

6
Managing Squid and Monitoring Traffic

In the previous chapter on log files, we learned about the different types of log messages generated by Squid and the various log files containing the different types of log messages. So, in the last few chapters, we have learned about running a Squid proxy server and interpreting the various log files. As it's not convenient to manually check log files every time, and as it's almost impossible to analyze traffic by manually going through the log files, it's time to explore Squid's cache manager which is a web interface which is used to monitor and manage the proxy server. We'll also look at a few log file analyzers that can directly parse log files generated by Squid and then present a statistical analysis of web pages browsed by clients.

In this chapter, we shall learn the following:

- Using cache manager (web interface)
- Installing the external log file analyzer software

So, let's get started.

Cache manager

As described briefly in the earlier chapters, cache manager (cachemgr) is a web interface for managing the Squid proxy servers. It is provided by default. This means that we don't have to install any additional module, or software, other than a web server to have a web interface to manage our proxy server. Also, cache manager is not just an interface to manage our proxy server. It provides various statistics about the usage of different resources that can help us in monitoring the proxy server from a web interface.

But before we can use the cache manager web interface, we need to configure Squid and our web server to use the `cachmgr.cgi` program for providing the web interface.

Installing the Apache Web server

Although this topic is out of the scope of this book, we'll have a quick look at installing Apache, which is a very popular open source Web server and is available for free from `http://httpd.apache.org/`. Apache is available in software repositories of most Linux/Unix-based operating systems under different names.

Time for action – installing Apache Web server

To install Apache on Red Hat Enterprise Linux, CentOS, or Fedora, we can use `yum`, the default package manager for these distributions, for example:

```
$ yum install httpd
```

To install Apache Ubuntu or Debian, we can use the `aptitude` package manager, as shown in the following example:

```
$ aptitude install apache2
```

For installing Apache on other operating systems, please check the package installation manual of the operating system.

What just happened?

We learned to install the very popular open source Web server, Apache, using the package manager for our operating system. This will help us in getting the web interface for the cache manager up and running.

Configuring Apache for providing the cache manager web interface

After installing Apache, we need to configure it to use `cachemgr.cgi`. The file `cachemgr.cgi` is generally located at `${prefix}/libexec/cachemgr.cgi` where `${prefix}` is the value specified for the `--prefix` option, before running `configure`.

> On some operating systems like OpenBSD, Apache is chrooted by default. Please visit `http://www.openbsd.org/faq/faq10.html#httpdchroot` for more information.

Time for action – configuring Apache to use cachemgr.cgi

To complete this task quickly we need to put the following lines in a file named
`squid-cachemgr.conf` and then move that file to our Apache installation's `conf.d`
directory (which is generally `/etc/httpd/conf.d/` or `/etc/apache2/conf.d/`).

```
ScriptAlias /Squid/cgi-bin/cachemgr.cgi /opt/squid/libexec/cachemgr.
cgi

# Only allow access from localhost by default
<Location /Squid/cgi-bin/cachemgr.cgi>
 order allow,deny
 allow from localhost
 # If we want to allow access to cache manager from 192.0.2.25,
 # uncomment the following line
 # allow from 192.0.2.25
 # Add additional allowed hosts as needed
 # allow from .example.com
</Location>
```

Once we have copied these lines in to a file called `squid-cachemgr.conf` and moved that
file to the appropriate directory, we need to restart or reload the Apache Web server using
the following command:

$ apachectl graceful

To learn more about configuring Apache, please check: `http://httpd.apache.org/
docs/current/configuring.html`.

What just happened?

We configured Apache to use `cachemgr.cgi` as a `cgi` script to provide the cache manager
web interface, which is a source of a lot of useful information about Squid's runtime.

Accessing the cache manager web interface

Before we can use the cache manager, we need to configure Squid to allow us to log in to
the cache manager interface. The cache manager specific directives are `cache_mgr` and
`cachemgr_passwd`. Let's learn how to use these directives.

Configuring Squid

The directive cache_mgr is used to specify the e-mail address of a local administrator who will receive an e-mail if the Squid proxy server stops functioning. The default is webmaster, however, we can change it to something better such as admin@example.com. For example:

```
cache_mgr admin@example.com
```

This configuration will set the administrators e-mail address to admin@example.com and an e-mail alert will be sent to this e-mail address if Squid stops functioning.

The directive cachemgr_passwd is used for controlling access to various parts of the cache manager web interface. The format for using the cachemgr_passwd directive is as follows:

```
cachemgr_passwd PASSWORD ACTION ACTION ...
```

The parameter PASSWORD in the configuration line is the password for the cache manager web interface in plain text format. There are two special values to the password named disable and none. The value disable will disable access to actions specified. The value none can be used if we want to give password less access to some actions.

The parameter ACTION can be replaced with the names one or more parts of the cache manager web interface. This parameter has a special value all, which means all parts of the cache manager web interface.

To allow access to all parts of the cache manager web interface using a password, we can use the following configuration line:

```
cachemgr_passwd s3cr3tP4sS all
```

This configuration will allow this password access to all parts of the cache manager web interface.

Log in to cache manger

To access the cache manager's web interface, we can launch a web browser and go to the URL http://localhost/Squid/cgi-bin/cachemgr.cgi. We should replace localhost with the IP address of the proxy server, if we are accessing the web interface from a different machine.

When we go to the previously mentioned URL, Squid will present us with a login screen, as shown in the following screenshot:

Cache Manager Interface

This is a WWW interface to the instrumentation interface for the Squid object cache.

Cache Server: localhost ⌄
Manager name: admin@example.com
Password: ••••••••••
Continue...

Here we can enter **admin@example.com** as **Manager name** and **Password** (which we set to s3cr3tP4sS in a previous example) and then click on the **Continue** button. Once we authenticate, we'll see a list of links that we can use to find out about the different statistics of Squid. The following screenshot shows some of the links:

Cache Manager menu for localhost:

- This Cachemanager Menu
- o Shut Down the Squid Process (hidden).
- o Reconfigure the Squid Process (hidden).
- o Toggle offline_mode setting (hidden).
- o Current Squid Configuration (hidden).
- AS Number Database
- CARP information
- peer userhash information
- peer sourcehash information
- Callback Data Registry Contents
- comm_incoming() stats
- Cache Client List
- Delay Pool Levels
- Async IO Function Counters
- DISKD Stats

The previous screenshot doesn't display all the links available and the number of links available in the cache manager menu will depend on the version of Squid installed, and the features which were enabled before compiling.

Now, let's go through some of the pages in the cache manager and see what they represent.

General Runtime Information

We can learn more about Squid and its resource usage from the **General Runtime Information** link in the **Cache Manager menu**. This link will take us to a page displaying information about the various components of our proxy server:

```
Start Time:    Mon, 20 Sep 2010 03:38:36 GMT
Current Time:  Tue, 25 Sep 2010 03:05:23 GMT

Connection information for squid:
        Number of clients accessing cache:      1146
        Number of HTTP requests received:       60396670
        Number of ICP messages received:        0
        Number of ICP messages sent:    0
        Number of queued ICP replies:   0
        Request failure ratio:   0.08
        Average HTTP requests per minute since start:   5257.9
        Average ICP messages per minute since start:    0.0
        Select loop called: 1978046739 times, 0.348 ms avg
Cache information for squid:
        Request Hit Ratios:     5min: 34.5%, 60min: 33.9%
        Byte Hit Ratios:        5min: 3.8%, 60min: 14.2%
        Request Memory Hit Ratios:      5min: 20.8%, 60min: 21.4%
        Request Disk Hit Ratios:        5min: 28.9%, 60min: 29.2%
        Storage Swap size:      357549416 KB
        Storage Mem size:       2097160 KB
        Mean Object Size:       55.60 KB
        Requests given to unlinkd:      0
```

The first table in the previous screenshot displays information about the time when Squid was started and the current time.

Following that, the first block of details gives out information about the client connections. So, according to the statistics, we have **1146** clients accessing our proxy server and the proxy server has received more than 60 million requests since starting. Also, we can see that our proxy server has been serving more than five thousand requests per minute, on average since it started.

The second block of details displays information about the performance of disk and memory caching. **Request Hit Ratios** is the ratio of requests served from the cache to the total number of requests in a particular interval of time. **Byte Hit Ratios** is the ratio of the bytes served from the cache to the total bytes served by the proxy server.

The previous screenshot is only a subset of the total information displayed on the page.

IP Cache Stats and Contents

Find **IP Cache Stats and Contents** in the **Cache Manager menu** and click on it. This will take us to a page containing statistics about the IP address cache which Squid has built over time (refer to the `ipcache_size`, `ipcache_low`, and `ipcache_high` directives in the Squid configuration file).

The statistics will be displayed on the top and should look similar to the following:

```
IP Cache Statistics:
IPcache Entries:  14550
IPcache Requests: 139729579
IPcache Hits:              119273350
IPcache Negative Hits:       2619823
IPcache Numeric Hits:        8339299
IPcache Misses:            9496827
IPcache Invalid Requests: 280
```

Next is an explanation of the previous statistics:

Entry name	Description
IPcache Entries	The total number of entries in the IP cache. This can be limited using the `ipcache_size` directive in `squid.conf`.
IPcache Requests	The total number of requests to resolve domain names that Squid has received so far.
IPcache Hits	The number of requests which could be satisfied from the IP cache itself, saving a DNS query.
IPcache Negative Hits	The number of hits for failed DNS requests due to various errors such as temporary routing issues.
IPcache Numeric Hits	Numeric hits occur when a request is for an IP address instead of a domain name which results in zero DNS queries.
IPcache Misses	IP cache misses is the number of DNS queries that Squid had to make because the IP addresses for those domain names were not present in the cache.
IPcache Invalid Requests	Invalid requests are caused by badly formatted domain names.

Apart from the aforementioned statistics, cache manager can also show detailed contents of IP cache. The following is an example of this:

```
IP Cache Contents:

Hostname           Flg lstref TTL N
chesscube.com          0    12 1(0) 174.129.143.69-OK
```

```
policy.chesscube.com      0    42 1(0)  75.101.157.73-OK
www.warez-bb.org          0  8084 1(0)  119.42.146.35-OK
rooms.chesscube.com       0    42 1(0)  174.129.144.56-OK
proxy.example.com     H 187749  -1 1(0)  127.0.0.1-OK
```

- The first column in the contents list is the `Hostname` or domain name seen in the request.

- The second column is `Flg` (flag) if present. Flag is blank most of the time. Other possible values of flag are `N`, representing a negatively cached entry and `H`, representing an entry used from host files generally located at `/etc/hosts` (refer to the `hosts_file` directive in `squid.conf`).

- The third column represents the number of seconds elapsed since the IP address for this domain name was last requested.

- The fourth column represents the time remaining after which the cached entry will expire.

- The fifth column represents the number of IP addresses cached for this domain name and number of addresses in the parentheses that can't be contacted due to temporary routing issues.

- The last column represents a list of IP addresses with suffix `OK` for good entries and `BAD` for corrupted entries.

FQDN Cache Statistics

FQDN (**Fully Qualified Domain Name**) is a domain name that specifies its exact location in the tree hierarchy of the Domain Name System (DNS). We can configure Squid to limit the FQDN entries in the cache using the `fqdncache_size` directive in the Squid `configure` file. From the list of links on the **Cache Manager** home page, go to **FQDN Cache Statistics**.

On this page, we'll see statistics similar to the IP cache statistics. The statistics should look like the following:

```
FQDN Cache Statistics:
FQDNcache Entries: 13499
FQDNcache Requests: 13252038
FQDNcache Hits: 7097795
FQDNcache Negative Hits: 2787241
FQDNcache Misses: 3367002
```

These stats are self descriptive, and in case of any problems, please refer to the IP cache statistics in the previous section. Now, let's have a look at a few FQDN cache contents.

```
Address          Flg TTL Cnt Hostnames
79.100.155.138       28678 1  79-100-155-138.btc-net.bg
209.197.11.179       22931 1  cds055.lo1.hwcdn.net
```

```
114.178.90.174     9099  1  p13174-ipngn501funabasi.chiba.ocn.ne.jp
190.228.215.10    36224  1  host10.190-228-215.telecom.net.ar
80.221.230.176     6887  1  cable-imt-fee6dd00-176.dhcp.inet.fi
190.178.245.105    6597  1  190-178-245-105.speedy.com.ar
187.36.54.232     -3809  1  bb2436e8.virtua.com.br
88.230.162.6   N -10941  0
```

The format of the FQDN cache contents is similar to the IP cache contents. The only differences are:

- Hostnames and IP addresses have swapped columns.

- The Count column doesn't have any entries for BAD or corrupt FQDN entries.

- There is no column representing the time since the entry was last referenced.

HTTP Header Statistics

We have learned about the various HTTP header fields in all requests and replies in the previous chapters. Squid maintains counters for all the header fields it encounters in the requests and replies. Click the link to **HTTP Header Statistics** in the **Cache Manager menu**.

On this page, we can see statistics about the various header fields in requests and replies, in a nicely formatted tabular form. Let's have a look at a few entries from one of the tables.

Header Stats: request

Field type distribution

id	name	count	#/header
0	Accept	80959818	0.88
1	Accept-Charset	74816256	0.81
2	Accept-Encoding	77445395	0.84
3	Accept-Language	76570620	0.83
4	Accept-Ranges	3250	0.00

These are a few entries for the counters of the header fields in client requests:

- The first column is id, which is for Squid's internal use.

- The second column represents the name of the HTTP header field.

- The third column represents the number of times a particular header field was found in the HTTP headers, in all client requests.

◆ The fourth column represents the percentage of cases when a particular header field occurred. For example, in the previous screenshot, the occurrence of the `Accept` header field is 88 percent.

Traffic and Resource Counters

Squid keeps tracks of all the requests and data flowing through it. A detailed view of these counters is available using the link **Traffic and Resource Counters** in the **Cache Manager menu**. Although a lot of data is available on this page, it's not nicely formatted and is really only meant for advanced users. Still, let's try to understand a few fields in the following screenshot of the page:

```
client_http.requests = 61265446
client_http.hits = 22386052
client_http.errors = 1334219
client_http.kbytes_in = 196353418
client_http.kbytes_out = 1726843361
client_http.hit_kbytes_out = 292757460
server.all.requests = 40989383
server.all.errors = 0
server.all.kbytes_in = 1417894692
server.all.kbytes_out = 184760475
server.http.requests = 35932317
server.http.errors = 0
server.http.kbytes_in = 1171528089
server.http.kbytes_out = 59247182
server.ftp.requests = 1249
server.ftp.errors = 0
server.ftp.kbytes_in = 4336291
server.ftp.kbytes_out = 228
```

Let's try and understand the meaning of a few of the counters in the previous screenshot:

Field	Description
`client_http.requests`	Total number of requests received by the proxy server so far, which is 61 million in this case.
`client_http.hits`	Total number of requests that could be served from the cache itself without making a request to the remote web servers. In this case, the total hits are 22 million which is quite significant.
`client_http.errors`	Total number of requests which resulted in an HTTP error like 404 (Page Not Found), 403 (Access Denied), and so on.
`client_http.kbytes_in`	Total data uploaded by clients in the form of requests or file uploads. In this case, 187 GB of data has been uploaded by clients so far.

Field	Description
client_http.kbytes_out	Total data downloaded by clients in the form of web pages or file downloads. In this case, 1.6 TB of data has been downloaded so far since Squid was started.
client_http.hit_kbytes_out	Total data sent to clients as a result of cache hits. In this case, a total 279 GB of data has been served as a result of cache hits.

All other fields are similar and can be interpreted easily.

Request Forwarding Statistics

When a request from a client is received by Squid, it identifies a set of possible servers and tries to forward the request to remote servers. If request forwarding fails, Squid will try again. A table containing complete statistics about the number of tries versus the HTTP status code received from the remote server can be accessed using the **Request Forwarding Statistics** link in the **Cache Manager menu**.

Status	try#1	try#2	try#3	try#4
0	1	0	0	0
200	26807801	19948	1137	0
201	13	0	0	0
202	1006	1	0	0
203	67	0	0	0
204	905129	79	0	0

The first column represents HTTP status code (for a list of HTTP status codes and their meanings, check http://en.wikipedia.org/wiki/List_of_HTTP_status_codes). The numbers in the cells represent the number of requests. For example, 26.8 million request forwards resulted in HTTP status code 200 in the first attempt.

 It's worth noting that small numbers of second or third tries are normal, but if these numbers get large in proportion, it's a sign of network trouble.

Cache Client List

Squid maintains a list of clients which have been served in the past 24 hours. The entries may fade out depending on the frequency of requests. It also maintains a few statistics related to each client, which may be of interest when we want to check what a particular client is up to. Find the **Cache Client List** link in the **Cache Manager menu** and browse to it. The page will contain a complete list of all the clients.

```
Cache Clients:
Address: 10.1.98.78
Name: 10.1.98.78
Currently established connections: 0
    ICP Requests 0
    HTTP Requests 2255
        TCP_HIT                     651   29%
        TCP_MISS                   1131   50%
        TCP_REFRESH_HIT              56    2%
        TCP_REFRESH_MISS              3    0%
        TCP_CLIENT_REFRESH_M          6    0%
        TCP_IMS_HIT                  26    1%
        TCP_MEM_HIT                 382   17%

Address: 10.1.40.190
Name: 10.1.40.190
Currently established connections: 0
    ICP Requests 0
    HTTP Requests 1510
        TCP_HIT                     227   15%
        TCP_MISS                    856   57%
        TCP_REFRESH_HIT             111    7%
        TCP_REFRESH_MISS             14    1%
        TCP_CLIENT_REFRESH_M         21    1%
        TCP_IMS_HIT                 183   12%
        TCP_NEGATIVE_HIT             13    1%
        TCP_MEM_HIT                  84    6%
        TCP_DENIED                    1    0%
```

Let's have a look at the details for the first client. The first line represents the IP address of the client. The second line represents the domain name corresponding to the client's IP address (will be omitted if domain name is not available or if reverse lookups are disabled).

The third line shows the **Currently established connections** to this client which is currently zero. The next line shows the total number of **ICP Requests** made by this client which is also zero.

The following line represents the number of HTTP requests made by that particular client. The list may also contain a line which will show the clients login username, if it's known. The next few lines in the HTTP requests block show the counts and percentages of various Squid statuses for those requests. For the latest list of Squid status codes, check `http://wiki.squid-cache.org/SquidFaq/SquidLogs#Squid_result_codes`.

Memory Utilization

Squid provides detailed statistics about its memory utilization. You will find a link to **Memory Utilization** in the **Cache Manager menu**, click and browse to it. The following table of information is a small section of the memory utilization page:

Pool	Obj Size (bytes)	Allocated			
		(#)	(KB)	high (KB)	high (hrs)
acl	64	35	3	3	199.06
acl_deny_info_list	32	1	1	1	199.06
acl_ip_data	24	98	3	3	170.29
acl_list	24	46	2	2	199.06
acl_name_list	40	1	1	1	199.06
acl_time_data	24	3	1	1	199.06

These statistics are mainly targeted at developers trying to analyze the memory utilized by various components. The first column represents the component occupying the memory. As we can see, the components are `acl`, `acl_deny_info_list`, `acl_ip_data`, and so on. Therefore, according to the previous table of information, a total of 3 KB of memory has been allocated to the `acl` component.

This table doesn't represent the total memory occupied by all of Squid's components. The actual memory utilization will be higher than shown in this table because this table doesn't contain the memory consumption by all components.

Internal DNS Statistics

As we learned in the previous chapters, Squid has its own built-in implementation of a DNS client, which helps it in resolving domain names to IP addresses. If we click on the **Internal DNS Statistics** link in the **Cache Manager menu**, we'll be presented with various statistics about the requests performed by the internal DNS client. See the following screenshot for an example of these statistics:

```
Internal DNS Statistics:

The Queue:
                            DELAY SINCE
   ID    SIZE SENDS FIRST  SEND LAST SEND
 ......  .... ..... ...........  .........
 0xaf24   34    1      0.157       0.157
 0xa717   42    1      0.542       0.542

Nameservers:
IP ADDRESS       # QUERIES # REPLIES
...............  .......... ..........
192.168.36.204     1255839    1254437
192.168.36.222       21820      21682

Rcode Matrix:
RCODE ATTEMPT1 ATTEMPT2 ATTEMPT3
    0  3011754     2209      283
    1        0        0        0
    2    75075    72051    71697
    3  1036829      810       66
    4        0        0        0
    5        0        0        0
```

The first table represents any DNS queries in the queue for which Squid has not received any response yet. This table is generally empty or has only a few entries. If this table has a lot of entries, then that may be an indication of a problem with our DNS servers.

The second table shows the number of queries and replies for each DNS server we have specified, which is pretty simple to understand.

The last table is a table representing the response code of a DNS query against the number of attempts to resolve a domain name. The count in the cell represents the number of DNS queries. **RCODE** value zero (**0**) means a successful completion of a DNS query. For more details on the various values of **RCODE**, check page 27 of **RFC 1035** at http://tools.ietf.org/html/rfc1035.

Have a go hero – exploring cache manager

There are a lot of other pages available through the cache manager web interface. Explore them and check what statistics they provide about your proxy server. Its also worth noting that the Squid components which we have disabled, are missing from the cache manager menu or have empty statistics pages.

So, we have learned about using cache manager to obtain information about resource utilization and general performance statistics over a period of time. Now it's time to install a Squid log file analyzer which can read and analyze Squid's access log file to generate interesting statistics.

Log file analyzers

In the previous chapter, we learned about Squid's access log file where every client request is logged unless configured otherwise. Over a period of time, it's not possible to evaluate this file manually as it may contain tens of thousands or even millions of entries. To parse and analyze this file, there are a lot of open source and free third party programs available. A list of these programs can be accessed at http://www.squid-cache.org/Scripts/.

In this book, we'll have a look at Calamaris, which is a Perl (http://www.perl.org/) based log fine analyzer and statistics generator. So, let's have a look at Calamaris.

Calamaris

Calamaris is a Perl-based script that can analyze Squid's access log files and generate interesting statistics about the usage and performance of the proxy server. The following are a few of the types reports that Calamaris can produce:

- A brief summary of the requests, clients served, bandwidth used, plus statistics about cache hits and hit rate
- Incoming requests by HTTP methods
- Incoming TCP/UDP requests by status
- Outgoing requests by status, destination
- Domain-level data flow
- Request analysis based on content type (audio, video, images, HTML, and so on) of the requests.

Calamaris proves to be a good choice because of the following features:

◆ It can cache the parsed data for the file which has already been parsed so we don't need to parse the same file again to generate reports

◆ It can produce nicely formatted printable plain text reports that look good

◆ It can also generate graphical reports which are a good way to analyze usage and performance

◆ It can be run using cron to periodically update the document root of a website, configured in a web server, to view the statistics in a web browser

For the most recent information on Calamaris, check the Calamaris official website at `http://cord.de/tools/squid/calamaris/`.

Installing Calamaris

We must have Perl installed on our server before we can install Calamaris. Perl is available in software repositories of almost all Linux/Unix operating systems. Check the installation manual for your operating system to install Perl.

Time for action – installing Calamaris

Calamaris can be installed using a package manager for our operating system. For installing Calamaris on Red Hat Enterprise Linux, CentOS, or Fedora, we can use `yum` as follows:

```
$ yum install calamaris
```

To install Calamaris on Debian, Ubuntu, or other Debian-like operating systems, we can use `aptitude` as follows:

```
$ aptitude install calamaris
```

If Calamaris is not available in our operating system's software repository, we can visit the Calamaris official website and download the latest version. Please follow the installation instructions in the software bundle. We'll be using version 2.99.4.0 in this book.

What just happened?

We learned how to install Calamaris using the package managers for several operating systems.

Using Calamaris to generate statistics

Once we have finished installing Calamaris, we can use it on the command line to parse our log files.

Time for action – generating stats in plain text format

Let's say we want to parse our current log file; we can use Calamaris as follows:

```
$ cd /opt/squid/var/logs/
$ cat access.log  | calamaris -a
```

By default, Calamaris generates stats in plain text format and prints them on a standard output. To output the stats to a text file, we can use Calamaris as follows:

```
$ cat access.log  | calamaris -a --output-file access_stats.txt
```

The content of `access_stats.txt` should look similar to the following:

```
# Summary
Calamaris statistics

------------------------------------------- ----------- --------

lines parsed:                               lines 50405872
invalid lines:                              lines        1
parse time:                                   sec     2456
parse speed:                            lines/sec    20524

------------------------------------------- ----------- --------

Proxy statistics

------------------------------------------- ----------- --------

Total amount:                           requests 50405872
unique hosts/users:                        hosts     1606
Total Bandwidth:                            Byte    1582G
Proxy efficiency:                         factor    54.85
(HIT [kB/sec] / DIRECT [kB/sec])
Average speed increase:                        %    15.81
TCP response time of 86.96% requests:       msec      241
(requests > 2000 msec skipped)

------------------------------------------- ----------- --------

Cache statistics

------------------------------------------- ----------- --------

Total amount cached:                    requests 17955880
```

```
Request hit rate:                          %      35.62
Bandwidth savings:                        Byte    220G
Bandwidth savings in Percent               %      13.90
(Byte hit rate):
Average cached object size:               Byte   13149
Average direct object size:               Byte   45056
Average object size:                      Byte   33690
------------------------------------------ ---------- --------
```

The previous output is self descriptive, we can analyze the bandwidth we have been saving by enabling disk caching and the requests we have served so far. We can also see the stats about object sizes we have in our cache.

What just happened?

We used Calamaris on the command line to generate plain text reports for our current access log file. We also learned that Calamaris will print the reports to standard output or the terminal by default, and we can use the `--output-file` option to output the reports to a file.

Have a go hero – exploring the reports

There will be stats using several other criteria in the stats file generated by Calamaris. Study them to see what the most popular websites are among your clients.

Time for action – generating graphical reports with Calamaris

Now, let's learn to generate HTML and graphical statistics using Calamaris. To generate graphical stats, we need to create a directory where Calamaris can dump image files. So, let's see how it works:

```
$ mkdir stats
$ cat access.log  | calamaris -a --output-file access_stats.html -F
html,graph --output-path ./stats/
```

The previous command will generate an `access_stats.html` file along with a few image files in the `stats` directory. Let's have a look at a few images from the `stats` directory:

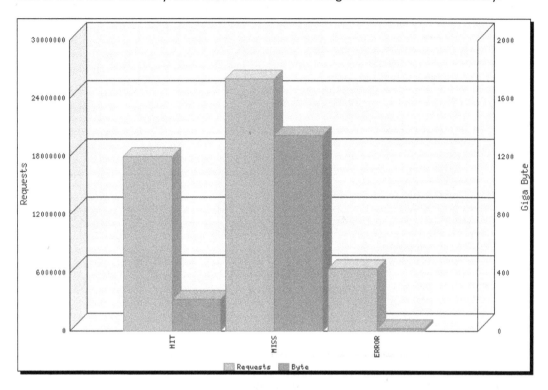

This image is a graph of TCP requests by the Squid status. On the left-hand side is a scale representing the number of requests, and on the right-hand side is a scale representing the data transferred in Gigabytes. As we can see from the previous graph, around 17 million requests resulted in a hit. This means that they could be served from the cache without fetching data from remote servers.

Let's have a look at another graph:

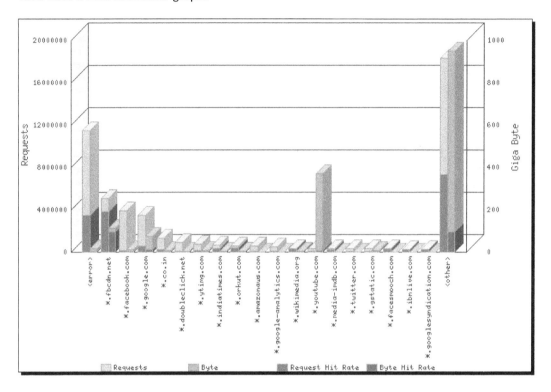

The previous screenshot shows is a graph of request destinations by the second level domain. As we can observe from the graph, a total of 9 million requests were sent to Facebook servers (*.fbcdn.net and *.facebook.com).

Calamaris generates a lot of interesting graphs like the ones shown, which can be helpful in analyzing and optimizing our proxy server to enable it to perform better.

What just happened?

We learned how to use the various options with Calamaris to generate HTML and graphical reports for better analysis.

Have a go hero – exploring Calamaris

Have a look at the Calamaris man page for more details about the different options which can be used on the command line.

Pop quiz

1. Which of the following is a correct choice for running the cache manager CGI program?

   a. Apache Web Server

   b. Lighttpd

   c. Roxen Web Server

   d. All of the above

2. Which of the following is the correct formula to calculate cache hit ratio?

   a. Number of cache hits * 100 / Number of requests

   b. Number of cache hits * 100 / Number of cache misses

   c. Number of bytes served as hits * 100 / Total Number of bytes served

   d. Number of cache misses * 100 / Number of requests.

3. Which of the following is the correct formula for calculating byte hit rate?

   a. Number of bytes served as cache hits * 100 / Total Number of requests served

   b. Number of bytes served in the past 24 hours * 100 / Total Number of bytes served

   c. Number of bytes served as cache hits * 100 / Total Number of requests served

   d. Number of bytes served as cache hits / Number of bytes served as cache misses

Summary

We have learned about using the cache manager to monitor our Squid proxy server for various statistics.

Specifically, we have covered the following:

- Installing and configuring Apache to use the `cachemgr.cgi` program to provide a web interface for the cache manager.
- Various types of information and statistics about our running proxy server
- An overview of log file analyzers
- Installing and using Calamaris to generate interesting statistics about the usage and performance of our proxy server.

Now that we have learned about monitoring the performance of our proxy server, we'll learn about protecting our proxy server with authentication in the next chapter.

7
Protecting your Squid Proxy Server with Authentication

In the previous chapters, we have learned about installing, configuring, running, and monitoring our Squid proxy server. In the last chapter, we also learned about analyzing the performance of our proxy server along with the usage statistics for different resources. In this chapter, we'll learn about protecting our Squid proxy server from unauthorized access, using the various authentication systems which are available. We'll also learn to develop a custom authentication helper, using which, we can design our own authentication system for our proxy server.

In this chapter, we will learn about:

- ◆ Squid authentication
- ◆ HTTP basic authentication
- ◆ HTTP digest authentication
- ◆ Microsoft NTLM authentication
- ◆ Negotiate authentication
- ◆ Using multiple authentication schemes
- ◆ Writing a custom authentication helper
- ◆ Making non-concurrent helpers concurrent
- ◆ Common issues with authentication

So let's get on with it.

HTTP authentication

So far we have learned about various ways of controlling access to our Squid proxy server. Using IP addresses and MAC addresses to identify clients provides significant access control, but these properties can be spoofed our proxy server can still be accessed by unauthorized people. Using Squid authentication helpers, we can enforce username/password/based authentication which can guarantee a higher level of access control.

Squid authentication helpers work in a simple way by which the user agent or browser sends out an `Authentication` HTTP header field, containing encoded credentials filled in by the user. Squid tries to decode the `Authentication` header field and passes the decoded fields to the helper, which then checks the credentials against a preconfigured service. If the credentials provided were valid, the client is allowed to access our proxy server; otherwise a HTTP status 407 (Proxy Authentication Required) is sent back. This is the complete process of authenticating a client using the Squid authentication helper against a preconfigured service.

Squid currently supports four types of authentication schemes named **Basic**, **Digest**, **NTML**, and **Negotiate**, which have their own advantages and disadvantages. Authentication schemes are configured using the `auth_param` directive in the Squid configuration file that supports various options for different authentication schemes. So let's move on and discuss the various authentication schemes and some of the corresponding helpers provided by Squid.

Basic authentication

Basic authentication is the simplest scheme to configure so that our proxy server enforces authentication, but it's the most insecure scheme. This is due to the fact that credentials are transmitted in a Base64-encoded string format, which can be decoded very easily to get the original credentials, such as, the username and password supplied by the client to authenticate with Squid.

This authentication scheme is generally discouraged because anyone who is able to sniff your user's network packets will be able to see that person's username and password and will be able to exploit it very easily. The authentication schemes Digest or Negotiate are recommended over the Basic authentication scheme.

This scheme can be used in small, isolated networks where the chances of packet sniffing are low and because of the simplicity of configuring Squid to use this scheme.

Time for action – exploring Basic authentication

HTTP Basic authentication supports the following `auth_param` options:

```
auth_param basic program COMMAND
auth_param basic utf8 on|off
auth_param basic children NUMBER [startup=N] [idle=N] [concurrency=N]
```

```
auth_param basic realm STRING
auth_param basic credentialsttl TIME_TO_LIVE
auth_param basic casesensitive on|off
```

Now let's discuss what each parameter specifies and what possible values can be passed with it.

 Please note that the options startup, idle, and concurrency are available only in Squid version 3.2 or later.

The program parameter specifies the absolute path to the authentication helper we are trying to configure. We should note that, we can also specify additional arguments to the program on the same line. By default, all the authentication helpers reside in ${prefix}/libexec/ where ${prefix} is the value supplied to the --prefix option while running the configure program.

The aforementioned code is given the username password string after decoding the Authentication HTTP header received from the client and the program should output either OK or ERR, depending on the validity of the credentials. The program should work in an endless loop following the logic just described.

The utf8 parameter specifies whether the credentials 'with' will be translated to UTF-8 encoding before they are passed to the authentication helper. This is because the HTTP uses ISO Latin-1 encoding and some authentication helpers may expect UTF-8.

The children parameter sets various options for the authentication helper. Normally, Squid will run more than one instance of the authentication helper, depending on the number of requests being received from clients. This ensures that the delay caused due to the authentication helper, while processing, can be minimized. NUMBER specifies the number of child helpers Squid is allowed to spawn. This number should be kept high enough, so that Squid will not be choked because of a high waiting time introduced by authentication helpers, and low enough so that the authentication helpers don't take all the system resources.

The startup and idle options with the children parameter specifies the number of the processes that should be started when Squid is started or reconfigured, and the maximum number of idle helpers present at any time. These numbers help Squid in spawning the appropriate number of authentication helpers depending on the current traffic.

The concurrency option specifies the number of concurrent credential validation requests one instance of an authentication helper can process at a time. Most authentication helpers will process only one request at a time, per instance, so the default value of concurrency is 0 (zero) to turn it off. If we are using an authentication helper that can process multiple requests concurrently, we can set this value accordingly. Please note that this feature is available only with Squid version 3.2 or later, we can however, make our existing helpers concurrent using helper -mux, which we'll discuss at the end of this chapter.

The `realm` parameter specifies the message presented to the user by the HTTP client.

The `credentialsttl` parameter sets the time after which Squid will ask the authentication helper whether the credentials provided by the client are still valid or the time for which they will remain valid. This value should be set high enough to ensure that the user is not prompted to enter their credentials time and time again. This should be set to a lower value if there is a short-lived password system in place.

The `casesensitive` parameter sets whether the usernames will be case sensitive or not. Most databases for storing user information are case insensitive and allow usernames in any case. Setting this parameter to on or off will affect the `max_user_ip` ACL type, so we should use it carefully.

Let's see a configuration example of an authentication helper using the Basic authentication scheme:

```
auth_param basic program /opt/squid/libexec/basic_pam_auth
auth_param basic utf8 on
auth_param basic children 15 start=1 idle=1
auth_param basic realm Squid proxy Server at proxy.example.com
auth_param basic credentialsttl 4 hours
auth_param basic casesensitive off
acl authenticated proxy_auth REQUIRED
http_access allow authenticated
http_access deny all
```

 Configuring authentication helpers is of no use unless we use the `proxy_auth` ACL type to control access.

What just happened?

We learned about the various options available for configuring HTTP Basic authentication. We also learned that we must construct ACL lists of the ACL type `proxy_auth` in order to enforce proxy authentication.

Now, we'll have a look at the various authentication helpers which implement the Basic authentication scheme.

Database authentication

The authentication helper `basic_db_auth` can validate credentials provided by a client against a database containing usernames and passwords. For every set of usernames and passwords supplied, `basic_db_auth` will try to match it against an existing database table containing the username and password columns.

Configuring database authentication

We need to pass additional options to this authentication helper to tell it about the database table which should be used for authentication. Let's have a quick look at the options that can be passed.

Option	Description
`--dsn`	The `--dsn` option is used to specify the Database Source Name (DSN) that will be used by the authentication helper to connect to a particular database. The default value is `DBI:mysql:database=squid` (replacing the word 'squid' with the name of the relevant database). So, if we set our database name as 'clients', the corresponding DSN will be `DBI:mysql:database=clients`. This helper uses Perl's database library, so any SQL style database can be used. For a database on a different server, we can set the DSN to `DBI:mysql:database=clients:example.com:3306`.
`--user`	The `--user` option specifies the username that will be used while connecting to the database.
`--password`	The `--password` option specifies the password that will be used while connecting to the database.
`--table`	The database table where Squid will look for usernames and passwords is specified using the `--table options`. The default table name used is `passwd`.
`--usercol`	The column name for the usernames is specified using the `--usercol` option. The default value is `user`.
`--passwdcol`	The `--passwdcol` option can be used to specify the password column name in the database table. The default value is `password`.
`--plaintext`	The `--plaintext` option determines whether the passwords stored in the database are plain text or encrypted. Then authentication helper assumes that they are encrypted by default. We can set this option's value to `1` if the passwords are stored in plaintext format.
`--cond`	The `--cond` option is quite handy when we want to temporarily deny access to certain clients using a flag or several conditions set using a database table. The default value of `--cond` is `enabled=1`, which means the authentication helper will add another condition, `AND enabled = 1`, in the SQL query before querying the database. We must set this option to " " (blank string) if we don't want any additional conditions to be used.
`--md5`	We can use the `--md5` option if the database contains unsalted passwords.
`--salt`	Using the `--salt` option, we can specify the salt to hash passwords.
`--persist`	The connections to the database will be persistent and will remain open in between queries if the `--persist` option is used.
`--joomla`	We can set the `--joomla` option to tell the helper that the database we are using is a Joomla database, so that it can use appropriate salt hashing. For more information on Joomla, please visit `http://www.joomla.org/`.

So, an example configuration for `basic_db_auth` will look like the following:

```
auth_param basic program /opt/squid/libexec/basic_db_auth --dsn "DBI:
mysql:database=squid_auth" --user 'db_squid' --password 'sQu1Dp4sS' --
table 'clients' --cond ''
```

This configuration line will configure `basic_db_auth` as a basic authentication helper and will also supply various options to the authentication helper `basic_db_auth`.

NCSA authentication

NCSA authentication is an authentication against a NCSA HTTPd style password file. To know more about NCSA HTTPd, refer to `http://en.wikipedia.org/wiki/NCSA_HTTPd`. Basic NCSA authentication is easy to set up and manage. All we need to do is, create a file containing usernames and passwords in a special format and use that password file as an option with the authentication helper program.

Time for action – configuring NCSA authentication

To create and manage users, we can use the `htpasswd` program, which is a part of `httpd` (Apache Web Server).

Let's say we are going to keep the passwords in the `/opt/squid/etc/passwd` file, then we can add some users as follows:

```
htpasswd /opt/squid/etc/passwd saini
New password:
Re-type new password:
```

We should enter the password when asked and a combination of a username and encrypted password will be written to the password file. To add more users, we can use the same command.

Now we need to configure the NCSA authentication helper to use this password file. We can do so using the following command:

```
auth_param basic program /opt/squid/libexec/basic_ncsa_auth /opt/
squid/etc/passwd
```

What just happened?

We learned to add new users to the password file, which is then used by the NCSA authentication helper to validate the credentials provided by the user.

NIS authentication

The network Information Service or NIS (previously Yellow Pages or YP) is a client-server directory protocol developed by Sun Microsystems. To be able to use NIS authentication with Squid, we need to provide the NIS domain name and the password database, as shown:

```
auth_param basic program /opt/squid/libexec/basic_nis_auth example.com
passwd.byname
```

LDAP authentication

The basic LDAP (Lightweight Directory Access Protocol) authentication helper (basic_ ldap_auth) provides authentication using an LDAP server. For this to work, we should have the OpenLDAP development libraries installed. Refer to http://www.openldap.org/ for details on installing and configuring an LDAP server.

The basic_ldap_auth helper has a large number of options available to configure different settings for authenticating against the LDAP server. However, in this book we will cover only the necessary options to get LDAP authentication working. For the details of all the available options, we can always refer to the basic_ldap_auth man page provided by Squid.

Therefore, an example configuration for proxy authentication against the LDAP server ldap.example.com will be as follows:

```
auth_param basic program /opt/squid/libexec/basic_ldap_auth -b
"dc=example,dc=com" ldap.example.com
```

In the configuration shown, ldap.example.com is our LDAP server. The domain example.com is the base distinguished name (DN).

SMB authentication

SMB authentication or basic_smb_auth is a very simple way to authenticate against SMB servers like Microsoft Windows NT or Samba. To be able to use basic_smb_auth, we should have Samba (http://www.samba.org/) installed on our machine or on another machine accessible to Squid. Samba is available in software repositories of most Linux/Unix distributions.

Once everything is installed and configured properly, we can add the following configuration line to use SMB authentication:

```
auth_param basic program /opt/squid/libexec/basic_smb_auth -W
WORKGROUP
```

The option -W specifies the Windows domain name.

PAM authentication

Pluggable Authentication Modules (PAM, `http://www.sun.com/software/solaris/pam/`) is a mechanism to integrate several low-level authentication schemes such as, fingerprint, smart cards, one time keys, and so on, into a high-level API. We should note that PAM is not available on systems such as BSD. Squid provides the `basic_pam_auth` helper, which provides authentication against the PAM database. However, to be able to use PAM authentication, we need to configure the Squid (or any other name) service in the `/etc/pam.d/` directory and configure the PAM modules we plan to use.

Time for action – configuring PAM service

An example `/etc/pam.d/` Squid file may look similar to the following:

```
#%PAM-1.0
auth     include     password-auth
account  include     password-auth
```

Once the Squid service is configured in `/etc/pam.d/`, we need to configure Squid to use the PAM authentication. The following configuration example will allow Squid to authenticate using the PAM database:

```
auth_param basic program /opt/squid/libexec/basic_pam_auth
```

For more information on configuring `basic_pam_auth`, refer to the `basic_pam_auth` man page.

What just happened?

We learned to configure PAM and to use the `basic_pam_auth` Squid helper for authentication.

MSNT authentication

The MSNT Basic authentication helper provides a way to authenticate against NT domain controllers on Windows or Samba.

Time for action – configuring MSNT authentication

Configuring the MSNT authentication helper is quite easy and is done by modifying the `/opt/squid/etc/msntauth.conf` file. The default configuration file looks as follows:

```
# NT domain hosts. Best to put the hostnames in /etc/hosts.
server myPDC          myBDC          myNTdomain
# Denied and allowed users. Comment these if not needed.
denyusers       /opt/squid/etc/msntauth.denyusers
allowusers      /opt/squid/etc/msntauth.allowusers
```

We should replace myPDC (Primary Domain Controller), myBDC (Backup Domain Controller), and myNTdomain (Windows NT Domain) with values for our environment. We can add as many as five different domains in this configuration file.

Also notice the denyusers and allowusers directives. The denyusers directive specifies a file that contains all the usernames that must not be allowed to access our proxy server. The helper will not even bother to check the credentials of the usernames in this file.

The directive allowusers specifies a file which contains a list of usernames that should always be allowed to access the proxy server, even if the credentials result in failed validation.

Once we have finished configuring the MSNT authentication helper, we can add the following line in our Squid configuration file:

```
auth_param basic program /opt/squid/libexec/msnt_auth
```

What just happened?

We just learned to create the configuration file for MSNT authentication. We have also learned to create exceptions (allow or deny) for certain users without validating the credentials provided by them.

MSNT multi domain authentication

The MSNT multi domain authentication works similar to the MSNT authenticator, except that with MSNT multi domain, the client has to enter the Windows NT domain name before the username, as follows:

```
workgroup\sarah
```

The configuration line for the MSNT multi domain authentication helper will look similar to the following:

```
auth_param basic program /opt/squid/libexec/basic_msnt_multi_domain_
auth
```

This authentication helper is a Perl script.

 This authentication helper needs the Authen::SMB Perl package. Moreover, Samba should be installed on the same system or any other system accessible to Squid. On the same system, we need the nmblookup and smbclient binaries.

SASL authentication

Simple Authentication and Secure Layer (SASL) is a framework for authentication that decouples the authentication mechanism from application protocols. The SASL authentication helper (basic_sasl_auth) for Squid is similar to the PAM authentication helper.

Time for action – configuring Squid to use SASL authentication

To configure the SASL authenticator, we need to create a file named basic_sasl_auth. conf with the following content:

```
pwcheck_method:sasldb
```

1. Move this file to the /usr/lib/sasl2/ directory.

2. Once we have placed the configuration file in the appropriate directory, we can add the following line in our configuration file to ensure the use of SASL authentication:

```
auth_param basic program /opt/squid/libexec/basic_sasl_auth
```

This command will configure Squid to use the basic_sasl_auth program as an SASL authentication helper.

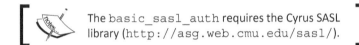 The basic_sasl_auth requires the Cyrus SASL library (http://asg.web.cmu.edu/sasl/).

What just happened?

We learned to configure the SASL authenticator and then configure Squid to use SASL authentication.

getpwnam authentication

The getpwnam authentication helper can allow Squid to authenticate local users. This authentication helper uses the getpwnam() Unix utility to locate users who have login accounts on the Squid server and authenticate them. Additionally, it can authenticate users against NIS, LDAP, and PAM databases.

To use the getpwnam authentication helper, we need to add the following line in our configuration file:

```
auth_param basic program /opt/squid/libexec/basic_getpwnam_auth
```

POP3 authentication

Squid can authenticate clients against an existing POP3 (Post Office Protocol Version 3) user database using the authentication helper `basic_pop3_auth`. To use POP3, we need to specify the IP address or domain name of the server running the POP3 service. We can configure Squid to use POP3 authentication, as shown:

```
auth_param basic program /opt/squid/libexec/basic_pop3_auth pop3.
example.com
```

 The `basic_pop3_auth` helper uses the `Net::POP3` Perl package. So, we should make sure that we have this package installed before using the authentication helper.

RADIUS authentication

The `basic_radius_auth` authentication helper allows Squid to connect to a RADIUS server (for more information on RADIUS servers, refer to `http://en.wikipedia.org/wiki/RADIUS`) and then validate the credentials provided by the HTTP client.

Time for action – configuring RADIUS authentication

We can add the following line to our Squid configuration file to use the RADIUS server for authentication:

```
auth_param basic program /opt/squid/libexec/basic_radius_auth -h
radius.example.com -p 1645 -i squid_proxy -w s3cR37 -t 15
```

In this configuration line, the option `-h` specifies the RADIUS server to connect to. The option `-p` identifies which port to use to connect to the RADIUS server. The option `-i` specifies the unique identifier for identifying the Squid proxy server on the RADIUS server. If option `-i` is not specified, the authentication helper will use the IP address of the proxy server. The shared secret with the RADIUS server is specified using the `-w` option. Finally, the option `-t` specifies the request timeout. The default request timeout is 10 seconds.

In order to avoid specifying a lot of options in the Squid configuration file, we can create a separate configuration file containing connection-related information. Let's say, we are going to place the configuration file at `/opt/squid/etc/basic_radius_auth.conf`, then we can write the following lines in the file:

```
server radius.example.com
port 1645
identifier squid_proxy
secret s3cR37
```

Now, we can replace the line in our Squid configuration file with the following line:

```
auth_param basic program /opt/squid/libexec/basic_radius_auth -f /opt/
squid/etc/basic_radius_auth.conf -t 15
```

The option -f is used to specify the configuration file that will be used by the basic_radius_auth helper to connect to the RADIUS server.

What just happened?

We learned two ways of using the basic_radius_auth helper. In one method, we can pass all options as arguments, and in the other, we can create a separate file containing information about the RADIUS server. Using a separate configuration file is the more convenient and recommended method.

Fake Basic authentication

Squid includes an interesting authentication helper called basic_fake_auth. This authentication helper is used for logging clients' credentials without actually checking them against any user database or service. This authentication helper is mainly used for testing and as a base helper which can be extended to implement complex Basic authentication helpers.

Digest authentication

HTTP Digest authentication is an improvement over the regular unencrypted HTTP Basic authentication mechanism, allowing user identity to be established securely without having to send a password over the network. HTTP Digest authentication is an application of MD5 cryptographic hashing with the use of the nonce value (for more information on the nonce value, refer to http://en.wikipedia.org/wiki/Cryptographic_nonce) to prevent cryptanalysis.

The following auth_param parameters are available for configuring HTTP Digest authentication helpers:

```
auth_param digest program COMMAND
auth_param digest utf8 on|off
auth_param digest children NUMBER [startup=N] [idle=N] [concurrency=N]
auth_param digest realm STRING
auth_param digest nonce_garbage_interval TIME
auth_param digest nonce_max_duration TIME
auth_param digest nonce_max_count NUMBER
auth_param digest nonce_strictness on|off
auth_param digest check_nonce_count on|off
auth_param digest post_workaround on|off
```

The parameters `program`, `utf8`, `children`, and `realm` have the same meanings as in HTTP Basic authentication. The following is a description of the remaining parameters:

Parameter	Description
nonce_garbage_interval	The parameter `nonce_garbage_interval` is used to specify the time interval after which the nonces that have been issued are checked for validity.
nonce_max_duration	The `nonce_max_duration` parameter specifies the time for which a given nonce will remain valid.
nonce_max_count	The parameter `nonce_max_count` defines the maximum number of times a nonce can be used.
nonce_strictness	The client may eventually skip some values while generating nonce counts like 3, 4, 5, 6, 8, 9, 11, and so on. The parameter `nonce_strictness` determines whether Squid should allow cases where the user agent or client misses a count value. The default value is off and the user agent is allowed to miss values.
check_nonce_count	The parameter `check_nonce_count` enforces Squid to check the nonce count, and in case of failure, the client will be sent the HTTP status 401 (Unauthorized). This is generally helpful against authentication replay attacks. For more information on authentication replay attacks, refer to `http://en.wikipedia.org/wiki/Replay_attack`.
post_workaround	Certain buggy HTTP clients send incorrect request digests in HTTP POST requests while utilizing the nonce acquired in an earlier HTTP GET request. The parameter `post_workaround` is a workaround for this situation.

Time for action – configuring Digest authentication

Therefore, an example HTTP Digest authentication with Squid will look similar to the following:

```
auth_param digest program /opt/squid/libexec/digest_file_auth
auth_param digest utf8 on
auth_param digest children 20 startup=0 idle=1
auth_param digest realm Squid proxy server at proxy.example.com
auth_param digest nonce_garbage_interval 5 minutes
auth_param digest nonce_max_duration 30 minutes
auth_param digest nonce_max_count 50
auth_param digest nonce_strictness on
auth_param digest check_nonce_count on
auth_param digest post_workaround on
acl authenticated proxy_auth REQUIRED
http_access allow authenticated
http_access deny all
```

Now, let's have a look at the available HTTP Digest authentication helpers provided by Squid.

What just happened?

We learned about the different options available while configuration HTTP Digest authentication. We also saw an example configuration that will fit most cases.

File authentication

The authentication helper `digest_file_auth` (previously known as `digest_pw_auth`) authenticates credentials provided by the client, against a password file containing passwords, either in plain text or MD5 encrypted.

If the passwords are stored in a plain text format, a line containing the username and password will look like the following:

```
username:password
```

However, if we store passwords in a plain text format we would not be helping ourselves in improving security. The only advantage is that we are not transmitting passwords in a plain text format over the network. So, there is another format using which we can store the passwords in the encrypted format. The format for storing the encrypted passwords is as follows:

```
username:realm:HA1
```

In this format code, `HA1` is `MD5 (username:realm:password)`. So, once we have our password file ready, we can proceed to configure Squid to use Digest authentication by adding the following line in our Squid configuration file:

```
auth_param digest program /opt/squid/libexec/digest_file_auth -c /opt/
squid/etc/digest_file_passwd
```

Note that we have used the option `-c` while specifying the digest password file because we are using encrypted passwords in our password file. In case where the digest password file contains passwords in a plain text format, we should not pass the option `-c`.

LDAP authentication

We can use LDAP authentication using the `digest_ldap_auth` helper for HTTP Digest authentication. The configuration and parameters are similar to the LDAP Basic authentication helper. To use `digest_ldap_auth` with Squid, we can add the following to the configuration file:

```
auth_param digest program /opt/squid/libexec/digest_ldap_auth
-b "ou=clients,dc=example,dc=com" -u "uid" -A "l"
-D "uid=digest,dc=example,dc=com"
-W "/opt/squid/etc/digest_cred" -e -v 3 -h ldap.example.com
```

The following is an explanation of the options used in the preceding configuration file addition:

Option	Description
-b	The option -b specifies the base distinguished name (DN)
-u	The option -u specifies the attribute that should be used along with base DN to generate user DN.
-A	The option -A identifies the password attribute.
-D	The option -D represents the DN to bind, to perform searches.
-W	The option -W represents a path to the file containing the digest password.
-e	The option -e enforces encrypted passwords.
-v	The option -v represents the LDAP version.
-h	The last option -h represents the LDAP server to connect to.

eDirectory authentication

Squid supports Digest authentication against Novell eDirectory using the digest_edirectory_auth authentication helper. The configuration options and usage of this authentication helper is similar to the digest_ldap_auth authentication helper. For more information on Novell eDirectory, refer to http://en.wikipedia.org/wiki/Novell_eDirectory.

Microsoft NTLM authentication

NTLM (NT LAN Manager) is a proprietary connection authentication protocol developed by Microsoft. The following are some important facts that we should know about NTLM authentication:

◆ NTLM authentication only authenticates a TCP connection and not the user using it.

◆ It requires a three-way handshake, which puts a limit on the speed and maximum client capacity.

◆ It is a binary protocol. So only the windows domain controller can be used.

For more details about NTLM, refer to http://en.wikipedia.org/wiki/NTLM. The following auth_param parameters are supported by the NTLM authentication helpers:

```
auth_param ntlm program COMMAND
auth_param ntlm children NUMBER [startup=N] [idle=N] [concurrency=N]
auth_param ntlm keep_alive on|off
```

The parameters `program` and `children` are similar to the ones in HTTP Basic and Digest authentication. If the parameter `keep_alive` is set to `off`, Squid will terminate the connection after the initial requests where browsers enquire about the supported schemes. Default value of the `keep_alive` parameter is `on`.

Therefore, an example configuration with NTLM authentication will be as follows:

```
auth_param ntlm program /opt/squid/libexec/ntlm_smb_lm_auth
auth_param ntlm children 20 startup=0 idle=1
auth_param ntlm keep_alive on
acl authenticated proxy_auth REQUIRED
http_access allow authenticated
http_access deny all
```

Samba's NTLM authentication

We can use NTLM authentication with the help of the `ntlm_auth` program, which is a part of Samba. To configure Squid to use `ntlm_auth` as an NTLM authentication helper, we need to add the following line to our Squid configuration file:

```
auth_param ntlm program /absolute/path/to/ntlm_auth
--helper-protocol=squid-2.5-ntlmssp
```

> Please make sure that the path to the `ntlm_auth` program provided by Samba is correct in the configuration line.

We can also force a group limitation with the `ntlm_auth` program using the `--require-membership-of` option, as shown as follows:

```
auth_param ntlm program /absolute/path/to/ntlm_auth
--helper-protocol=squid-2.5-ntlmssp
--require-membership-of="WORKGROUP\Domain Users"
```

This configuration will allow users to log in if they are members of a particular group. To explore all of the options available with the `ntlm_auth` program, refer to http://www.samba.org/samba/docs/man/manpages/ntlm_auth.1.html.

Fake NTLM authentication

Similar to the `basic_fake_auth` authentication helper, we have the `ntlm_fake_auth` authentication helper, which acts as a fake NTLM authenticator. This authentication helper doesn't authenticate credentials provided by the client. It is generally used for logging purposes while testing NTLM authentication.

Negotiate authentication

Negotiate authentication is a wrapper of GSSAPI, which in turn is a wrapper over Kerberos or NTLM authentication schemes. This protocol is used in Microsoft Active Directory enabled environments with modern versions of the Microsoft Internet Explorer, Mozilla Firefox, and Google Chrome browsers. In this protocol, the credentials are exchanged with the Squid proxy server using the Kerberos mechanism. This authentication scheme is more secure compared to NTLM authentication and is preferred over NTLM.

Time for action – configuring Negotiate authentication

Negotiate/Kerberos authentication is provided by the `negotiate_kerberos_auth` authentication helper. Next, we'll learn to configure the system running Squid to enable Negotiate authentication.

1. First of all, we need to generate a `keytab` file using the `ktpass` utility on a Windows machine, as shown:

   ```
   ktpass -princ HTTP/proxy.example.com@REALM
   -mapuser proxy.example.com -crypto rc4-hmac-nt pass s3cr3t
   -ptype KRB5_NT_SRV_HST -out squid.keytab
   ```

   We should make sure that we have a `proxy.example.com` user account on our Windows machine before generating the `keytab` file. Once the `keytab` file is generated, move it to an appropriate location on the Squid server, for example, `/opt/squid/etc/squid.keytab`. We should make sure that only the Squid user has access to the `keytab` file on our system.

2. Now, we need to configure Kerberos on our Squid proxy server. For that, we need to change the `libdefaults` section in our Kerberos configuration file, which is generally located at `/etc/krb5.conf`, to the following:

   ```
   [libdefaults]
    default_realm = REALM
    dns_lookup_realm = true
    dns_lookup_kdc = true
    ticket_lifetime = 24h
    renew_lifetime = 7d
    forwardable = true
   ```

3. After making changes to the Kerberos configuration file, we need to make changes to our Squid startup file. Please refer to *Chapter 3, Running Squid* for determining the location of the startup script. We should add the following line to our startup script:

   ```
   export KRB5_KTNAME=/etc/squid/squid.keytab
   ```

4. Finally, we need to add the following lines to our Squid configuration file:

```
auth_param negotiate program /opt/squid/libexec/negotiate_
kerberos_auth
auth_param negotiate children 15
auth_param negotiate keep_alive on
acl authenticated proxy_auth REQUIRED
http_access allow authenticated
http_access deny all
```

This configuration will enable Squid to use Negotiate authentication using the `negotiate_kerberos_auth` authentication helper.

What just happened?

We just learned about Negotiate authentication using Kerberos and how we can configure our Squid proxy server to use Negotiate authentication for stronger security.

Using multiple authentication schemes

We can configure Squid to use multiple authentication schemes by using the `auth_param` directive for each authentication scheme. If we use multiple authentication schemes, then Squid will present the clients with a list of available authentication schemes. According to RFC 2617 (`http://www.ietf.org/rfc/rfc2617`), a client must select the strongest authentication scheme that it understands. However, due to bugs in various user agents, they generally pick the first one.

So, while adding the configuration lines with the `auth_param` directive in our configuration file, we should consider the following order (strongest first) for the different authentication schemes:

1. Negotiate/Kerberos Authentication

2. Microsoft NTLM Authentication

3. Digest Authentication

4. Basic Authentication

Also, it's not compulsory to use configure helpers for all authentication schemes. We can configure helpers for any number of authentication schemes. All we need to do is preserve the aforementioned order so that even the buggy clients will pick up a stronger authentication scheme to authenticate the users.

Writing a custom authentication helper

There is no need to worry if none of the existing authentication helpers seem to fit your needs. It is possible to write your own HTTP Basic authentication helper relatively quickly. The HTTP Basic authentication helpers are very simple programs that read `username password` strings from standard input, extract the username and password from the string, match them against an existing user database, and then write `OK` or `ERR` on the standard output in a never ending loop.

Time for action – writing a helper program

So, let's write a dummy Python script that can act as a Basic authentication helper:

```python
#!/usr/bin/env python

import sys

def validate_credentials(username, password):
    """
    Returns True if the username and password are valid.
    False otherwise
    """
    # Write your own function definition.
    # Use mysql, files, /etc/passwd or some service you want
    return False

if __name__ == '__main__':
    while True:
        # Read a line from stdin
        line = sys.stdin.readline()
        # Remove '\n' from line
        line = line.strip()

        # Check if string contains two entities
        parts = line.split(' ', 1)
        if len(parts) == 2:
            # Extract username and password from line
            username, password = parts
            # Check if username and password are valid
            if validate_credentials(username, password):
                sys.stdout.write('OK\n')
            else:
                sys.stdout.write('ERR Wrong username or password\n')
        else:
            # Unexpected input
            sys.stdout.write('ERR Invalid input\n')

        # Flush the output to stdout.
        sys.stdout.flush()
```

What just happened?

In the previous program, we are reading one line from the standard input at a time. Then we go on to extracting the username and password from the input provided. Then, we try to validate the username and password using our validate_credentials method, which is a skeleton method and can be implemented to validate the username and password provided against any system. Depending on the return value of the validate_ credentials method, we write either OK or ERR on the standard output, which is read by Squid and it authenticates the client accordingly.

We can save the preceding program in a file named basic_generic_auth.py and move it to the /opt/squid/libexec/ directory. Now, we can add the following lines to our Squid configuration file to use this as a Basic authentication helper:

```
auth_param basic program /opt/squid/libexec/basic_generic_auth.py
auth_param basic children 15 startup=0 idle=1
auth_param basic realm Squid proxy server at proxy.example.com
auth_param basic credentialsttl 4 hours
auth_param basic casesensitive on
acl authenticated proxy_auth REQUIRED
http_access allow authenticated
http_access deny all
```

Have a go hero – implementing the validation function

Implement the validate_credentials method in the previous program such that when a user enters a password that is a palindrome, the program will consider the supplied username and password valid.

Making non-concurrent helpers concurrent

Helper concurrency is a relatively new concept in Squid and is supported only within Squid versions 3.2 or later. However, there is a contributed script called helper-mux that can convert our old style non-concurrent helper programs into a concurrent helper, thus improving the overall helper performance by a significant amount.

The purpose of the helper-mux program is to share some of the load that Squid has to handle while dealing with relatively slower helper programs. The helper multiplexer program acts as a medium through which Squid and actual helper programs exchange messages. So, the helper multiplexer's interface with Squid is totally concurrent and while talking to the actual helper program, it uses a non-concurrent interface.

The helper-mux program can start helper programs on demand and can handle up to 1000 helpers per instance. The helper-mux program doesn't know anything about the messages being exchanged between Squid and the actual helper program.

Therefore, we can use the `helper-mux` program to make our Basic NCSA authentication helper concurrent, as demonstrated:

```
auth_param basic program /opt/squid/libexec/helper-mux.pl /opt/squid/
libexec/basic_ncsa_auth /opt/squid/etc/passwd
auth_param basic children 1 startup=1 idle=1 concurrency=5
auth_param basic realm Squid proxy-caching web server
auth_param basic credentialsttl 2 hours
```

The previous configuration is equivalent to the following configuration without concurrency:

```
auth_param basic program /opt/squid/libexec/basic_ncsa_auth /opt/
squid/etc/passwd
auth_param basic children 5
auth_param basic realm Squid proxy-caching web server
auth_param basic credentialsttl 2 hours
```

We'll have five helper processes running if the concurrent configuration is used.

So, we learned how we can make the old style non-concurrent helpers concurrent using the helper multiplexer program available with Squid.

Common issues with authentication

Sometimes, we may run into problems with authentication helpers due to incorrect configuration. Next, we'll have a look at a few commonly known issues that can be fixed easily by modifying our main configuration file.

Whitelisting selected websites

Depending on our environment, there may be some websites which can be accessed by our users without authenticating with the proxy server. We can create special ACL lists for such websites and allow non-authenticated users access to those websites. Let's have a look at the configuration lines we need to add to our configuration file:

```
acl whitelisted dstdomain .example.com .news.example.net
acl authenticated proxy_auth REQUIRED

# Allow access to whitelisted websites.
# But only from our local network.
# localnet is default ACL list provided by Squid.
http_access allow localnet whitelisted

# Allow access to authenticated users.
http_access allow authenticated

# Deny access to everyone else.
http_access deny all
```

This configuration will allow users in our LAN access to `whitelisted` websites, and they will not have to authenticate with our proxy server to use or browse these websites. To browse websites other than ones which are `whitelisted`, all users will have to be authenticated.

Challenge loops

Squid asks HTTP clients for login credentials if the client is denied access by a proxy authentication-related ACL (`proxy_auth`, `proxy_auth_regex`, external ACL using `%LOGIN`). The order of ACLs in an `http_access` rule determines whether Squid will ask for login credentials again. This will result in continuous login pop ups by the browsers, which can get really annoying.

Normally, a user will see a login pop up once when they open or re-open (after closing) their browser for Basic or Digest authentication. A login pop up may not appear or may appear once in case of NTLM or Kerberos authentication. A login pop up may appear again if the user changes his/her password in the master system. If there are more pop ups than described here, then we might have some configuration issues.

Let's have a look at two different configurations.

First of all, let's consider the following configuration:

```
# Below auth_acl is of type proxy_auth, proxy_auth_regex
# or externl_acl using %LOGIN
http_access deny non_auth_acl auth_acl
```

Squid will prompt for new login credentials if the preceding `http_access` rule is matched and access is denied because of `auth_acl`.

Now, consider the following configuration:

```
# Below auth_acl is of type proxy_auth, proxy_auth_regex
# or externl_acl using %LOGIN
http_access deny auth_acl non_auth_acl
```

According this configuration, Squid will not prompt for new login credentials if this `http_access` rule is matched and access is denied because of `non_auth_acl`. In this case, the client will be presented with a simple access denied page if the authentication fails.

To prevent challenge loops, we can keep `all` as the last ACL element in our `http_access` rule, as shown:

```
http_access deny !authenticated all
```

This configuration will prevent challenge loops as the last ACL element `all` in the `http_access` rule will always match.

Authentication in the intercept or transparent mode

It is not possible to achieve proxy authentication when Squid is operating in intercept or transparent mode because the HTTP client is not aware that there is a proxy in between the client and remote server and hence it doesn't send the credentials required for authenticating a user.

Pop quiz

1. In what format are usernames and passwords transmitted over the network while using HTTP Basic authentication?

    a. Plain text

    b. HTML

    c. Encrypted text which can't be decrypted

    d. Encoded in `base64`

2. Why should we use case insensitive usernames when using database authentication?

    a. Squid can't differentiate between upper and lower case characters

    b. Browser's can't differentiate between upper and lower case characters

    c. String comparisons in most databases are case insensitive

    d. There is no such limitation. We can use case-sensitive usernames with all the databases.

3. Which of the following is the correct command line utility to change a user's password in an NCSA HTTPd style password file?

    a. `passwd`

    b. `chpasswd`

    c. `htpasswd`

    d. `kpasswd`

Summary

We have learned the various authentication schemes supported by Squid. We also learned about the various authentication helpers available for different authentication schemes.

Specifically, we have covered:

- A lot of different ways to authenticate using the HTTP Basic authentication
- HTTP Digest authentication and helpers supporting Digest authentication
- Microsoft NTLM authentication
- Negotiate authentication
- Writing our own custom authentication helper, using which we can authenticate against various types of user databases.

Now, we know several ways to protect our Squid proxy server from unauthorized access. In the next chapter, we'll learn about building a hierarchy of Squid proxy servers to distribute load and optimize performance.

8

Building a Hierarchy of Squid Caches

In the previous chapters, we learned that the Squid proxy server can talk to other proxy servers over the network to share information about cached content, to fetch content from remote servers on behalf of other proxy servers, or to use other proxy servers to fetch content from remote servers. In this chapter, we will explore cache hierarchies in detail. We'll also learn to configure Squid to act as a parent or a sibling proxy server in a hierarchy, and use other proxy servers as parent or sibling proxy servers.

In this chapter, we will learn about the following:

- ◆ Cache hierarchies
- ◆ Reasons to use hierarchical caching
- ◆ Problems with hierarchical caching
- ◆ Related Squid configuration
- ◆ Controlling communication with peers
- ◆ Peer communication protocols

So let's get started.

Cache hierarchies

A cache hierarchy is the name given to an arrangement of proxy servers which can communicate with each other to forward requests. The arrangement is typically a tree structure in which the proxy servers have a parent-child or sibling relationship. Parent proxy servers are closer to the remote servers, compared to the child servers, and the child servers typically use the parent servers to fetch content for their clients. Child servers can act as a parent server to other proxy servers. Let's have a look at the following diagram:

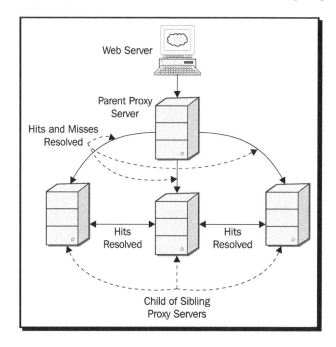

Siblings are the proxy servers at the same level in the tree structure. In a cache hierarchy, proxy servers use protocols like ICP, HTCP, Cache Digests, and CARP to identify a useful source. The other peering types are origin server, which is generally a special type of parent and multicast, which in essence is a special type of sibling.

Reasons to use hierarchical caching

Sometimes, it's necessary to be a part of a cache hierarchy. For example, in a large network where all packets must pass through a firewall proxy we will be forced to use the firewall proxy server as a parent proxy, as it's the only point of contact with the Internet. So, all our cache misses will be fetched by the firewall proxy.

Sometimes, we join a cache hierarchy to reduce the average page load time. It helps only when the fetch time from neighbors is significantly less than the fetch time from remote servers. Therefore, if some requests result in a cache MISS in our proxy's cache, it may be a cache HIT in one of our neighbors caches.

Another example may be, a network where we have a large number of clients and one proxy server is not able to handle all the traffic. In this case, we'll split the load by deploying two proxy servers as siblings. Two servers will be able to serve HITs from each other's cache, which will further enhance the performance.

An example that is becoming increasingly popular and important for scalability and availability of modern day websites, in a hierarchy of proxy servers, is the reverse proxy mode. Reverse proxy mode is more commonly known as **Content Delivery Networks (CDNs)**. The main purpose of a CDN is to replicate the content of one or more websites to various geographic locations across the Internet and then transparently direct the client web browsers to the nearest or most responsive cache. For more information on CDN, refer to `http://en.wikipedia.org/wiki/Content_delivery_network`.

We can also join a cache hierarchy to redirect traffic, based on different criteria such as, domain names, content type, request origins, and so on. We'll see examples later in this chapter.

Problems with hierarchical caching

When we are a part of a cache hierarchy, we serve the content received from neighbors directly to our clients. So, there is a serious problem if content received from neighbors is not genuine. For example, let's say we are a part of a cache hierarchy and one of our neighbor proxy servers is compromised. In such a scenario, the compromised proxy server can serve any content for the requests we are forwarding. This generally leads to propagation of viruses and worms on a network. Therefore, all our neighbors should be properly secured and up-to-date so that we don't end up compromising our client for the sake of increasing our hit ratio.

We'll essentially be forwarding a lot of our client's requests to our neighbor proxy servers. This may result in leakage of private information of our clients. For example, a lot of data is sent as a part of the URL in HTTP GET requests. If a neighbor cache is not properly striping query terms from the URL before logging, then the complete URL will be logged in the access log file, which can be later parsed for retrieving sensitive information about clients. Hence, client privacy is also one of the problems we face when we are a part of cache hierarchy.

Another common problem with hierarchical caching is forwarding loops as a result of misconfiguration. The following is an example scenario:

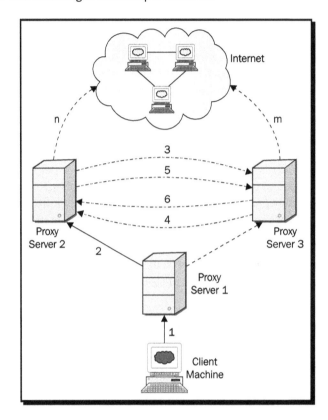

In the preceding diagram, a request is sent from a client machine to the proxy server 1, which may in turn, forward the request to proxy server 2 or 3. Let's say the request is forwarded to proxy server 2, as shown in this scenario. Also, as proxy servers 2 and 3 are siblings, proxy server 2 will check if proxy server 3 has a cached response for the current request. Now, if the request results in a cache miss in proxy server 3, then it'll again forward the request to proxy server 2 to check for a cache hit. This will go on forever, resulting in a forwarding loop.

Avoiding a forwarding loop

We can avoid such situations easily by configuring our proxy server properly. We don't have to forward a request to a proxy server if that proxy server itself was the source of the request.

One quick and partial solution for this problem is to set the value of the directive via to on. If via is set to on, then Squid will include a via header in requests and replies as required by RFC 2616. In the presence of a via header, peers will abort early and log an error message instead of consuming network bandwidth and memory on the proxy servers.

Another foolproof solution is to have a proper configuration. Consider the following Squid configuration on the proxy server s1.example.com (192.0.2.25):

```
cache_peer s2.example.com sibling 3128 3130
```

And the following configuration on a proxy server s2.example.com (198.51.100.86):

```
cache_peer s1.example.com sibling 3128 3130
```

This configuration may result in a forwarding loop. Now we'll edit the configuration on both the servers to avoid forwarding loops.

The configuration on s1.example.com should be:

```
cache_peer s2.example.com sibling 3128 3130
acl sibling2 src 198.51.100.86
cache_peer_access s2.example.com deny sibling2
```

And the configuration on s2.example.com should be:

```
cache_peer s1.example.com sibling 3128 3130
acl sibling1 src 192.0.2.25
cache_peer_access s2.example.com deny sibling1
```

These configurations will prevent any possible forwarding loops.

Joining a cache hierarchy

In the previous chapters, we learned about the cache_peer directive in the Squid configuration file and how to use cache_peer to add other proxy servers in our configuration file, so that our proxy server can forward requests to neighbors. However, we only had a brief overview of the options used along with cache_peer. In this chapter, we'll explore cache_peer and its various options in detail.

The following is the format to add a proxy server in a configuration file using cache_peer:

```
cache_peer HOSTNAME TYPE HTTP_PORT ICP_OR_HTCP_PORT [OPTIONS]
```

The parameter HOSTNAME is the IP address or domain name of the proxy server we are trying to add to the configuration file. The TYPE parameter takes one of the values parent, sibling, or multicast, and specifies the type of the proxy server, which further determines the type of communication between the two servers.

Please note that DNS resolution must be working if you want to use domain name as a value for the HOSTNAME parameter. Also note that future releases will support `originserver` as a type for the TYPE parameter.

The HTTP_PORT parameter specifies the port on which a neighbor or peer accepts HTTP requests on the hostname specified with the HOSTNAME parameter. Normally it's 3128.

The ICP_OR_HTCP_PORT parameter specifies the ICP or HTCP port for peer communication. The default ICP port is 3130, but we still need to specify it. Also, if we specify the HTCP port (default 4827), we must append `htcp` so that Squid can send HTCP queries to the peer. We can set this to 0 if we don't want any ICP or HTCP communication with the peer.

Time for action – joining a cache hierarchy

Let's add two proxy servers to our Squid configuration file:

```
cache_peer parent.example.com parent 3128 3130 default
cache_peer sib.example.com sibling 3128 3130 proxy-only
```

So, according to this configuration, `parent.example.com` is a parent proxy server and `sib.example.com` is a sibling proxy server.

What just happened?

We just learned how to add a proxy server or neighbors to our Squid configuration file, so that our proxy server can be a part of a cache hierarchy.

Now, let's have a look at the options which can be used to control ICP or HTCP communication.

ICP options

When we configure a peer with ICP communication, we must configure the `icp_port` and `icp_access` directives properly. Next, we'll have a look at the ICP-related options for the `cache_peer` directive.

no-query

If we use the option `no-query`, then Squid will never send any ICP queries to this peer.

multicast-responder

The option `multicast-responder` specifies that this peer is a member of a multicast group and Squid should not send ICP queries directly to this peer, however, we can receive ICP replies from this host.

closest-only

When the `closest-only` option is used, and in case there are `ICP_OP_MISS` replies, Squid will not forward requests resulting in `FIRST_PARENT_MISS`. However, Squid can still forward requests resulting in `CLOSEST_PARENT_MISS`.

background-ping

The `background-ping` option instructs Squid to send ICP queries to this peer in the background only and that too infrequently. This is generally used to update the round trip time.

HTCP options

When we configure a peer with HTCP communication, we must properly configure the `htcp_port` and `htcp_access` directives in the Squid configuration file. Let's have a look at the additional options for HTCP communication. Refer to `http://tools.ietf.org/html/rfc2756` for details on the HTCP protocol.

htcp

If we want Squid to use HTCP instead of ICP for communication, we must append the `htcp` option with the `ICP_PORT` parameter, while adding a neighbor using the `cache_peer` directive. Also, we should specify the port 4827 instead of 3130. This directive accepts a comma-separated list of the options described below.

htcp=oldsquid

If we use the option `htcp=oldsquid`, Squid will treat this neighbor as Squid version 2.5 or earlier and send HTCP queries accordingly.

htcp=no-clr

When the `htcp=no-clr` option is used, Squid is allowed to send HTCP queries to this neighbor, but CLR requests will not be sent. This option conflicts with the `htcp=only-clr` option and they should not be used together.

htcp=only-clr

The option `htcp=only-clr` instructs Squid to send only HTCP CLR requests to this neighbor.

htcp=no-purge-clr

When the option `htcp=no-purge-clr` is used, Squid is allowed to send HTCP queries including CLR requests, only when CLR requests don't result from PURGE requests.

htcp=forward-clr

If the option `htcp=forward-clr` is used and our proxy server receives a HTCP CLR request, they will be forwarded to this peer.

Peer or neighbor selection

If we add more than one cache peer or neighbor to our Squid configuration file, then we may be concerned about how Squid should select the peer to forward misses or send ICP or HTCP queries to. Squid provides the following options or methods for peer selection, depending on our environment or needs. By default, ICP is used for peer selection.

default

If we specify the option `default` while adding a peer or neighbor, then this parent will be used when no other peer can be located using any other peer selection algorithm. We should not use this option with more than one peer because this will mean that only the first one with the `default` option will be used.

round-robin

The option `round-robin` can be used to enable a very simple form of load balancing. The requests will be forwarded to cache peers marked with the `round-robin` option in an alternate order. This option is useful only when we use it with at least two peers. The option `weight`, which we'll see in the next section, biases the request counter which results in biased peer selection.

weighted-round-robin

The option `weighted-round-robin` instructs Squid to load balance requests among peers based on the round trip time, calculated by the `background-ping` option which we saw earlier. When this option is used, closer parents are used more often than other peers. We can also use the `weight` option which biases the round trip time, resulting in a biased peer selection.

userhash

The option `userhash` load balances requests on the basis of the client `proxy_auth` or the `ident` username.

sourcehash

The option `sourcehash` is similar to `userhash`, but the load balancing is done on the basis of the clients source IP address.

carp

The **Cache Array Routing Protocol** (**CARP**) is used to load balance HTTP requests across multiple caching proxy servers by generating a hash for individual URLs. For more information about CARP protocol, please visit `http://icp.ircache.net/carp.txt`. The option `carp` makes a parent peer a part of the cache array. The requests will be distributed uniformly among the parents in this cache array based on the CARP load balancing hash function. The option `weight` will cause biased peer selection in this case also.

multicast-siblings

The option `multicast-siblings` can be used only with multicast peers. The members of the multicast group must have a sibling relationship with this cache peer. This option is particularly useful when we want to configure a pool of redundant proxies that are members of the same multicast group, which are also known as a cluster of siblings, where multicast is used to speed up and reduce the ICP query overhead.

Options for peer selection methods

Along with the various peer selection methods we discussed previously, there are various options that can be combined with peer selection methods to further optimize the load balancing. Let's have a look at the available options.

weight

The option `weight` (`weight=N`) is used to affect the peer selection in methods that perform a weighted peer selection. The larger value of `weight` means that we are favoring a cache peer more over other cache peers with smaller values of `weight`. By default, the value of weight is 1, which means that all peers are equally favored.

basetime

The option `basetime` (`basetime=N`) is used to specify an amount of time that will be subtracted from the round trip time of all the parents, before dividing it by the weight to decide or select the parent to fetch from.

ttl

The option `ttl` (`ttl=N`) is specific to multicast groups. This option can be used to specify a Time to Live (TTL) when sending ICP queries to the multicast group. Other peers or the members of the multicast group must be configured with the `multicast-responder` option so that they can receive ICP replies properly. For more information on TTL, please check `http://en.wikipedia.org/wiki/Time_to_live`.

no-delay

If we are using Squid delay pools and we have added several peers to our configuration file, then the cache hits from peer proxy servers will be included in the client's delay pools. We don't want cache hits from other peers to be limited and they should not affect the delay pools. To achieve such behavior, we can use the `no-delay` option to ensure maximum speed.

digest-URL

If cache digests are enabled, Squid will try to fetch them using the standard location for cache digests. However, if we want Squid to fetch cache digests from an alternate URL, we can use the option `digest-URL` (`digest-URL=URL`) to instruct Squid to fetch digests from a different URL.

no-digest

The option `no-digest` disables fetching of cache digests from this peer.

SSL or HTTPS options

We can encrypt our connections to a cache peer with SSL or TLS. Squid provides a series of related options using which we can customize the connection parameters. Later, we'll have a look at these options.

ssl

When the option `ssl` is set, the communication to this cache peer will be encrypted with SSL or TLS.

sslcert

The option `sslcert` (`sslcert=FILE`) is used to specify the absolute path of a file containing the client SSL certificate, which should be used while connecting to this cache peer.

sslkey

We can optionally use the `sslkey` (`sslkey=FILE`) option to specify the absolute path to a file containing private SSL key, corresponding to the SSL certificate, specified using the `sslcert` option. If this option is not specified, then the SSL certificate file specified using the `sslcert` option is assumed to be a combined file containing the SSL certificate and the private key.

sslversion

The option `sslversion` (`sslversion=NUMBER`) can be used to specify the version of the SSL/TLS protocols we need to support. The following are the possible values of `sslversion`:

> 1: Automatic detection. This is the default value.
>
> 2: SSLv2 only.
>
> 3: SSLv3 only.
>
> 4: TLSv1 only.

sslcipher

We can specify a colon separated list of supported ciphers using the `sslcipher` (`sslcipher=COLON_SEPARATED_LIST`) option. Please check man page for `ciphers(1)` or visit `http://www.openssl.org/docs/apps/ciphers.html` for more information on ciphers supported by OpenSSL. Please note that the availability of ciphers depends on the version of OpenSSL being used.

ssloptions

We can specify various SSL engine-specific options in the form of a colon separated list using the ssloptions (ssloptions=LIST) parameter. Please check the SSL_CTX_set_ options(3) man page or visit http://www.openssl.org/docs/ssl/SSL_CTX_set_ options.html for a list of supported SSL engine options.

sslcafile

We can specify a file containing additional CA certificates using the option sslcafile (sslcafile=FILE), which can be used to verify the cache peer certificates.

sslcapath

The option sslcapath (sslcapath=DIRECTORY) is used to specify the absolute path to a directory containing additional certificates and **CRL (Certificate Revocation List)** lists that should be used while verifying the cache peer certificates.

sslcrlfile

The option sslcrlfile (sslcrlfile=FILE) is the absolute path to a file containing additional CRL lists, which should be used to verify cache peer certificates. These CRL lists will be used in addition to the CRL lists stored in sslcapath.

sslflags

Using the option sslflags (sslflags=LIST_OF_FLAGS), we can specify one or more flags, which will modify the usage of SSL. Let's have a look at the available flags:

- ◆ DONT_VERIFY_PEER: Accept the peer certificates, even if they fail to verify.
- ◆ NO_DEFAULT_CA: If the flag NO_DEFAULT_CA is used, the default CA lists built in OpenSSL will not be used.
- ◆ DONT_VERIFY_DOMAIN: If the DONT_VERIFY_DOMAIN flag is used, the peer certificate will not be verified if the domain matches the server name.

ssldomain

The option ssldomain (ssldomain=DOMAIN_NAME) can be used to specify the peer domain name, as mentioned in the peer certificate. This option is used to verify the received peer certificates. If this option is not specified, then the peer hostname will be used.

front-end-https

Using the option front-end-https will enable the Front-End-Https: On header when Squid is used as a SSL frontend in front of **Microsoft Outlook Web Access (OWA)**. For more information on why this header is needed, please check http://support.microsoft. com/kb/307347.

Other cache peer options

Until now, we have learned about various options that can be specified for optimizing peer selection and hence optimizing the flow of traffic. Now, let's have a look at the other important options provided by Squid.

login=username:password

Some of our peers may require proxy authentication for access. For such scenarios, we can use `login` option (`login=username:password`) to authenticate our cache so that it can use this peer.

login=PASS

The option `login=PASS` is used when we want to pass on login details received from the client to this particular peer. Proxy authentication is not a requirement for using this option. Also, if Squid didn't receive any authentication headers from the client but the username and password are available from external ACL `user=` and `password=` result tags, then they may be sent instead.

If we want to use proxy authentication on our proxy server as well as with this peer, then both the proxies must share the same user database, as HTTP allows only a single login (one for the proxy server and one for the origin server).

login=PASSTHRU

The option `login=PASSTHRU` is used when we want to forward HTTP authentication (`Proxy-Authentication` and `WWW-Authorization`) headers to this peer without any modification.

login=NEGOTIATE

We can use the option `login=NEGOTIATE` if this is a personal or a workgroup proxy server and the parent proxy server requires a secure proxy authentication. The first **Service Principal Name** (**SPN**) from the default keytab or defined by the environment variable `KRB5_KTNAME` will be used.

connect-timeout

The option `connect-timeout` determines the connection timeout to this peer. This can be different for different peers. If this option is not used, then Squid will determine the timeout from the `peer_connect_timeout` directive.

connect-fail-limit

The option `connect-fail-limit` (`connect-fail-limit=N`) determines the number of connection failures to this peer or neighbor, after which it will be declared dead or unreachable. The default value of `connect-fail-limit` is 10.

max-conn

The number of parallel connections that can be opened to this peer is determined by the option `max-conn` (max-conn=N).

name

There may be cases when we have multiple peers on the same host listening on different ports. In such cases, the hostname will not be able to uniquely identify a peer or neighbor. So, we can use the `name` (name=STRING) option to specify a unique name for this peer. Also, this option is always set and defaults to either the hostname, the IP address, or the cache peer. The name specified using this option is used with directives like `cache_peer_access` and `cache_peer_domain`.

proxy-only

Normally, Squid will try to store the responses locally if the requests are cacheable. However, if the request is fetched from peers in the local area network, then this will result in the unnecessary waste of disk space on our proxy servers if the responses can be fetched at a very high speed from our peers. Specifying the `proxy-only` option will instruct Squid not to cache any responses from this peer. Please note that we should use this option only when the cache peer is connected with a low latency and high speed connection to our proxy server.

allow-miss

The client requests are forwarded to a sibling only when they result in hits. We can use the `allow-miss` option to forward cache misses to siblings. We should use this option carefully as this may result in forward loops.

Controlling communication with peers

Unil now we have learned about various options that can be used to configure cache peers or neighbors as parents or siblings. Now, we'll learn about controlling access to different peers and sending a variety of requests to different peers, depending on various rules. Access control over peer communication is achieved via various directives in the Squid configuration file. We have learned about these directives briefly, but we'll explore them in detail now.

Domain-based forwarding

Squid provides a directive `cache_peer_domain`, using which we can restrict the domains for which a particular peer or neighbor will be referred. The general format for the `cache_peer_domain` directive is:

```
cache_peer_domain NAME [!]domain [[!]domain] ...
```

In the preceding format, NAME is the name of the neighbor cache, which will be either the values of the name option, the hostname, or the IP address specified while declaring it as a peer using the `cache_peer` directive.

We can specify any number of domains with the `cache_peer_domain` directive, either on the same line or multiple lines. Prefixing a domain name with '!' will result in all domains being matched except the specified one.

Time for action – configuring Squid for domain-based forwarding

Let's see an example configuration:

```
cache_peer parent.example.com   parent 3128 3130 default proxy-only
cache_peer acad.example.com     parent 3128 3130 proxy-only
cache_peer video.example.com    parent 3128 3130 proxy-only
cache_peer social.example.com   parent 3128 3130 proxy-only
cache_peer search.example.com   parent 3128 3130 proxy-only

cache_peer_domain acad.example.com     .edu
cache_peer_domain video.example.com    .youtube.com .vimeo.com
cache_peer_domain video.example.com    .metacafe.com .dailymotion.com
cache_peer_domain social.example.com   .facebook.com .myspace.com
cache_peer_domain social.example.com   .twitter.com
cache_peer_domain search.example.com   .google.com .yahoo.com .bing.com
```

According to the previous configuration example, the proxy server `acad.example.com` can be used to forward requests for the `.edu` domains only. A cache peer can only be contacted for the domain names matching the ones specified with `cache_peer_domain`. If we don't specify any domain name for a peer (`parent.example.com` in the above example), then it can be used to forward all requests.

So, we can see how straight forward it is to partition traffic by using some simple rules such as those in the previous configuration.

What just happened?

We learned to use the directive `cache_peer_domain` to partition the traffic or client requests based on domain names so that the requests can be forwarded to different proxy servers.

Cache peer access

Squid provides another directive named `cache_peer_access`, which is a more flexible version of `cache_peer_domain` as we can control request forwarding using powerful access control lists. The format of the `cache_peer_access` directive is as follows:

```
cache_peer_access NAME allow|deny [!]ACL_NAME [[!]ACL_NAME] ...
```

The `NAME` parameter is the same as the one used with `cache_peer_domain` and specifies the name of the cache peer or neighbor. The options `allow` or `deny` will determine whether a request will be forwarded or not to this cache peer.

Time for action – forwarding requests to cache peers using ACLs

Let's say we have three parent proxy servers (`p1.exmaple.com`, `p2.example.com`, and `p3.example.com`). The proxy server `p3.example.com` is connected to the internet with a highly reliable, but expensive connection, with a fair usage policy. The proxy servers p1 and p2 are cheaper but unreliable. Also, we have three subnets (academic, research, and finance) on our local area network, according to the following diagram:

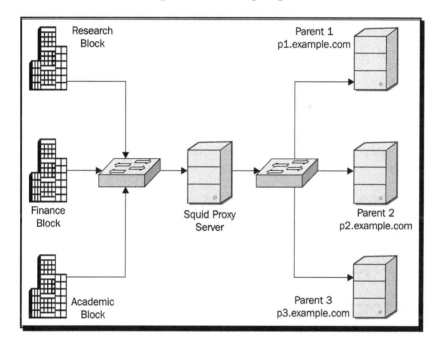

Now, let's have a look at the following configuration:

```
cache_peer p1.example.com parent 3128 3130 round-robin
cache_peer p2.example.com parent 3128 3130 round-robin
cache_peer p3.example.com parent 8080 3130

acl academic src 192.0.2.0/16
acl finance src 198.51.100.0/16
acl research src 203.0.13.0/16

acl imp_domains dstdomain .corporate.example.com .edu
```

```
acl ftp proto FTP

cache_peer_access p3.example.com deny ftp
cache_peer_access p3.example.com allow research
cache_peer_access p3.exmaple.com allow academic imp_domains
cache_peer_access p3.exmaple.com allow finance imp_domains
cache_peer_access p3.example.com deny academic
cache_peer_access p3.example.com deny finance
```

As we can see in the previous example, we have allowed request forwarding to the parent proxy server p3.example.com for the requests originating from the research subnet only. We have allowed other subnets to access some important domains using the highly reliable connection and we have completely disabled the use of this connection for the FTP protocol. Also, note that the requests will be forwarded to the proxy server p3.example.com only when both p1.example.com and p2.example.com are not reachable. The requests will be forwarded to the p1.example.com and p2.example.com proxy servers in a round robin fashion.

We can achieve even better control by using ACL lists of different ACL types.

What just happened?

We just explored the power of the cache_peer_access directive, which in combination with Squid's access control lists, provides a powerful way to forward requests to different peers. We can further improve the request forwarding by using the time-based ACLs along with cache_peer_access.

Have a go hero – join a cache hierarchy

Make a list of proxy servers on your network. Add these proxy servers to the Squid configuration file and then partition traffic to these proxy servers in such a way that the requests go to one group of servers in the day time, and to a different group at night.

Switching peer relationship

As we saw earlier, we have to specify the peer relationship while adding a peer to our Squid configuration file. However, there may be cache peers who can offer to serve cache misses only for certain domains, while serving cache hits for all domains. The misses and hits mentioned above are corresponding to the ICP, Cache Digest, or HTCP, misses and hits. An ICP, Cache Digest, or HTCP miss means that the peer does not have the required object. The peer relationship switch for certain domains can be achieved using the neighbor_type_domain directive in the configuration file. The following format uses the neighbor_type_domain directive:

```
neighbor_type_domain CACHE_HOST parent|sibling domain [domain] ...
```

Time for action – configuring Squid to switch peer relationship

For example, let's say we have configured `sibling.example.com` as a sibling proxy server but `sibling.example.com` allows us to forward requests to `.edu` domains, even if there are cache misses. So, we can have the following configuration:

```
cache_peer parent.example.com parent 3128 3130 default proxy-only
cache_peer sibling.example.com sibling 3128 3130 proxy-only
neighbor_type_domain sibling.example.com parent .edu
```

In accordance with the previous configuration, we can fetch cache misses for `.edu` domains using `sibling.example.com`.

What just happened?

In this section, we learned to switch the peer relationship, from sibling to parent, dynamically for certain domains.

Controlling request redirects

We have just seen a list of directives, using which, we can use different peers to forward requests based on various parameters. In addition to the previously mentioned directives, Squid provides a few more directives, using which we can force certain requests to be forwarded to remote servers directly or to always pass through peers. Let's have a look at these directives.

hierarchy_stoplist

We normally use cache peers to increase the cache hit ratio, but there are certain requests which can't be cached as the content served in response to these requests is dynamic and changes every time it's requested. It's of no use to query our cache peers for such requests. We can instruct Squid to stop forwarding requests to peers and instead contact the remote servers directly using the directive `hierarchy_stoplist`. The directive `hierarchy_stoplist` essentially takes a list of words, which if found in a request URL, will mean that the URL will be handled by this cache and will not be forwarded to any of the neighbors.

```
hierarchy_stoplist cgi-bin ? jsp
```

 We should note that `never_direct` overrides the directive `hierarchy_stoplist`.

always_direct

There may be certain requests which we always want to forward to remote servers instead of forwarding them to neighbor caches. We can use the directive `always_direct` to direct or forward such requests directly to remote servers. This is generally helpful in retrieving the content on the local area network directly because cache peers will introduce unnecessary delay.

For example, consider the following configuration:

```
acl local_domain dstdomain .local.example.com
always_direct allow local_domain
```

The requests destined to `.local.example.com` will be sent directly to the corresponding servers instead of routing them through cache peers.

never_direct

Using the directive `never_direct`, we can control the requests which must not be sent to remote servers directly and must be forwarded to a peer cache. This is generally helpful when all the packets going to internet must pass through a proxy firewall, which is normally configured as a default parent.

Let's say we have `firewall.example.com` as a firewall proxy which must be used for forwarding all requests, but we can still forward all requests for local servers directly. So, we can have the following configuration:

```
cache_peer firewall.example.com parent 3128 3130 default
acl local_domain dstdomain .local.example.com
always_direct allow local_domain
never_direct allow all
```

The previous configuration will configure Squid so that all requests to the local servers are forwarded directly to the destination servers and that all external requests pass through the firewall proxy server `firewall.example.com`.

prefer_direct

Any requests which are cacheable by Squid are routed via peers so that we can utilize neighbor caches to improve the average page load time. However, in case we are willing to forward the cacheable requests directly to remote servers, we can set the value of the `prefer_direct` directive to on. The default value of this directive is off and Squid will try to use neighbor caches first instead of forwarding the requests directly to remote servers.

The directive `prefer_direct` modifies Squid's behavior only for cacheable requests. If we want to route all requests through a firewall proxy, we should use `never_direct` instead.

nonhierarchical_direct

Non-hierarchical requests are the requests that are either identified by the `hierarchy_stoplist` directive or can't be cached by Squid. Such requests should not be sent to cache peers because they will not result in cache hits. Therefore it's a good idea to forward these requests directly to remote servers. We achieve this behavior by setting the value of the directive `nonhierarchical_direct` to `on`. If we set this directive's value to `off`, these requests will not be sent to remote servers directly. Please note that although HTTPS requests are not cacheable, `nonhierarchical_direct` must be set to `off` for HTTPS requests to be relayed through a firewall parent proxy.

 It's not recommended to set the value of `nonhierarchical_direct` to off. If we want to direct all requests via a firewall proxy, we should use the `never_direct` directive instead.

Have a go hero – proxy server behind a firewall

Configure your proxy server so that it forwards all the requests to a parent proxy server and never contacts the remote servers directly.

Peer communication protocols

We have learned about configuring Squid to be a part of a cache hierarchy. When many proxy servers are a part of cache hierarchy, they need to communicate to share information about the objects present in their cache so that neighbors can utilize these cached objects as hits. For communication among peers, Squid implements ICP, HTCP, and Cache Digest protocols. Later on, we'll have a brief look at ICP, HTCP, and Cache Digest protocols.

Internet Cache Protocol

ICP or **Internet Cache Protocol** is a simple web-caching protocol used to query proxy servers (cache peers) about the existence of a particular object in their cache. Depending on the replies received from the neighbors, Squid will decide the forwarding path for the particular request.

As we saw in the peer selection algorithms, ICP is also used to calculate the round trip time and also for detecting dead peers in a hierarchy. The round trip time calculation is an important measure as it can help Squid in dynamically rerouting the traffic to a less congested network route.

Although ICP is a simple protocol and it's very easy to configure proxy servers to communicate with each other using it, ICP also suffers from a lot of problems. The first one is latency. Squid doesn't know whether an object is present in a peer cache or not. It has to query all the peer caches for each object, which in some cases (if the number of peers is large), will introduce a significant delay as it will take time to query all of them. So, if we have a large number of peers, there will be a lot of ICP packets floating around on the network which may end up causing congestion. To get around the congestion issue here, we can use the multicast ICP protocol.

Other flaws in the ICP protocol are false hits, security, and so on. For more details on the ICP protocol, please visit `http://icp.ircache.net/rfc2186.txt`. Another interesting read about the application of the ICP protocol is at `http://tools.ietf.org/html/rfc2187`.

The HTCP protocol is recommended over the ICP protocol to avoid problems like latency, false hits, and so on.

Cache digests

Squid keeps a list of all the cached objects in the main memory in the form of a hash, so that it can quickly guess whether a URI will result in a hit or miss without actually searching for the files on disk. Cache digest is a summary of these cached objects into a compact bitmap using the Bloom Filter data structure (for more information on the Bloom Filter, please visit `http://en.wikipedia.org/wiki/Bloom_filter`). The value of the bit determines whether a particular object is present in the cache or not. If the bit is on or set to 1, the object is present in the cache, otherwise it's not in the cache. This summary is available to other peers via a special URL over the HTTP protocol. When a cache digest is retrieved by peers they can determine, by checking the digest, whether a particular URI is present in the cache or not.

So, cache digests significantly reduce the number of packets flowing on the network which are just for querying the other peers, but the total data transfer amount increases as the cache digests are fetched by all the peers periodically. However, this helps in significantly decreasing the delay introduced by ICP queries.

With the cache digest protocol, the problem of false hits get worse as the digest grows older. The digest is rebuilt only periodically (hourly by default). This also introduces the problems of false misses. The false misses are for web objects which were cached after the cache digest was built.

Squid and cache digest configuration

To be able to use cache digests, we must enable cache digests using the `--enable-cache-digests` option with the `configure` program before compiling Squid. Let's have a look at the cache digest related directives available in the Squid configuration file.

Digest generation

It makes sense to generate cache digests only when we plan to use cache digests for peer communication. Therefore, we can use the `digest_generation` directive in the configuration file to select whether the digest will be generated or not. The possible values for this directive can be on or off. By default, this directive is set to on and Squid generates cache digests.

Digest bits per entry

The data structure, Bloom Filter, which is used to build cache digest, provides a lossy encoding and there may be false hits even in the cache digests. The directive `digest_bits_per_entry` determines the number of bits that will be used for encoding one single entry or a cached object. The larger value of bits per entry will result in higher accuracy and hence lesser false hits, but will this consume more space in the main memory and more bandwidth while transferring over the network. The default value of `digest_bits_per_entry` is 5 but we can safely push it to 7 for more accuracy if we have a large cache.

Digest rebuild period

We can use the directive `digest_rebuild_period` to set the time interval, after which the cache digest will be rebuilt. One hour is the default, which will result in a not so up-to-date cache digest, but rebuilding a cache digest is a CPU-intensive job and this time interval should be set depending on the hardware capabilities and load on the proxy server. We can safely set it to 10 or 15 minutes to keep things fresh.

> Digest rebuild period implies the time after which the cache digest will be rebuilt in memory. This time doesn't imply the time after which the cache digest will be written to disk.

Digest rebuild chunk percentage

The directive `digest_rebuild_chunk_percentage` determines the percentage of the cache which will be added to the cache digest every time the rebuild routine is called on schedule. The default behavior is to add 10 percent of the cache to the cache digest every rebuild.

Digest swapout chunk

The amount or number of bytes of the cache digest that will be written to the disk at a time is determined by the directive `digest_swapout_chunk`. The default behavior is to write 4096 bytes at a time.

Digest rewrite period

The digest rewrite period is the time interval after which the cache digest is written to disk, which then can be served to other peers. We can configure this time interval using the `digest_rewrite_period` directive. Generally, it should be equal to digest the rebuild period.

Hypertext Caching Protocol

HTCP or **Hypertext Caching Protocol** is similar to ICP but has advanced features and generally results in better performance compared to the ICP protocol. Both the ICP and HTCP protocols use UDP for communication and TCP communication is optionally allowed for HTCP for protocol debugging. HTCP has the following advantages over the ICP protocol:

◆ ICP queries include only URI while HTCP queries include full HTTP headers. HTCP also includes HTTP headers in a request, which helps the server avoid false hits, but would be true only for a URL key and would be false if more headers are known.

◆ HTCP allows third party replies, using which a peer can inform us about an alternate location of a cached object. ICP doesn't have a similar provision.

◆ HTCP supports monitoring of peers for cache additions or deletions while ICP doesn't.

◆ HTCP uses a variable sized binary message format, which can be used for extending the protocol, while ICP uses a fixed size binary message format rendering ICP to be very difficult to extend.

◆ HTCP provides optional message authentication using shared secret keys while ICP doesn't.

For more details on the HTCP protocol, please visit `http://tools.ietf.org/html/rfc2756`.

Pop quiz

1. Consider the following configuration and then select the most appropriate answer from the following selection:

```
cache_peer p1.example.com parent  3128 3130 default weight=1
cache_peer p2.example.com parent  3128 3130 default weight=10
cache_peer s1.example.com sibling 3128 3130 default
cache_peer s2.example.com sibling 3128 3130 default
```

If all siblings are dead, then which parent proxy servers will be used for forwarding requests?

a. `p1.example.com`

b. `s1.example.com`

c. `p2.example.com`

d. `s2.example.com`

2. Consider the following Squid configuration and then select the most appropriate answer from the following selection:

```
cache_peer sibling.example.com sibling 3128 0 no-query no-digest
```

Which of the following directives can be used for forwarding all requests, except requests to `local.example.com`?

a. `cache_peer_domain`

b. `cache_peer_access`

c. Both a and b

d. None

Summary

In this chapter, we have learned about configuring the Squid proxy server to join a cache hierarchy. We also learned about the various relationships between cache peers or neighbors. We also learned about various peer selection mechanisms for forwarding requests.

Specifically, we covered:

◆ Advantages and disadvantages of joining a cache hierarchy

◆ Various configuration options while adding peers

◆ Ways to restrict access to cache peers

◆ Various configuration directives to control request forwarding to peers

◆ The protocols used for communication among cache peers

In the next chapter, we'll learn about configuring Squid in the reverse proxy mode.

9
Squid in Reverse Proxy Mode

So far, we have learned to use Squid for caching the requests to various websites on the Internet, and for hiding a number of clients behind a single or a hierarchy of proxy servers. The Squid proxy server can also act as an origin server accelerator in which it accepts normal HTTP requests and forwards the cache misses to the origin servers. This is commonly known as surrogate mode. In this chapter, we'll learn about configuring Squid in reverse proxy mode.

In this chapter, we will learn about:

- ◆ Reverse proxy mode
- ◆ Configuring Squid as a server surrogate (also known as an accelerator)
- ◆ Access controls in reverse proxy mode
- ◆ Example configurations

So let's get started...

What is reverse proxy mode?

In previous chapters, we have learned to use Squid to cache the web documents locally so that we can enhance the user experience. This is done by serving the cached web documents from the proxy server, which is generally on the same local network as the clients. So, we can visualize this behavior using the following diagram:

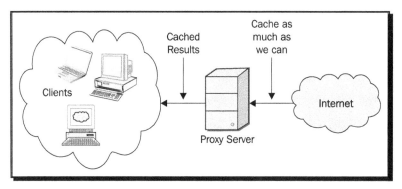

As we can see in the previous diagram, we try to cache the responses received from various web servers on the Internet and then use those cached responses to serve the subsequent requests for the same web documents. In short, we are using Squid to improve the performance of our Internet connection.

Exploring reverse proxy mode

Now, consider the scenario from a point of view of a web server. Let's say that the website `www.example.com` is hosted on a web server and there are tens of thousands of clients browsing the website. So, in the scenario where a website gets way too many visitors, the web server will be overloaded and we would have to distribute the load by deploying more servers. We can visualize this situation using the following diagram:

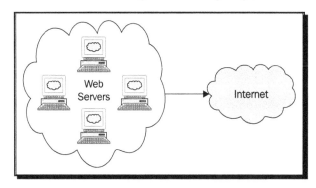

In the previous diagram, a group of web servers are hosting the domain `www.example.com` and serving the responses to the requests from all over the internet.

As we know, most of the content served to clients by a web server hosting a website doesn't change frequently. For example, the additional files like JavaScript files, CSS style sheets, and images embedded in a web page, which constitute the major part of a web page, don't change frequently. So, we can introduce a Squid proxy server in a reverse proxy mode (also known as a surrogate or an accelerator), which will cache the content that doesn't change frequently. It will also try to help the otherwise overloaded web server by responding to the majority of requests targeted to the web server, by serving the content from its cache. Let's have a look at the following diagram:

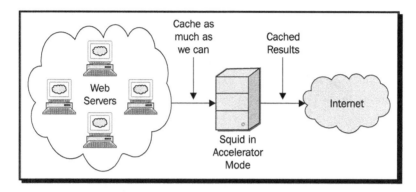

In the preceding diagram, we placed a Squid proxy server in front of the web servers so that all the requests to the web servers are passing through the proxy server. Therefore in this scenario, Squid will be accepting the HTTP requests. Squid will forward all the requests to the origin web servers, except the requests that it has already cached. So, web servers will not have to deal with the requests that are already cached on the proxy server. This mode of Squid is called reverse proxy mode or server accelerator mode.

Now that we have understood the reverse proxy mode, it's time to learn to configure Squid as a server accelerator.

Configuring Squid as a server surrogate

To configure Squid as a server surrogate, we need to provide the appropriate options with various directives, depending on the requirements. We can configure Squid to act as a forward proxy and server surrogate at the same time. However, the access control rules must be written very carefully in such cases, which we will cover in our special section on Access Control Configuration for surrogate servers. However, to omit any possible confusion, it's always better to have a dedicated instance of Squid for server acceleration and a separate instance for the forward proxy.

Also, as Squid will be listening on port 80 to accept HTTP requests, our web server can't listen on the same IP address as Squid. In this scenario, we have the following options:

◆ Squid can listen on port 80 on the public IP address and the web server can listen on port 80 on the loopback (127.0.0.1) address.

◆ The web server can listen on port 80 on a virtual network interface with an IP address from the private address space. If the web server and Squid are on different machines, then this is not going to be a problem at all.

HTTP port

As we learned that Squid will be accepting HTTP requests on behalf of the web servers sitting behind it, the most important configuration directive is http_port. We need to set the HTTP port with the appropriate options. Let's have a look at the general format of http_port for configuring Squid in the reverse proxy mode.

```
http_port 80 accel [options]
```

So, we need to specify a port number, such as 80. Apart from the port, we need to use the option accel, which will tell Squid that port 80 will be used for server acceleration. Also, there are additional options that are required to properly configure Squid so that it can communicate with the web servers.

 Please note that while configuring Squid in surrogate mode, we need to specify at least one option from defaultsite, vhost, or vport. We should also note that the CONNECT requests are blocked from receiving accel flagged ports.

HTTP options in reverse proxy mode

Let's have a look at the other options that can be used with the http_port directive.

defaultsite

The option defaultsite (defaultsite=domain_name) specifies the domain name or site that will be used to construct the Host HTTP header if it is missing. The domain name here is the public domain name that a visitor types in his/her browser to access the website.

vhost

If we specify the option vhost, Squid will support domains hosted as virtualhosts.

vport

To enable IP-based virtual host support, we can use the vport option. The option vport can be specified in the following two ways:

If we specify the vport option, Squid will use the port from the Host HTTP header. If the port in the Host header is missing, then it'll use http_port (port) for virtual host support.

If we specify the vport option along with the port (vport=PORT_NUMBER), Squid will use PORT_NUMBER instead of the port specified with http_port.

allow-direct

The direct forwarding of requests is denied in reverse proxy mode, by default, for security reasons. When we have direct forwarding enabled in reverse proxy mode, a rogue client may send a forged request with any external domain name in the Host HTTP header and Squid will fetch and forward the response to the client. This will permit relay attacks. A very strict access control is required to prevent such attacks when direct forwarding is enabled. If we want, we can enable direct forwarding by specifying the option allow-direct.

protocol

The protocol (protocol=STRING) option can be used to reconstruct the requests. The default is HTTP.

ignore-cc

The HTTP requests carry Cache-Control HTTP headers from the clients which determine whether the cached response should be flushed or reloaded. If we use the option ignore-cc, the Cache-Control headers will be ignored and Squid will serve the cached response if it's still fresh.

The following are a few examples showing the usage of http_port.

```
http_port 80 accel defaultsite=www.example.com
http_port 80 accel vhost
http_port 80 accel vport ignore-cc
```

HTTPS port

Let's consider a scenario where we are serving a website or a few pages on a website over an encrypted secure connection using secure HTTP or HTTPS. We can outsource the encryption and decryption work to the Squid proxy server, which can handle HTTPS requests. So, when we configure Squid to accept HTTPS connections or requests, it'll decrypt the requests and forward the unencrypted requests to the web server.

 Please note that we should use the --enable-ssl option with the configure program before compiling, if we want Squid to accept HTTPS requests. Also note that several operating systems don't provide packages capable of HTTPS reverse-proxy due to GPL and policy constraints.

HTTPS options in reverse proxy mode

Let's have a look at the syntax for the `https_port` directive.

```
https_port [IP_ADDRESS:]port accel cert=certificate.pem [key=key.pem]
[options]
```

In the preceding configuration line, the `IP_ADDRESS` to which Squid will bind to can be optionally specified. The option `port` determines the port on which Squid will listen for HTTPS requests.

The `cert` parameter is used to specify the absolute path to either the SSL certificate file or an OpenSSL-compatible combined certificate and private key file. The `key` parameter is optional and is used to specify the absolute path to the SSL private key file. If we don't specify the `key` parameter, Squid will assume the file specified by the `cert` parameter as a combined certificate and private key file.

> Please note that we should have OpenSSL installed on our system. Please check `http://www.openssl.org/` for more information on OpenSSL. It is also recommended to keep an eye on the latest OpenSSL vulnerabilities and to apply the patches as soon as they are available at `http://www.openssl.org/news/vulnerabilities.html`.

Let's have a quick look at the other options available with the `https_port` directive.

defaultsite

The option `defaultsite` (`defaultsite=domain_name`) can be used to specify the default HTTPS website which should be used in case HTTP `Host` header is missing.

vhost

Identical to `http_port`, the `vhost` option can be used to support virtually-hosted domains. Please note that if the `vhost` option is used, the certificate specified should be either a wildcard certificate or one that is valid for more than one domain.

version

The option `version` (`version=NUMBER`) can be used to specify the version of the SSL/TLS protocols which we need to support. The following are the possible values of `version`:

- 1: Automatic detection. This is the default value.
- 2: SSLv2 only.
- 3: SSLv3 only.
- 4: TLSv1 only.

cipher

We can specify a colon separated list of supported ciphers using the `cipher` (`cipher=COLON_SEPARATED_LIST`) option. Please check the man page for ciphers(1) or visit `http://www.openssl.org/docs/apps/ciphers.html` for more information on ciphers supported by OpenSSL. Please note that this list of ciphers is directly passed to OpenSSL libraries and we should check the availability of ciphers for our version of OpenSSL before specifying them.

options

We can specify various SSL engine-specific options in the form of a colon separated list using the `options` (`options=LIST`) parameter. Please check the `SSL_CTX_set_options(3)` man page or visit `http://www.openssl.org/docs/ssl/SSL_CTX_set_options.html` for a list of supported SSL engine options. Please note that these options are directly passed to OpenSSL libraries and we should check the availability of these options for our OpenSSL version.

clientca

The option `clientca` (`clientca=FILE`) is used to specify the absolute path to the file containing a list of **Certificate Authorities** (**CA**s) to be used while requesting a client certificate.

cafile

We can specify a file containing additional CA certificates using the option `cafile` (`cafile=FILE`), which can be used to verify client certificates.

capath

The option `capath` (`capath=DIRECTORY`) is used to specify the absolute path to a directory containing additional certificates and **CRL** (**Certificate Revocation List**) lists that should be used while verifying the client certificates.

 Please note that if we don't specify the `clientca`, `cafile`, or `capath` options, then SSL library defaults will be used.

crlfile

The option `crlfile` (`crlfile=FILE`) is the absolute path to a file containing additional CRL lists, which should be used to verify client certificates. These CRL lists will be used in addition to the CRL lists stored in `capath`.

dhparams

We can specify a file containing DH parameters for DH key exchanges using the option `dhparams` (`dhparams=FILE`). For more information on DH parameter generation, please check the `dhparam(1)` man page or visit `http://www.openssl.org/docs/apps/dhparam.html`.

sslflags

Using the option `sslflags` (`sslflags=LIST_OF_FLAGS`), we can specify one or more flags, which will modify the usage of SSL. Let's have a look at the available flags:

NO_DEFAULT_CA

If the flag `NO_DEFAULT_CA` is used, the default CA lists built in OpenSSL will not be used.

NO_SESSION_REUSE

When `NO_SESSION_REUSE` is used, every new connection will be a new SSL connection and no connection will be reused.

VERIFY_CRL

The CRL lists contained in the files specified using `crlfile` or `capath` options will be used to verify the client certificates before accepting them, if the `VERIFY_CRL` flag is used.

VERIFY_CRL_ALL

If we use the `VERIFY_CRL_ALL` flag, then all the certificates in the client certificate chain will be verified.

sslcontext

Using the option `sslcontext` (`sslcontext=ID`) we can set the SSL session ID context identifier.

vport

The option `vport` is used to enable the IP-based virtual host support. Its usage is identical to the `vport` option in the `http_port` directive.

Let's see a few examples showing the usage of the `https_port` directive:

```
https_port 443 accel defaultsite=secure.example.com cert=/opt/squid/
etc/squid_combined.pem sslflags=NO_DEFAULT_CA

https_port 443 accel vhost cert=/opt/squid/etc/squid.pem key=/opt/
squid/etc/squid_key.pem
```

Have a go hero – exploring OpenSSL

Try to read the OpenSSL documentation for generating various certificates and private keys.

Adding backend web servers

So far, we learned about configuring Squid to accept HTTP or HTTPS connections on behalf of our web servers. Once Squid has received a HTTP or HTTPS request, it needs to forward it to a web server so that it can fetch content from the web server. It will then pass that content back to the client requesting the content. So, we need to tell Squid about our backend servers to which it will connect to satisfy the client requests. We can add one or more web servers using the `cache_peer` directive in the Squid configuration.

Cache peer options for reverse proxy mode

Let's have a look at the options for the `cache_peer` directive specifically meant for Squid in reverse proxy mode.

originserver

If the option `originserver` is used with a cache peer, Squid will treat it as an origin web server.

forcedomain

The `forcedomain` (`forcedomain=domain_name`) can be used to configure Squid to always send the host header with the domain name specified. This option is generally used to fix broken origin servers which are publicly available over multiple domains. This option should be avoided if the origin server is capable of handling the multiple domains.

Time for action – adding backend web servers

We learned about `cache_peer` in detail in the previous chapter and previously, we saw two options specifically meant for Squid in reverse proxy mode. Now, let's see a few examples showing the usage of the `cache_peer` directive to add backend web servers.

```
cache_peer 127.0.0.1 parent 80 0 no-query no-digest originserver
cache_peer local_ip_of_web_server parent 80 no-query originserver
forcedomain=www.example.com
```

What just happened?

We learned to add backend web servers in our Squid configuration file as cache peers or neighbors so that Squid can forward them the requests which it receives from clients.

Support for surrogate protocol

The requests and responses for a web document may pass through a series of server surrogates (reverse proxies or origin server accelerators) and forward caching proxies. While the server surrogates are used for scaling individual or a group of websites, the forward proxies are used to provide a better browsing experience by caching the content locally. The server surrogates act on behalf of the origin server and they act with the same authority as the origin server. So, we need a different cache control mechanism or a different way to control these server surrogates to achieve higher performance while maintaining the data accuracy.

Surrogate protocol extensions to the HTTP protocol provides a way to assign controls to server surrogates, which can be different from controls assigned to the intermediary forward proxies or the HTTP clients. Now, we'll explore the surrogate protocol and a few related aspects.

Understanding the surrogate protocol

Let's see how the surrogate protocol works and how the surrogate capabilities and controls are passed using HTTP header fields.

◆ When a surrogate receives a request, it builds a request which will look similar to the following:

```
GET / HTTP/1.1
...
Surrogate-Capability: mirror.example.com="Surrogate/1.0"
...
```

Notice the special header field Surrogate-Capability. The Squid proxy server is advertising itself as a surrogate (`mirror.example.com`). Now this request will be forwarded to the origin web server.

◆ Upon receiving the request from a surrogate, the web server will construct a response with the appropriate surrogate control HTTP header, shown in the following example:

```
HTTP/1.1 200OK
...
Cache-Control: no-cache, max-age=1800, s-max-age=3600
Surrogate-Control: max-age=43200;mirror.example.com
...
```

Let's see what controls are being passed by the origin server to surrogates, forward proxies, and HTTP clients. The end clients (HTTP clients) can store the response for a maximum time of half an hour, as determined by `Cache-Control: max-age=1800`. The forward proxies on the way can store the response for an hour, as determined by `Cache-Control:s-max-age=3600`. The surrogate known by the identification token `mirror.example.com` can store the response for half a day, as defined in `Surrogate-Control: max-age=43200`.

So, as we can see from the previous examples, the surrogate protocol extensions to HTTP have facilitated the different controls for the HTTP clients, the intermediary forward proxies and server surrogates. For more details on the surrogate protocol, please visit `http://www.w3.org/TR/edge-arch`.

Configuration options for surrogate support

We have two directives in the Squid configuration file related to surrogate protocol. Let's have a look at these directives.

httpd_accel_surrogate_id

All server surrogates need an identification token, which is sent to origin servers so that they can send appropriate controls to a surrogate gateway. This identification token can be unique for a surrogate or can be shared among a cluster of proxy servers, depending on the gateway design.

The default value of this identification token is the same as the value of `visible_hostname`. To set it to a different value, we can use the `httpd_accel_surrogate_id` as shown in the following example:

```
httpd_accel_surrogate_id mirror1.example.com
```

The previous configuration line will set the surrogate ID to `mirror1.example.com`.

httpd_accel_surrogate_remote

The remote surrogates (such as those in a **Content Delivery Network** or **CDN**) honor the `Surrogate-Control: no-store-remote` directive in the HTTP header, which means that the response should not be stored in cache. Such a response can only be sent in a reply to the original request. We can advertise our proxy server as a remote surrogate by setting the directive `http_accel_surrogate_remote` to `on`, which is shown in the following example:

```
http_accel_surrogate_remote on
```

We should only set this option to `on` when our proxy server is two or more hops away from the origin server.

Support for ESI protocol

ESI or **Edge Side Includes** is an XML-based markup language that can facilitate the dynamic assembling of HTML content at the edge of the Internet or near the end user. ESI is designed for processing on surrogates capable of processing the ESI language. Its capability token is `ESI/1.0`. The following are a few advantages of the ESI protocol:

- Allows surrogates to cache parts of web documents, which result in a better HIT ratio.

- Reduces processing overhead on the origin servers as the resource assembling can be performed by the surrogates or HTTP clients themselves.

◆ Enhances the availability of content.

◆ Improves the performance for the end user as content can be fetched from multiple caches.

For more information on the ESI protocol and the ESI language, please visit `http://www.akamai.com/html/support/esi.html`.

Configuring Squid for ESI support

To enable ESI support, we need to use the `--enable-esi` option with the configure program before compiling Squid. If Squid is built with ESI, then we can use the `esi_parser` directive in the Squid configuration file to choose the appropriate parser for ESI markup.

We can use the `esi_parser` directive, as shown in the following example:

```
esi_parser libxml2
```

This configuration line will set `libxml2` as the parser for ESI markup. We can choose a parser from `libxml2`, `expat`, or `custom`. The default parser is `custom`.

We should note that ESI markup is not strictly XML compatible. The `custom` ESI parser provides higher performance compared to the other two, however it can't handle non ASCII character encoding, which may result in unexpected behavior.

Logging messages in web server log format

When we use Squid in reverse proxy mode, most of our web server log messages will go missing as the requests which can be satisfied from Squid's cache will never make it to the web server. So, Squid's access log will be our source of web server logs now. However, the problem is that, by default Squid's access log format is completely different to the log format used by most web servers. To get rid of this problem, we can use the `common` log format with the `access_log` directive and this will allow Squid to start logging messages in the Apache web server log format.

Ignoring the browser reloads

Most browsers have a reload button, which if used, sets the `Cache-Control` HTTP header to `no-cache`. This will force Squid to purge the cached content and fetch it from the origin server even if the content in the cache was still valid, which results in a waste of resources.

Time for action – configuring Squid to ignore the browser reloads

There are three ways to fix this issue using `http_port` and `refresh_pattern` directives in the Squid configuration file. Please note that the `refresh_pattern` rules apply to both server and client headers and can pose issues if we ignore certain headers and clients may receive stale replies.

Using ignore-cc

We have seen the `ignore-cc` option in the HTTP port section previously. If we use this option while specifying the HTTP port, Squid will ignore the `Cache-Control` HTTP header from clients and will completely depend on the `Cache-Control` headers supplied by the backend web servers. For example:

```
http_port 80 accel defaultsite=example.com vhost ignore-cc
```

Using ignore-reload

Using the option `ignore-reload` with the `refresh_pattern` directive, we can completely ignore the browser reloads and serve the content from cache anyway. However, this may result in serving stale content in some cases. For example:

```
refresh_pattern .    0 20% 4320 ignore-reload
```

Using reload-into-ims

If we don't want to completely ignore the browser reloads using the previously explained `ignore-reload` option, we can use the `reload-into-ims` option. This will downgrade the reload into an `IfModifiedSince` check, allowing less bandwidth to be wasted while retaining the data accuracy. For example:

```
refresh_pattern .    0 20% 4320 reload-into-ims
```

What just happened?

We learned about three available options using which we can configure Squid to properly handle the reloads forced by the browser reload button.

Access controls in reverse proxy mode

When Squid is configured in reverse proxy mode or our proxy server is acting as a surrogate, it'll be accepting requests from all over the Internet. In this case, we can't form a list of clients or subnets to allow access to HTTP via our proxy server, as we did in forward proxy mode. However, we'll have to make sure that our proxy server doesn't accept requests for origin servers that we are not accelerating.

We should note that we'll have to be clever while constructing access rules when we are using the same Squid instance for reverse proxying as well as forward proxying. We'll have to allow access to foreign origin servers so that our clients can access foreign websites using our proxy server. Later, we'll have a look at the access control configuration for various types of setups.

Squid in only reverse proxy mode

When we have configured Squid to work only as a reverse proxy, we need to restrict access to the origin server which we are accelerating. Let's say, the origin servers configured for our proxy servers are `www.example.com` and `www.example.net`, then we can have the following access control rules:

```
acl orign_servers dstdomain www.example.com www.example.net
http_access allow origin_servers
http_access deny all
```

The preceding configuration will allow all requests destined for `www.example.com` and `www.example.net`.

 Please note that these access control rules should be above Squid's default access controls, otherwise requests from clients will be denied by the default Squid access controls.

Squid in reverse proxy and forward proxy mode

When Squid is configured to operate in reverse proxy and forward proxy modes simultaneously, we need to be careful while designing our access controls. We need to keep the following points in mind:

- Clients using our proxy server as a forward proxy should be able to access all the websites, except the ones that we have blacklisted.
- Squid should accept all the requests destined to the origin servers we are accelerating, except the requests from the clients that we have blacklisted.

Let's say our clients in subnet `192.0.2.0/24` will be using our proxy server as a forward proxy and they are allowed to access all the websites except `www.example.net`. We can therefore, write the access rules as follows:

```
acl our_clients src 192.0.2.0/24
acl blacklisted_websites dstdomain www.example.net
http_access allow our_clients !blacklisted_websites
http_access deny all
```

Now, let's say we have configured our proxy server to accelerate the origin server www.
example.com. However, we have found some suspicious activity on our origin server from
the subnet 203.0.113.0/24 and don't want these visitors to access our website. So, we
can have the following access rules:

```
acl origin_servers dstdomain www.example.com
acl bad_visitors src 203.0.113.0/24
http_access allow origin_servers !bad_visitors
http_access deny all
```

We can combine the preceding two configurations into one configuration as follows:

```
# ACLs for Forward Proxy
acl our_clients src 192.0.2.0/24
acl blacklisted_websites dstdomain www.example.net

# ACLs for Reverse Proxy
acl origin_servers dstdomain www.example.com
acl bad_visitors src 203.0.113.0/24

# Allow local clients to access allowed websites
http_access allow our_clients !blacklisted_websites

# Allow visitors to access origin servers
http_access allow origin_servers !bad_visitors

# Deny access to everyone else
http_access deny all
```

The preceding configuration will allow our local clients to access all websites except
www.example.net. Also, it'll allow all visitors (except from the subnet 203.0.113.0/24)
to access our origin server www.example.com. We can extend this configuration according
to our environment.

Example configurations

Let's have a look at a few common examples of Squid in reverse proxy mode. For the access
control configuration for the following examples, please refer to the section on access
controls in reverse proxy mode.

Web server and Squid server on the same machine

In this example, we'll write the Squid configuration for accelerating a web server hosting www.example.com. As we will run Squid and the web server on the same machine, we must ensure that the web server is bound to the loopback address (127.0.0.1) and listening on port 80. Let's write this configuration.

```
http_port 192.0.2.25:80 accel defaultsite=www.example.com

cache_peer 127.0.0.1 parent 80 0 no-query originserver name=example

cache_peer_domain example .exmaple.com
```

In the first configuration line of the previous example, we have configured Squid to bind to the IP address 192.0.2.25 and it'll listen on port 80 where it will be accepting visitor requests on behalf of our origin web server. In the second line, we have added 127.0.0.1 (port 80) as a cache peer where our web server is listening for requests. In the last configuration line, we are allowing a cache peer named example to be used for fetching only example.com and its sub-domains.

Accelerating multiple backend web servers hosting one website

In this example, we have three servers with IP addresses 192.0.2.25, 192.0.2.26, and 192.0.2.27, which host the same website www.example.com. All web servers are listening on port 80. Squid is hosted on a different machine with a public IP address and www.example.com points to the public IP address of the Squid server. Let's see an example of this configuration:

```
http_port 80 accel defaultsite=www.example.com

cache_peer 192.0.2.25 parent 80 0 no-query originserver round-robin
name=server1
cache_peer 192.0.2.26 parent 80 0 no-query originserver round-robin
name=server2
cache_peer 192.0.2.27 parent 80 0 no-query originserver round-robin
name=server3

cache_peer_domain server1 .example.com
cache_peer_domain server2 .example.com
cache_peer_domain server3 .example.com
```

As we have used the round-robin option with cache_peer in the preceding configuration, this will also load balance the requests between the three web servers.

Accelerating multiple web servers hosting multiple websites

In this example, we have example.com and its sub-domains hosted on 192.0.2.25, example.net and its sub-domains hosted on 192.0.2.26, and example.org and its sub-domains hosted on 192.0.2.27. We have a Squid server installed on a different machine with a public IP address and all the domains (example.com, example.net, example.org, and their sub-domains) point to the public IP address of the Squid server. The following is an example of such a configuration:

```
http_port 80 accel vhost defaultsite=www.example.com ignore-cc

cache_peer 192.0.2.25 parent 80 0 no-query originserver name=server1
cache_peer 192.0.2.26 parent 80 0 no-query originserver name=server2
cache_peer 192.0.2.27 parent 80 0 no-query originserver name=server3

cache_peer_domain server1 .example.com
cache_peer_domain server2 .example.net
cache_peer_domain server3 .example.org
```

Note that we can't use the round-robin option with the cache_peer directive here because different web servers are hosting different domains. We have also restricted request forwarding using the cache_peer_domain directive so that we contact only the relevant web server for forwarding the requests.

Have a go hero – set up a Squid proxy server in reverse proxy mode

Try to set up a Squid proxy server in reverse proxy mode as a server accelerator for your website on the same server as web server.

Pop quiz

1. When the ignore-cc option is used while specifying http_port as follows:

    ```
    http_port 80 accel vhost ignore-cc
    ```

    What will happen when a client clicks on the reload button in the browser?

    a. Squid will not receive the Cache-Control HTTP headers.

    b. The ignore-cc option doesn't affect client requests.

    c. Squid will ignore the Cache-Control HTTP header from the request.

    d. The backend web server will ignore the Cache-Control HTTP header.

2. Consider the following configuration:

```
http_port 80 accel defaultsite=www.example.com

cache_peer 192.0.2.25 parent 80 0 no-query originserver
forcedomain=example.com name=example
```

What will the contents of the `Host` HTTP header sent to the backend web server when a client requests `http://www.example.com/` be?

a. `www.example.com`

b. `example.com`

c. `example`

d. `192.0.2.25`

Summary

In this chapter, we learned about Squid's reverse proxy mode, which can be used to share the load of a very busy web server or a cluster of web servers. We also learned about the various configuration options to configure Squid in reverse proxy mode.

Specifically, we covered:

◆ What is a web server accelerator and how does Squid fit in this model.

◆ Configuring Squid to accept HTTP and HTTPS requests from clients on behalf of our web servers.

◆ Adding backend web servers to Squid so that it can forward requests to origin servers appropriately.

◆ We also saw a few configuration examples in which we tried to accelerate various web servers hosting different websites.

In the next chapter, we'll learn about configuring Squid in intercept mode.

10
Squid in Intercept Mode

In previous chapters, we have learned about using Squid in the forward proxy and accelerator or reverse proxy modes. In this chapter, we are going to learn about configuring Squid in the intercept (or transparent) mode. We'll learn about Squid's behavior in the intercept mode and also the basic configuration required for achieving interception caching.

In this chapter, we shall discuss:

- ◆ Interception caching
- ◆ Advantages of running Squid in the intercept mode
- ◆ Problems with the intercept mode
- ◆ Diverting HTTP traffic to Squid
- ◆ Implementing interception caching

So let's get started...

Interception caching

When the requests from clients are intercepted by a proxy server or are redirected to one or more proxy servers, without configuring the HTTP clients on the client machines or without the knowledge of clients, it's known as interception proxying. As proxying is mostly accompanied by caching, it's known as interception caching. Interception caching is also known by several other names, such as, transparent caching, cache redirection, and so on. Squid can be configured to intercept requests from clients so that we can leverage the benefits of caching without explicitly configuring each one of our clients.

Time for action – understanding interception caching

Interception caching is generally implemented by configuring a network device (router or switch) on our network perimeter to divert client requests to our Squid server. Other components that need to be configured include packet filtering software on the operating system running Squid, and finally Squid itself. First of all, let's see how the interception of requests occurs:

1. A client requests a web page `http://www.example.com/index.html`.

2. First of all, the client needs to resolve the domain name to determine the IP address, so that it can connect to the remote server. Next, the client contacts the DNS server and resolves the domain name `www.example.com` to `192.0.2.10`.

3. Now, the client initiates a TCP connection to `192.0.2.10` on port 80.

4. The connection request in the previous step is intercepted by the router/switch and is directed to the Squid proxy server instead of sending it directly to a remote server.

5. On the Squid proxy server, the packet is received by the packet filtering tool, which is configured to redirect all packets on port 80 to a port where Squid is listening.

6. Finally the packet reaches Squid, which then pretends its the remote server and establishes the TCP connection with the client.

7. At this point, the client is under the impression that it has established a connection with the remote server when it's actually connected to the Squid server.

8. Once the connection is established, the client sends a HTTP request to the remote server asking for a specific URL (`/index.html` in this case).

9. When Squid receives the request, it then pretends to be a client and establishes a connection to the remote server, if the client request can't be satisfied from the cache, and then fetches the content the client has requested.

So, the idea is to redirect all our HTTP traffic to the Squid server using router/switch and host-based IP packet filtering tools.

What just happened?

We just learned how HTTP packets flow from clients to a router or a switch, which redirects these packets to the server running Squid. We also saw how these packets are redirected to Squid by the IP filtering tools on the server and finally how Squid reconstructs clients' requests using the HTTP headers.

Advantages of interception caching

There are several advantages to using Squid in the intercept mode instead of the normal caching mode. A few of them are as follows:

Zero client configuration

As we discussed previously, we don't need to configure HTTP clients at all, as all the request redirection magic is performed by the switch and routers. This is one of the most prominent reasons for using interception caching in networks where we have thousands of clients, and it's not possible to configure each and every client to use the proxy server.

Better control

As a user cannot configure their HTTP clients to bypass a proxy server, it's easy to enforce network usage policies as only administrators can control network devices and the Squid proxy servers. However, the policies can still be bypassed by clients using tunnels or using specially designed software.

Increased reliability

We can configure our router or switch to forward the client requests directly to the internet in case our Squid proxy server goes down, which will mean that clients can still access the internet without any problems. This results in better uptime and increased reliability.

These few advantages are the reasons for the popularity of interception caching among organizations with a large number of clients and a requirement for higher uptime.

Problems with interception caching

Although interception caching is attractive and there are a few advantages as well, it has got some serious disadvantages, which can make it painful to manage or debug if something goes wrong. Let's have a look at a few disadvantages of interception caching:

Violates TCP/IP standards

The routers or switches in a network are supposed to forward packets to the hosts to which they are destined. Diverting packets to proxy servers violates the TCP/IP standards. Also, the proxy server accepts TCP/IP packets which are not destined for it, which is another violation of the TCP/IP standards.

The proxy server often has a different OS to the client, which confuses the end-to-end packet management outside of the HTTP packets. Which in turn can cause servers and the remote networks to become completely inaccessible or the transfer rates may drop down considerably.

Susceptible to routing problems

Interception caching relies on stable routed paths and the diversion of the traffic to caching proxies by a router or a switch. As routes or network paths are determined dynamically, requests may flow via a different path, which may not have a router that will divert the traffic to a caching proxy and a user's session will be lost. Also, sometimes the replies may not return to a proxy server, resulting in long timeouts and unavailable websites.

No authentication

Proxy authentication doesn't work as browsers and HTTP clients are not aware that they are connected to remote servers via a proxy server, and will refuse to send credentials to the unknown middleware. The IP-based authentication doesn't work because the proxy server is initiating connections on behalf of all the clients and the remote server thinks that only one client is trying to access the website.

Supports only HTTP interception

Squid can intercept only HTTP traffic as the HTTP request contains Host header and Squid can fetch content on behalf of the client using the Host and other HTTP headers. It can't intercept other protocols, as it will not be able to process them.

Client exposure

Since we will be able to intercept only HTTP traffic, clients will still need to go on the internet directly to make DNS queries or use other protocols like HTTPS, FTP, and so on. So, essentially we'll have all our clients exposed on the internet, which is not desirable in most networks.

IP filtering

Interception caching is incompatible with IP filtering, which prevents IP address spoofing. We must create exceptions in our network devices to allow address spoofing.

Protocol support

Although this is not a major issue with the modern browsers and newer versions of the legacy browsers, it may be a significant problem with older browsers supporting only HTTP/1.0 (or older) or buggy HTTP clients. As we learned previously, that Squid in intercept mode totally depends on the `Host` HTTP header supplied within the HTTP request by the client, if a client doesn't send the HTTP header, Squid will have no idea what to do with the HTTP request.

The protocol support problem may be present the other way around as well. This occurs when the client uses a HTTP feature, which is still not implemented in Squid or if Squid doesn't know how to handle the feature. For example, chunked encoding HTTP/1.1 was not supported by Squid 3.0 or earlier and hence cannot be intercepted.

Security vulnerabilities

We learned that Squid in intercept mode is totally dependent on the Host HTTP header supplied by the clients. The Host header can be easily forged by malware or rouge applications to poison our proxy server's cache, which can result in the spread of the poisoned (cached) content across the whole network.

So, as we can see, there are a lot of disadvantages of using interception caching, but it's up to us to analyze our network and see if the advantages outweigh the disadvantages. Please also have a look at other alternative solutions such as, **Web Proxy Auto-Discovery Protocol** (**WPAD**, http://en.wikipedia.org/wiki/Web_Proxy_Autodiscovery_Protocol), **Proxy auto config** (**PAC**, http://en.wikipedia.org/wiki/Proxy_auto-config), and **Captive portal** (http://en.wikipedia.org/wiki/Captive_portal).

Have a go hero – interception caching for your network

Based on the advantages and disadvantages of interception caching we saw previously, check if it will be beneficial to implement interception caching in your network. Also, check whether you'll be using a router or switch to divert traffic to the Squid server.

Diverting HTTP traffic to Squid

We learned in previous sections that we need to divert all HTTP traffic from our clients to our proxy server. Later, we'll have a look at the ways in which we can divert HTTP traffic to our Squid proxy server.

Using a router's policy routing to divert requests

If we have an arrangement where all our client requests are passing through a router, we can utilize the router's ability to divert the packets, to redirect them to our Squid proxy server. Therefore if we set our router's policy to redirect all the packets with port 80 to the Squid server and all other traffic is sent to the internet directly, it will look like the following diagram:

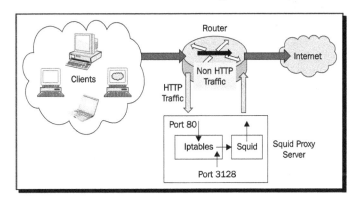

In the previous diagram, we can see that the router is passing all the HTTP requests to the Squid proxy server and all the non-HTTP traffic is going to the internet directly. A router can only modify the IP address of a packet. So, we must configure an IP packet filtering tool (`iptables`, `ipfw`) to redirect traffic on port 80 to the port on which Squid is listening.

Using rule-based switching to divert requests

We can also use a Layer 4 (L4) or Layer 7 (L7) switch to divert HTTP requests from our clients to the Squid proxy server, as shown the in the following diagram:

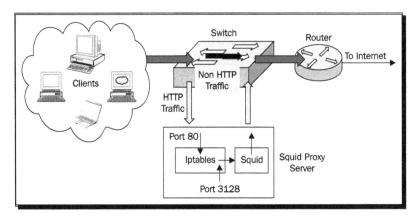

In the previous diagram, we can see that the switch is passing HTTP traffic to the Squid proxy server based on rules configured in the switch. All the non-HTTP traffic is directly forwarded to the internet.

Using Squid server as a bridge

In this scenario, the machine running Squid proxy server also acts as a gateway to the internet for all the clients. So, all the packets or requests to remote servers pass through the Squid server. The IP packet filtering tool can be configured to redirect all HTTP traffic to the Squid process and all the non-HTTP traffic can be forwarded to the Internet directly.

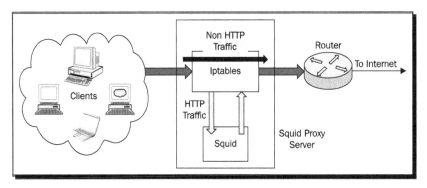

In the preceding diagram, we can see that we are not using any switch or router to direct HTTP traffic to the Squid server. Instead, all the traffic is passing through the Squid server and the `iptables` direct HTTP traffic to the Squid process, and passes the rest to the router connected to internet. This is the easiest of the three ways to achieve interception caching as we don't have to configure our router or switch, which is generally a relatively complex task.

Using WCCP tunnel

Web Cache Coordination Protocol (WCCP) is a protocol developed by Cisco to route content with a mechanism to redirect traffic in real-time. We can utilize WCCP in the absence of a Layer4 switch . It is sometimes preferred over **Policy-based Routing** as it allows multiple proxy servers to participate compared to **Policy-based Routing**, which allows only one server. WCCP has built-in features such as scaling, load balancing, fault tolerance, and failover mechanisms.

When using WCCP, a **GRE (Generic Routing Encapsulation)** tunnel is established between the router and the machine running the Squid proxy server. The redirected requests from the router are encapsulated in GRE packets and sent to the proxy server through the GRE tunnel. The job of decapsulating the GRE packets and redirecting them to Squid is done by the host machine using iptables. Then Squid will either fetch the content from the original server or pull it from the cache and deliver the content back to the router. The router then sends the response to the HTTP client. For configuring various Cisco devices, the host operating system, and Squid to use WCCP, please visit `http://wiki.squid-cache.org/Features/Wccp2`.

Implementing interception caching

After going through the advantages and disadvantages of interception caching, if we choose to go with the interception caching, then as described previously, we need to configure three different components to implement interception caching. We need to configure a network device (not needed if we are using the Squid server as a gateway or bridge), the IP filtering tool (`iptables`, `ipfw`, and so on.) on a server running Squid and then Squid itself. Let's have a quick look at the configuration of the different components.

Configuring the network devices

If we are using a network device to divert traffic to our Squid proxy server, then we need to configure the network device so that it can identify all the HTTP traffic and redirect it to our Squid proxy server. As different routers and switches have different configuration tools, please refer to the documentation or instruction manual for the router or switch which is going to divert the traffic.

Configuring the operating system

Once the packets or HTTP requests reach our machine running Squid, they'll have a destination port 80. Now we need to configure an IP filtering tool, which goes by the different names of different operating systems, to divert these packets to the port where Squid is configured to listen. We should note that the port on which Squid is listening, is used between the filtering tool and Squid. So, we should firewall this port from external access.

However, before configuring that, we need to configure our operating system to accept packets that are not destined to it. This is because the packets diverted by the routers or switches will have a destination IP of the remote server. These packets will be dropped immediately by the kernel because the destination IP address doesn't match the address of any of the interfaces. We need to use the IP forwarding feature in the kernel so that our server can accept packets that are not destined to it.

Enabling IP forwarding

There are different ways to enable IP forwarding for different operating systems. Let's have a look at few of them:

Time for action – enabling IP forwarding

1. To enable IP forwarding on Linux-based operating systems, we can use any of the following methods.

   Using the `sysctl` command:

   ```
   sysctl -w net.ipv4.ip_forward=1
   ```

   This method doesn't need a reboot and will enable IP forwarding on the fly but will not be preserved after a reboot.

   Using the `sysctl` configuration file, we can add the following line in the `/etc/sysctl.conf` file:

   ```
   net.ipv4.ip_forward = 1
   ```

2. To enable the changes made to the `/etc/sysctl.conf` file, we need to run the following command:

   ```
   sysctl -p /etc/sysctl.conf
   ```

   These changes will be preserved after a reboot.

3. Enabling IP forwarding on BSD operating systems is almost similar. We can use any of the following methods:

   Using the `sysctl` command.

   ```
   sysctl -w net.inet.ip.forwarding=1
   ```

This method doesn't need a reboot and will enable IP forwarding on the fly but will not be preserved after a reboot. Please note that we don't need the `-w` option on **OpenBSD** and **DragonFlyBSD**.

We can add the following line in the `/etc/rc.conf` file:

```
gateway_enable="YES"
```

4. To enable these changes made to the `/etc/rc.conf` file, we need to reboot our server. The changes made will be preserved after further reboots. Note that we don't need to perform this step for OpenBSD.

What just happened?

We learned about various commands and methods, using which we can enable IP forwarding on our operating system so that it can accept packets which are not destined for it.

For other operating systems, please check the respective instruction manual.

Redirecting packets to Squid

Once we have enabled our operating system to accept packets on behalf of others, we'll start getting packets diverted by the router or switch. Now, we need to get these packets to our Squid process. For this we need to configure `iptables` (Linux), `ipf/ipnat/ipfw` (BSD variants) to redirect the packets which we have received on port 80 to port 3128.X.

Time for action – redirecting HTTP traffic to Squid

Let's have a quick look at the configuration we need to perform. For the following, we'll assume that the IP for the Squid proxy server is `192.0.2.25`.

1. Working with Linux:

To redirect traffic destined to port 80, we can use `iptables` as follows:

```
iptables -t nat -A PREROUTING -s 192.0.2.25 -p tcp --dport 80 -j
ACCEPT
iptables -t nat -A PREROUTING -p tcp --dport 80 -j DNAT --to-
destination 192.0.2.25:3128
iptables -t nat -A POSTROUTING -j MASQUERADE
```

In the previous list of commands, the first command prevents the redirecting HTTP traffic from the Squid server itself. If we don't have the first line in place, we'll face forwarding loops and requests will not be satisfied. The second command captures all the traffic on port 80 and redirects it to the IP address to which Squid is bound and port 3128 where Squid is listening. The last command allows **Network Address Translation** (**NAT**, for more details, please check `http://en.wikipedia.org/ wiki/Network_address_translation`).

We can achieve a fully transparent setup using the Tproxy feature. However, we should note that we'll need a relatively newer Linux kernel version and iptables with support for Tproxy version 4.1 or later. Please check `http://wiki.squid-cache.org/Features/Tproxy4` for details.

2. Working with BSD:

   There are many packet filtering programs available for various flavors of BSD but OpenBSD's Packet Filter (`pf`) is one of the most popular programs. Please refer to the Packet Filter manual at `http://www.openbsd.org/faq/pf/`. The Packet Filter has been integrated in NetBSD as well. Please have a look at the NetBSD's manual for `pf` at `http://www.netbsd.org/docs/network/pf.html`.

What just happened?

We learned how we can redirect HTTP traffic destined to port 80 to port 3128 (to Squid) using `iptables` on Linux. We also learned that we have to create an exception for the IP address to which Squid is bound, to avoid any forwarding loops.

Have a go hero – testing the traffic diversion

Once you have finished enabling IP forwarding and configuring the appropriate rules in the firewall to redirect traffic to port 3128, try accessing any website from a client machine. Now, check if packets are being directed properly using `tcpdump` or `wireshark`.

Configuring Squid

So far, we have configured our environment to divert all HTTP traffic to port 3128 on the Squid server. Finally, it's time to check what configuration we need to do in Squid so that it can intercept all the diverted traffic.

Configuring HTTP port

Finally, we need to tell Squid that we will be intercepting the client requests. We can do so by using the appropriate option with the `http_port` directive as follows:

```
http_port 3128 intercept
http_port 8080
```

If we use the previous configuration, the requests on port 3128 will be intercepted and port 8080 will be used for normal forward proxying. It's not necessary to have the port 8080 configuration above, but it's useful for proxy management access, which will not work through the intercept port.

So, that's all we need to do for interception caching. Now, Squid will handle all the requests normally and cached responses will be served from the cache.

Pop quiz

1. Which of the following protocols can be intercepted by Squid?

    a. HTTP

    b. FTP

    c. Gopher

    d. HTTPS

2. Which one of the following is an essential HTTP header for the proper functioning of Squid in intercept mode?

    a. Cache-Control

    b. Proxy-Authorization

    c. Host

    d. User-Agent

3. Why can't we use proxy authentication with Squid in intercept mode?

    a. Squid is not responsible for providing authentication in intercept mode.

    b. HTTP clients are not aware of a proxy and don't send the Proxy-Authorization HTTP header.

    c. It's not possible to assign usernames and passwords to thousands of clients.

    d. Proxy-Authorization HTTP headers are removed by the routers or switches on the way, when using interception caching.

Summary

We have learned about the basics of interception caching in this chapter. We have also learned how the requests flow and packets are diverted to our Squid server so that Squid can fetch content on behalf of clients, without explicitly configuring all the clients on our network.

Specifically, we have covered:

- Interception caching and how it works.
- Different ways in which to implement interception caching.
- Advantages and drawbacks of interception caching.
- Configuring our operating systems to forward IP packets.
- Configuring IP filtering tools for our operating systems to redirect web traffic to the Squid server.
- Various compile options that can be used to implement interception caching on different operating systems.

In the next chapter, we'll learn about writing Squid plugins or helpers to customize Squid's behavior.

11
Writing URL Redirectors and Rewriters

In the previous chapters, we have learned about installing and configuring the Squid proxy server for various scenarios. In this chapter, we'll learn about writing our own URL redirectors or rewriters to customize Squid's behavior. We'll also see a few examples that can be helpful in enhancing the caching performance of Squid or enforcing the access control.

In this chapter, we shall learn about:

- ◆ URL redirectors and rewriters
- ◆ Writing our own URL helper
- ◆ Configuring Squid
- ◆ A special URL redirector - deny_info
- ◆ Popular URL helpers

So let's get started....

URL redirectors and rewriters

URL redirectors are external helper processes that can redirect the HTTP clients to alternate URLs using HTTP redirect messages. Similarly, URL rewriters are also external helper processes that can rewrite the URLs requested by the client with another URL. When a URL is rewritten by a helper process, Squid fetches the rewritten URL transparently and sends the response to the end client as if it was the one originally requested by the client.

The URL redirectors can be used to send HTTP redirect messages like 301, 302, 303, 307, or 3xx, along with an alternate URL to the HTTP clients. When a HTTP client receives a redirect message, the client will request the new URL. So, the major difference between URL redirectors and URL rewriters is that the client is aware of a URL redirect, while rewritten URLs are fetched transparently by Squid, and the client remains unaware of a rewritten URL. Let's try to understand the workings of URL redirector and rewriter helper programs in detail.

Understanding URL redirectors

Now, we'll try to see what happens when we are using a URL redirector helper with the Squid proxy server and a client tries to access a webpage at `http://example.com/index.html`.

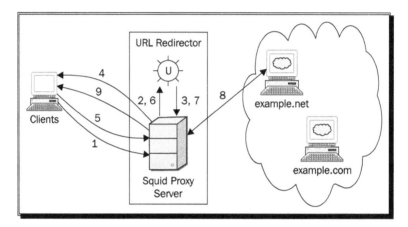

The previous diagram shows the flow of requests and responses using numbered steps. Let's try to learn what is happening at each step in the previous diagram:

1. The **Client** requests the webpage `http://example.com/index.html`.

2. The **Squid Proxy Server** receives the requests and forwards the essential details related to the request to the URL redirector helper program.

3. The URL redirector helper program processes the details and issues a 303 HTTP redirect with an alternate URL `http://example.net/index.html`. In other words, the URL redirector program suggests to Squid that the client should be redirected to a different URL.

4. Squid, as suggested by the URL redirector helper, sends the redirect message to the client with the alternate URL.

5. The client, on receiving the redirect message, initiates another request for the new URL `http://example.net/index.html`.

6. When Squid receives the new request, it is again sent to the URL redirector helper program.

7. The URL redirector program processes the request and suggests to Squid that this URL can be fetched and we don't need to redirect the client to an alternate URL.

8. Squid fetches the URL `http://example.net/index.html`.

9. The response received by Squid from the origin server at `example.net` is delivered to the client.

We have just learned how the client initiated a request, which was redirected to an alternate URL by the URL redirector helper program. We'll learn about the logic followed by the URL redirector program for redirecting URLs at a later stage in this chapter. Now, let's try to understand the useful HTTP status codes for redirection and where they can be used.

HTTP status codes for redirection

We have learned that we can use various HTTP redirect codes for redirecting clients to a different URL. Now let's try to understand when and where we can use these HTTP redirect codes.

Code	Description and usage
301	The HTTP status code 301 means that the URL requested by the client has moved permanently and all the future requests should be made to the redirected URL. This status code should be used in reverse proxy setups only.
302	The HTTP status code 302 means that the content can be fetched using an alternate URL. This status code should be used with `GET` or `HEAD` requests.
303	The code 303 means that the request can be satisfied with an alternate URL but the alternate URL should be fetched using a `GET` request. This status code can be used with `POST` or `PUT` requests.
305	The status code 305 indicates that the client should use a proxy for fetching the content. This status code is intended to be used by interception proxies needing to switch to a forward proxy for the request.
307	The status code 307 means a temporary HTTP redirect to a different URL but the future requests should use the original URL. In this case, the request method should not be changed while requesting the redirected URL. This status code can be used for `CONNECT/HTTPS` requests.

For more information on HTTP status codes for redirection, please visit `http://en.wikipedia.org/wiki/List_of_HTTP_status_codes#3xx_Redirection`.

It's now time to learn how the URL rewriter helper programs rewrite URLs.

Understanding URL rewriters

URL rewriters are almost similar to URL redirectors, with a major difference being that they never tell the client about the change of URLs. Let's say, a client is trying to retrieve the webpage at `http://example.com/index.html` and we have a URL rewriter program working on our proxy server. Now, have a look at the following diagram:

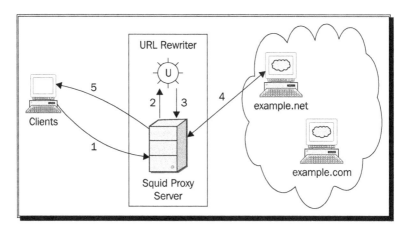

The numbered steps in the previous diagram represent the flow of requests and responses. Let's try to understand the steps shown in the diagram as follows:

1. The client requests a URL `http://example.com/index.html` using our proxy server.

2. Squid receives the request and forwards the essential details about the request to the URL rewriter helper program.

3. The URL rewriter helper program processes the details received from Squid and suggests to Squid that it should fetch `http://example.net/index.html` instead of `http://example.com/index.html`. In other words, the rewriter program has rewritten the URL with a new URL.

4. Squid receives the rewritten URL (`http://example.net/index.html`) from the rewriter program and contacts the origin server at `example.net` instead of contacting `example.com`.

5. Squid delivers the response returned by the origin server at `example.net` to the client.

So, we have seen how client requests are rewritten by the URL rewriter helper programs and the client is not even informed about it. The client still thinks that the response was fetched from the origin server `example.com` and not `example.net`.

So far, we have learned about URL redirector and rewriter programs. The basic difference between the two is the presence or absence of a 3xx HTTP redirect code. When a 3xx redirect code is present, the client is redirected to a new URL. On the other hand, in the absence of a 3xx redirect code, the URL is simply rewritten by Squid transparently.

Issues with URL rewriters

There are some known issues when rewriting URLs, which can result in unexpected behavior from original servers or the proxy server itself. Let's have a look at a few possible issues with URL rewriters.

- Rewriting URLs on a criterion other than the URL may result in unpredictable cached responses. Moreover, the same response may be cached for several URLs. This may expose our proxy server to cache poisoning attacks. This is not a problem when redirecting URLs as the client will request the redirected URL, and the response if cached, will correspond to the correct URL.

- Rewriting upload, POST, or WebDAV requests may result in unpredictable alterations on origin servers.

- If a rewriter passes an invalid URL back to Squid, it may result in unexpected behavior from Squid. For example, we may consider that a hash (#) character is valid in a URL as our browser understands it. However, when we rewrite a URL with a different URL containing a hash (#) character, the proxy doesn't know what to do with it. Hence, Squid will reject the new URL and will either send an error message to the client or bypass the rewrite depending on the Squid version. A HTTP redirect to a URL with a hash (#) in it will work as the browser understands what to do with fragments.

- Rewriting CONNECT/HTTPS requests may result in HTTPS errors breaking the security channels.

As we saw previously, rewriting URLs poses more problems compared to URL redirection. Hence, URL redirectors are recommended over URL rewriters, as the client is fully aware in case of redirections.

This ability of a redirector to rewrite the originally requested URL exposes a lot of power to the developers or administrators. We can use this feature to redirect clients to alternate access-denied pages, help, or documentation pages, block ads from well known ad networks, implement more affective filters, or redirect clients to a locally mirrored content.

Squid, URL redirectors, and rewriters

Squid and URL redirector (or rewriter) programs work closely and every request is passed through the specified URL redirector (or rewriter) program and then Squid acts accordingly (redirects the HTTP client to the rewritten URL or fetches the rewritten URL). Let's have a look at a few details about Squid and URL redirectors.

Communication interface

The URL redirectors and rewriters communicate with Squid using a similar and simple interface, which is very easy to understand as well as implement. For each request, the following details are passed to a helper program in one line.

```
ID URL client_IP/FQDN username method myip=IP myport=PORT [kv-pairs]
```

The following table gives a brief explanation of the fields passed by Squid to the redirectors:

Field	Description
ID	The ID is used for identifying each request that Squid passes on as the standard input to the redirector program. The redirector program is supposed to pass the ID back to Squid so that it can relate the returned URL to an appropriate request. This ID is used to achieve concurrency. This field will be missing with non-concurrent helpers.
URL	The URL field is the actual URL requested by the client and is passed to rewriters as it is.
client_IP	The field client_IP represents the IP address of the client.
FQDN	The FQDN (Fully Qualified Domain Name) field contains the fully qualified domain name of the client, if present. If FQDN is not set, a hyphen (-) is put in its place. Please note that FQDN will not be available at all when reverse DNS lookup is not set for the IP address.
username	The username field contains the username of the client for the current request, as determined by Squid. The username field will be replaced by a hyphen (-) if Squid was unable to determine the username.
method	The method field contains the HTTP request method used by the client to request the current URL. The values will be GET, POST, DELETE, and so on.
myip=IP	The myip (myip=IP_ADDRESS) represents the Squid receiving IP address to which the client request was sent. It is helpful if there is more than one network interface on the server and Squid is bound to more than one IP address.
myport=PORT	The field myport (myport=PORT_NUMBER) represents the Squid port on which the client request was sent. It is helpful in case Squid is listening on more than one port.
kv-pairs	There may be other key value pairs which may be made available to rewriter programs in the future.

The URL helper program can process the previous fields and take appropriate actions according to a predefined login in the helper program. Now, it's time to explore how the messages are passed between Squid and URL helpers.

Time for action – exploring the message flow between Squid and redirectors

Let's try to understand the message flow between Squid and the redirector (or rewriter) programs.

1. A line containing the fields shown previously (separated by spaces) is passed by Squid to the URL redirector program using a single line for each client request. Once the helper program has finished processing the fields, it must write one of the following messages on the standard output. Please note that the new line (\n) at the end of the message is important and must not be omitted:

2. The line containing the fields is read by the URL redirector program from the standard input.

3. After reading the line from the standard input, the redirector (or rewriter) program can process the fields and make decisions based on the values of different fields.

    - A line containing only the identifier (ID \n).
    - A modified URL with an HTTP redirect code followed by a new line.
    - (ID 3XX:URL \n). The HTTP redirect code and the URL should be separated by a colon.
    - A modified URL followed by a new line (ID URL \n)

4. The message written by the helper program on the standard output is read by Squid for further processing. It then takes one of the following actions:

    - If the helper program wrote a blank line on the standard output, Squid treats it as if we didn't modify the URL at all and the original URL will be used by Squid to fetch the content.
    - If the helper program wrote a different URL with a redirect code, then Squid will send a response to the client redirecting it to the alternate URL.
    - If a different URL without a redirect code was written, Squid will treat it as if that was the original URL requested by the client, will fetch the content transparently, and return it to the client.

So, as we have seen previously, a single program can act as a URL redirector as well as a URL rewriter program by executing conditional redirection or rewriting URLs. In the following sections, we'll be using the URL redirector to mean both URL redirector and URL rewriter, unless specified otherwise.

What just happened?

We have just learned how Squid communicates with URL redirector programs using standard I/O. Squid sends some details about each request to the URL redirector program. Then the URL redirector program processes the fields sent by Squid and makes a decision accordingly. After making the decision, the redirector sends back the appropriate message, which is then read by Squid.

Now, let's have a look at a few example fields sent by Squid to a URL redirector program:

```
http://www.example.com/ 127.0.0.1/localhost - GET myip=127.0.0.1
myport=3128

http://www.example.net/index.php?test=123 192.0.2.25/- john GET
myip=192.0.2.25 myport=8080

http://www.example.org/login.php 198.51.100.86/- saini POST
myip=192.0.2.25 myport=8080
```

As shown in the previous examples, the entire URL is passed to a URL redirector program along with the query parameters, if any. The fragment identifiers are removed from the URL, while Squid passes the URL to the redirector program.

 We should be careful while using URL redirector programs because Squid passes the entire URL along with query parameters to the URL redirector program. This may lead to leakage of sensitive client information as some websites use HTTP GET methods for passing clients' private information.

The URL redirector program has to read lines, as shown in above examples, in an endless loop unless an EOF (end of file) occurs on the standard input. The program should not exit. However, if the program exits prematurely, Squid tries to respawn another instance of the redirector program and writes a message (as shown in the following example) to the Squid cache log, warning the user of a probable problem with the redirector program:

```
2010/11/08 22:01:19| WARNING: redirector #1 (FD 8) exited
```

Time for action – writing a simple URL redirector program

Let's see a very simple Perl script that can act as a URL redirector program.

```
$|=1;
while (<>) {
  s@http://www.example.com@303:http://www.example.net@;
  print;
}
```

The previous code is a URL redirector program in its simplest form. It redirects all URLs containing the URL www.example.com to www.example.net without inspecting values of any of the fields by Squid.

What just happened?

We have just seen a simplistic Perl script which can act as a URL redirector program and can be used with Squid.

Have a go hero – modify the redirector program

Modify the previous URL redirector program so that all requests to google.co.uk can be redirected to google.com.

Concurrency

We can make our URL redirector programs concurrent for better performance. When we configure Squid to use a concurrent URL redirector program, it passes an additional field, ID, on the standard input to the redirector program. This is used to achieve concurrency as we learned in the previous section.

 It's always better to have more concurrency than more children helpers for better performance.

Handling whitespace in URLs

There are different ways to handle whitespaces in URLs. A few techniques that can be used are as follows:

Using the uri_whitespace directive

We can use the uri_whitespace directive to drop, truncate, or encode the whitespaces in URLs. Let's have a look at the format for using the uri_whitespace directive.

```
uri_whitespace OPTION
```

The possible values that OPTION can have are as follows:

Strip whitespaces

When we use the strip option, the whitespace characters are completely stripped from the URL. This behavior is recommended.

Deny URLs with whitespaces

The requests to URLs containing whitespaces are denied and the user gets an `Invalid Request` message when the `deny` option is used.

Encode whitespaces in URLs

When the `encode` option is used, the whitespaces in the URLs are encoded. This is a violation of HTTP protocol as proxies should not make changes to a URL. It is however, what the browser should have sent, so it is relatively safe to do if needed.

Chop URLs

When the `chop` option is used, the URL is chopped at the first whitespace. This is not recommended and may lead to unexpected behavior. This is also a violation of HTTP protocol.

Allow URLs with whitespaces

The request URL is not changed at all when the `allow` option is used.

So, to remove whitespaces from the URLs before they are passed to the URL redirector programs, we can use the `strip`, `encode`, `deny`, or `chop` options with the `uri_whitespace` directive, and the redirector program will never have to worry about whitespaces in the URLs. For example:

```
uri_whitespace deny
```

 Please note that the default Squid behavior is to strip whitespaces from all the URLs in compliance with RFC 2396.

Making redirector programs intelligent

Just in case we choose to allow whitespaces in URLs, then we'll need to make our redirector programs a bit more intelligent. In non-concurrent redirectors, we can remove the five fields from the end and whatever is left will be the URL (with or without whitespaces). For concurrent redirector programs, the logic will be a bit different and we'll need to remove one field (ID) from the beginning, five fields from the end, and whatever is left will be the URL (with or without whitespaces).

Writing our own URL redirector program

Based on the concepts we learned earlier about the URL redirector helper programs, we can write a program that can redirect/rewrite URLs conditionally. So, let's have a look at an example:

Time for action – writing our own template for a URL redirector

Now, let's have a look at an example URL redirector program in Python, which can be extended to fit any scenario:

```python
#!/usr/bin/env python

import sys

def redirect_url(line, concurrent):
  list = line.split(' ')
  # 1st or 2nd element of the list
  # is the URL depending on concurrency
  if concurrent:
    old_url = list[1]
  else:
    old_url = list[0]

  # Do remember that the new_url
  # should contain a '\n' at the end.
  new_url = '\n'
  # Take the decision and modify the url if needed
  if old_url.endswith('.avi'):
    # Rewrite example
    new_url = 'http://example.com/' + new_url
  elif old_url.endswith('.exe'):
    # Redirect example
    new_url = '302:http://google.co.in/' + new_url
  return new_url

def main(concurrent = True):
  # the format of the line read from stdin with concurrency is
  # ID URL ip-address/fqdn ident method myip=ip myport=port
  # and with concurrency disabled is
  # URL ip-address/fqdn ident method myip=ip myport=port
  line = sys.stdin.readline().strip()

  # We are to keep doing this unless there is EOF
  while line:
    # new_url will be a URL, URL prefixed with 3xx code
    # or just a blank line.
    new_url = redirect_url(line, concurrent)
```

```
        id = ''
        # Add ID for concurrency if concurrency is enabled.
        if concurrent:
            id += line.split(' ')[0] + ' '
        new_url = id + new_url
        # Write the new_url to standard output and
        # flush immediately so that it's available to Squid
        sys.stdout.write(new_url)
        sys.stdout.flush()
        # Read the next line
        line = sys.stdin.readline().strip()

if __name__ == '__main__':
    # Check if concurrency is enabled or not
    main(len(sys.argv) > 1 and sys.argv[1] == '-c')
```

The previous program is a bit more powerful than the Perl script we saw before. In the previous program, we first read the data (a single line) from a standard input and removed any unwanted characters from it. Then we call the `redirect_url` function using the data obtained from a standard input. Then we split the data on whitespace and extract the URL from it (the second element).

If the URL ends with `.avi`, we rewrite the URL with a URL to our custom access denied page. If the URL ends with `.exe`, then we redirect the user to a different URL, warning them of a probable virus.

We can extend the `redirect_url` function according to our needs and return a rewritten URL.

What just happened?

We wrote our own URL redirector program, which is more of a template, and can be extended to fit any scenario. We can use any programming language to write such URL redirector programs.

Have a go hero – extend the redirector program

Extend the URL redirector program, shown previously, to redirect all requests from flash animation files to a tiny GIF image located at `http://www.example.com/ban.gif`.

Configuring Squid

Once we have finished writing the redirector program, we need to configure Squid to use it properly. There are a few directives in the Squid configuration file using which we can control how Squid will use our URL redirector program. Let's have a quick look at these directives.

Specifying the URL redirector program

We can specify the absolute path to our URL redirector program using the url_rewrite_program directive. We can also specify any additional interpreter or command line arguments that the program expects. The following are a few examples:

```
url_rewrite_program /opt/squid/libexec/custom_rewriter

url_rewrite_program /usr/bin/python /opt/squid/libexec/my_rewriter.py

url_rewrite_program /usr/bin/python /opt/squid/libexec/another_
rewriter.py --concurrent
```

 Squid can use only one URL redirector program at a time, so we should specify only one program using the url_rewrite_program directive.

Controlling redirector children

Once we have specified the redirector program, we need to use the url_rewrite_children directive to specify the number of instances of the redirector program (children) that Squid is allowed to spawn. The format of the url_rewrite_children directive is given as follows:

```
url_rewrite_children CHILDREN startup=N idle=N concurrency=N
```

In the previous configuration line, the parameter CHILDREN represents the maximum number of children or the maximum number of instances of the redirector program that Squid is allowed to spawn.

We should choose this value carefully because if we keep this value very low, Squid may have to wait for the redirector programs to process and write data to a standard output, which may lead to significant delays in processing client requests. Also, if we keep this value very high, then the redirector programs will consume a significant amount of resources (RAM, CPU) on the server, which in turn may slow down the server, leading to delays in processing client requests. The default value is 20.

The argument startup (startup=N) is used to specify the minimum number of children that will be spawned when Squid is started or reconfigured. If we set the value of startup to zero (0), the first child will be spawned on the first request. The default value of the startup argument is zero (0).

 Setting startup to a low value will cause initial slowdown if Squid receives a large number of requests, as it'll have to spawn a lot of children.

The argument `idle` (`idle=N`) is used to set the minimum number of children processes that should be idle at any point of time. The number of children processes rises with the traffic up to the maximum number, set previously. The minimum and default value of `idle` argument is 1.

The value of the argument `concurrency` (`concurrency=N`) determines the number of concurrent requests that each redirector program can process in parallel. The default value of `concurrency` is zero (0) which means that the rewriter program is single threaded.

Controlling requests passed to the redirector program

By default, all the requests are passed to the URL redirector program. However, this may not be the desired behavior. We can control what requests Squid passes to the redirector program using the `url_rewrite_access` directive. The format and usage of the `url_rewrite_access` directive is similar to `http_access`.

Let's say our URL redirector program redirects/rewrites URLs only for the domain `example.com`. Now, we can add the following configuration lines to our Squid configuration file:

```
acl rewrite_domain dstdom .example.com
url_rewrite_access allow rewrite_domain
url_rewrite_access deny all
```

In accordance to the previous configuration, Squid will only pass requests whose domain is `example.com` or any of its sub-domains. Similarly, we can create powerful filters by combining Access Control Lists and the `url_rewrite_access` directive.

 Please note that certain request types such as `POST` and `CONNECT` must not be rewritten as they may lead to errors and unexpected behavior. It's a good idea to block them using the `url_rewrite_access` directive.

Bypassing URL redirector programs when under heavy load

When the redirector programs are under heavy load (receiving more requests than they can process), Squid will have to wait until a redirector program returns the redirected or rewritten URL. This will introduce significant delays in processing the user requests. In such situations, we can use the `url_rewrite_bypass` directive to skip passing the requests to the redirector program so that Squid can handle them on its own. So, to bypass the redirector program, we can add the following configuration line to our Squid configuration file.

```
url_rewrite_bypass on
```

The default Squid behavior is not to bypass any request and wait for a redirector to become free, if all of them are busy.

 Bypassing redirector programs may not be desirable in some cases, especially if the redirector program is being used to limit access to certain resources, because it may give clients access to resources which are not accessible otherwise.

Rewriting the Host HTTP header

When we use a URL redirector program to send HTTP redirect messages to the client, Squid rewrites the Host HTTP header in the redirected requests. This may work when Squid is configured in the forward proxy mode. However, when in reverse proxy mode, rewriting the Host header may cause problems. To prevent the rewriting of the Host header, we can use the url_rewrite_host_header directive. When set to off, the url_rewrite_host_header will stop Squid from rewriting the Host HTTP header.

 The default Squid behavior is to rewrite the Host HTTP header in all redirected requests.

A special URL redirector – deny_info

The deny_info option is a directive in the Squid configuration file, which can be used to:

- Present clients with a custom access denied page.
- Redirect (HTTP 302) the clients to a different URL, displaying more information about why access was denied or containing help messages.
- Reset the TCP connection.

Let's have a look at the three syntaxes of the deny_info directive:

```
deny_info CUSTOM_ERROR_PAGE ACL_NAME
deny_info ALTERNATE_URL ACL_NAME
deny_info TCP_RESET ACL_NAME
```

The syntaxes shown previously correspond to the uses we have just discussed. In the first syntax, the parameter CUSTOM_ERROR_PAGE specifies a custom error page written in HTML or plain text, which will be displayed instead of Squid's default access denied page. The error page written in English should be placed in the ${prefix}/share/errors/en-us/ directory or another appropriate location for other languages. We can also place this errors file in a custom location such as /etc/squid/local-errors/.

In the second syntax, the client will be redirected (HTTP 302) to an alternate URL specified using the ALTERNATE_URL parameter. In the last syntax, the connection with the client will be reset.

In all of the previous syntaxes, ACL_NAME represents the ACL name that must match for rendering the corresponding access denied page or resetting the TCP connection.

When the http_access rules result in denied access, Squid remembers the last ACL it evaluated in the http_access rules. If a deny_info line exists for the ACL last evaluated, then Squid will render the corresponding error page. Now, let's try to understand this in detail using examples.

Consider the following configuration:

```
acl example_com dstdomain .example.com
acl example_net dstdomain .example.net
acl png_file    urlpath_regex -i \.png$

http_access allow example_net
http_access deny example_com png_file
http_access deny all

deny_info TCP_RESET example_com
deny_info http://example.net/ png_file
```

Now, let's say a client tries to access http://www.example.com/default.png. According to the previous configuration, the first access rule with the example_net ACL doesn't match. So, we proceed to the second access rule. The URL mentioned here is matched by both the example_com and png_file ACLs. However, note that the last ACL evaluated by Squid which resulted in denied access is png_file. So, Squid will try to find a deny_info line corresponding to the png_file ACL. As a result, the HTTP client will be sent a HTTP 302 redirect, redirecting the client to http://example.net/.

Now, we are going to modify our configuration by switching the position of ACL names in the access rule, shown as follows:

```
acl example_com dstdomain .example.com
acl example_net dstdomain .example.net
acl png_file    urlpath_regex -i \.png$

http_access allow example_net
# Notice the switch
http_access deny png_file example_com
http_access deny all

deny_info TCP_RESET example_com
deny_info http://example.net/ png_file
```

If a client tries to access the same URL `http://www.example.com/default.png`, the result will be a TCP connection reset. This is because the last ACL resulting in denied access will be `example_com` and not `png_file`.

The `deny_info` directive is preferred over custom URL redirects when we need to redirect our client to alternate URLs pointing to custom error pages.

Popular URL redirectors

So far, we have learned about how URL redirector programs communicate with Squid and how we can write our own URL redirector programs. Now, let's have a look at a few popular URL redirectors. For a full list of available redirector programs, please visit `http://www.squid-cache.org/Misc/related-software.html`.

SquidGuard

SquidGuard is a combination of filter, URL rewriter, and an access control plugin for Squid. The main features of SquidGuard includes the fact that it is fast, free, flexible, and ease of installation. Below are a few use cases of SquidGuard:

- Limiting access for some users to a list of well known web servers or URLs
- Blocking access for some users based on blacklists
- Redirect blocked URLs to pages containing helpful information
- Redirect unregistered users to registration pages
- And much more...

For more details on SquidGuard, please see `http://www.squidguard.org/`.

Squirm

Squirm is a fast and configurable URL rewriter for Squid. Please check `http://squirm.foote.com.au/` for more details. A few features of Squirm are as follows:

- It is very fast and uses almost no memory
- It can read the configuration file again even when running
- It can run in bypass mode in case the configuration file contains errors
- It has an interactive mode for testing new configuration files

Ad Zapper

Ad Zapper is another popular Squid URL rewriter for removing ad banners, flash animations, pop-up windows, page counters, and other web bugs. Ad zapper maintains a list of regular expressions for well known ad networks. For more details on ad zapper, please check `http://adzapper.sourceforge.net/`.

Pop quiz

1. If a client requests a URL `http://www.example.com/users/list.php?start=10&end=20#top`, then which one of the following is the URL which will be received by a URL rewriter program?

   a. `http://www.example.com`

   b. `http://www.example.com/users/list.php`

   c. `http://www.example.com/users/list.php?start=10&end=20`

   d. `http://www.example.com/users/list.php?start=10&end=20#top`

2. How many different URL rewriter programs can be used by Squid at any time?

   a. Unlimited

   b. Depends on the RAM and CPU power of the machine

   c. Depends on the number of network interfaces available on the server

   d. 1

3. Consider the following snippet from a Squid configuration file:

   ```
   url_rewrite_program /opt/squid/libexec/rewriter

   acl rewrite_domain dstdom example.com
   url_rewrite_access allow rewrite_domain
   url_rewrite_access deny all

   url_rewrite_bypass off
   ```

   Now, consider a situation when all the URL rewriter programs are busy and a client requests a URL `http://www.example.com/index.html`. What will Squid do?

   a. Return an access denied message

   b. Wait for a rewriter program to become free

   c. Crash

   d. Will not wait for the rewriter and will process the request normally

Summary

In this chapter, we have learned about URL redirector and rewriter programs, which are very helpful in extending the basic Squid functionality. We have also learned about the `deny_info` directive which is a better fit for redirecting users to better and more understandable error pages. We also learned how Squid communicates with URL helpers.

Specifically, we covered:

+ URL redirectors and their use
+ How Squid communicates with the URL redirector programs
+ Writing our own URL redirector program
+ Configuring Squid to use our URL redirector program
+ A few popular URL redirectors that are helpful in saving bandwidth and providing better access control

Now that we have learned about most of the components of Squid, we need to learn about troubleshooting in case a component doesn't behave appropriately, and that is the topic of our next chapter.

12
Troubleshooting Squid

In the previous chapters, we have learned about installing and configuring the Squid proxy server in different modes. Then we moved on to learning about and further customizing Squid using the powerful URL redirector programs. Though we may take utmost care while configuring Squid and testing everything before deploying changes in production mode, sometimes we may face issues which can affect our clients. The issues may be a result of configuration glitches, Squid bugs, operating system limitations, or even because of the network issues. In this chapter, we'll learn about common known issues and how we can go about the troubleshooting of these issues in a strategic manner.

In this chapter, we shall learn about:

- ◆ Some common issues
- ◆ Debugging problems
- ◆ Getting help online and reporting bugs

So let's begin...

Some common issues

Most of the issues which arise are due to configuration errors and ambiguous configurations, which are known as Squid bugs or operating system issues. You can fix these issues quickly if you are aware of the issues which are commonly faced by Squid users, as these types of issues generally have standard solutions. So, let's have a look at a few common problems.

Cannot write to log files

Sometimes, while starting Squid, we may get a warning similar to the following:

```
WARNING: Cannot write log file: /opt/squid/var/logs/cache.log
/opt/squid/var/logs/cache.log: Permission denied
  messages will be sent to 'stderr'.
```

This generally happens when the user running Squid doesn't have write permissions to the directory containing log files or the log files themselves. This error can be avoided to a large extent if we use binary packages for our operating system because the permissions and ownerships will be set up properly by the packet installer during installation.

Time for action – changing the ownership of log files

This issue can be quickly fixed by changing the ownership of the log directory and files within. Squid is either run by the user `nobody` or by the user mentioned using the `cache_effective_user` directive in the Squid configuration file. So, to change the ownership of the log directory and files within, we can use the `chown` command as follows:

```
chown -R nobody:nobody /opt/squid/var/logs/
```

 Don't forget to replace username, group name, and log directory in accordance with your Squid installation.

What just happened?

We learned that Squid should have the ownership of the directory containing log files to be able to log messages properly. We also learned how to change the ownership using the `chown` command.

Could not determine hostname

Another error encountered commonly is shown as follows:

```
FATAL: Could not determine fully qualified hostname.  Please set
'visible_hostname'
Squid Cache (Version 3.1.10): Terminated abnormally.
```

This happens when Squid is not able to determine the fully-qualified hostname for the IP address it's binding to.

Please note that with Squid version 3.2 onwards, this error will be converted from FATAL to WARNING and Squid will still run using the name `localhost`.

This issue can be resolved quickly by setting an appropriate hostname using the
`visible_hostname` directive in the Squid configuration, demonstrated in the
following example:

```
visible_hostname proxy.example.com
```

The hostname provided previously should now have DNS records resolving it to the
IP address of the proxy server. In a cluster of proxies, this hostname should be unique
for every proxy server to tackle IP-forwarding issues.

Cannot create swap directories

When we try to create new swap directories using the Squid command, we may get an error
shown as follows:

```
[root@saini ~]# /opt/squid/sbin/squid -z
2010/11/10 00:42:34| Creating Swap Directories
FATAL: Failed to make swap directory /opt/squid/var/cache: (13)
Permission denied
[root@saini ~]#
```

As it is clear from the previous error message, Squid didn't have enough permission to create
the swap directories.

Time for action – fixing cache directory permissions

We can fix this issue by creating the cache directory and then transferring the ownership
to the Squid user manually.

```
mkdir /opt/squid/var/cache
chown nobody:nobody /opt/squid/var/cache
```

The previous commands will create the cache directory and will transfer the ownership
to the Squid user.

If we try to create the swap directories now, the command will succeed and will output
something like this:

```
[root@saini etc]# /opt/squid/sbin/squid -z
2010/11/10 00:44:16| Creating Swap Directories
2010/11/10 00:44:16| /opt/squid/var/cache exists
2010/11/10 00:44:16| Making directories in /opt/squid/var/cache/00
2010/11/10 00:44:16| Making directories in /opt/squid/var/cache/01
...
```

What just happened?

We learned how to create the cache directory with proper ownership, so that Squid can create the swap directories without any problems.

Failed verification of swap directories

In most cases, we'll be using Squid as a caching proxy server and we'll have disk caching enabled. A common error related to cache or swap directories is as follows:

```
2010/11/10 00:33:56| /opt/squid/var/cache: (2) No such file or
directory
FATAL:  Failed to verify one of the swap directories, Check cache.log
        for details.  Run 'squid -z' to create swap directories
        if needed, or if running Squid for the first time.
Squid Cache (Version 3.1.10): Terminated abnormally.
```

This error generally occurs when:

- We run Squid for the first time without creating swap directories
- We run Squid after updating (adding/modifying) the existing swap directories using the `cache_dir` directive.

Time for action – creating swap directories

This error can be fixed by running the following command:

```
squid -z
```

This should be run every time we add new swap directories or modify the existing `cache_dir` lines in our configuration file. If we run Squid after running the previous command, everything will be fine.

What just happened?

We learned that we should run Squid with the `-z` option whenever we make changes to the Squid cache directories, so that Squid can create swap directories properly.

Address already in use

Another commonly encountered error is `Address already in use`, `Cannot bind socket`, or `Cannot open HTTP port`, shown as follows:

```
2010/11/10 01:04:20| commBind: Cannot bind socket FD 16 to [::]:8080:
(98) Address already in use
FATAL: Cannot open HTTP Port
Squid Cache (Version 3.1.10): Terminated abnormally.
```

When we start Squid, it tries to bind itself to one or more network interfaces, on the port mentioned using the `http_port` directive in the Squid configuration file. The error mentioned previously occurs when another program is already listening on the port Squid is trying to bind to.

Time for action – finding the program listening on a specific port

To resolve this issue, we first have to find out which program is listening on the port in question. The process of finding out the program listening on a port depends the operating system we are using. The following methods are used for popular operating systems:

For Linux-based operating systems

For Linux-based operating systems, we can use the following command:

```
lsof -i :8080
```

Don't forget to replace 8080 with the appropriate port number.

For OpenBSD and NetBSD

For OpenBSD and NetBSD, we can use the `fstat` command as follows:

```
fstat | grep 8080
```

This will give us a list of connections involving port 8080.

For FreeBSD and DragonFlyBSD

The program for determining a program listening on a port for FreeBSD and DragonFlyBSD is `sockstat` and can be used as follows:

```
sockstat -4l | grep 8080
```

The previous command will show us the program listening on port 8080.

Once we have identified the program listening on port 8080, we can resolve the issues in the following two ways:

♦ If the program is important, we may need to change the Squid HTTP port using the `http_port` directive and then restart Squid.

♦ Close the program already listening on port 8080 and then start Squid. However, this may affect the clients using the services offered by the other program.

This issue can also occur if we configure the same port twice in the configuration file with an IP and/or wildcard. So, it's a good idea to double the configuration file also.

What just happened?

We learned about the usage of the `lsof`, `fstat`, and `sockstat` commands to find out the program listening on a particular port on our system. We also learned about the possible ways to make Squid work when another program is listening on the same port.

URLs with underscore results in an invalid URL

This error doesn't occur with the default Squid configuration, but may occur when we enforce Squid to check URLs against standards. In the public DNS system, an underscore is not allowed. It is only workable for locally-resolved hosts when the local resolver has been configured to allow it. There are two important directives related to this issue. Let's have a look at them.

Enforce hostname checks

The directive that enforces Squid to check every hostname against standards is `check_hostnames`. The default Squid behavior is not to restrict hostnames to standards only, but when this directive is set to `on`, Squid will enforce checks and requests to URLs with illegal hostnames, and this will result in an `Invalid URL` message. To resolve this issue, we can simply reset this directive to `off` so that Squid doesn't enforce checks.

Allow underscore

Another directive that determines whether underscores in domains names will be allowed or not is `allow_underscore`. The default Squid behavior is to allow underscores. If we don't want to allow underscores in domain names, we can set this option to `off`. To resolve the issue mentioned previously, this option should be reset to its default value, namely, `on`.

 Please note that the directive `allow_underscore` is used only when the `check_hostnames` directive is set to on.

Squid becomes slow over time

This is another common issue faced when we try to get too much out of our system. In most cases, it happens because we have set `cache_mem` to a very high value and there is not enough memory available for other processes to perform normally, and the system as a whole is running short of memory.

As we have learned in the previous chapters, `cache_mem` is the amount of memory used for caching web documents in the main memory and the total memory occupied by Squid will always be more than `cache_mem`.

We can resolve this issue in three incremental steps.

♦ We should analyze the total memory available on our system besides the memory consumed by the operating system and other essential processes. Then we should set `cache_mem` accordingly so that there will enough free memory for Squid and other processes to perform without any swapping.

♦ Secondly, we can try turning off the memory pools using the `memory_pools` directive as follows:

```
memory_pools off
```

♦ We know that Squid keeps an index of all the cached documents on disk in the main memory. So, if we have large disk caches, the index will be proportionally large and will take a significant amount of memory. If neither of the previous two techniques work, we can try reducing the size of our cache directories.

The request or reply is too large

Sometimes, clients may report that they are periodically getting the error message `"The request or reply is too large"`. This error occurs when either the reply, the request headers, or body size exceeds the maximum permitted values.

This error is related to the directives `request_header_max_size`, `request_body_max_size`, `reply_header_max_size`, and `reply_body_max_size` in the Squid configuration file. Adjusting the values of these directives will fix this issue.

Access denied on the proxy server

Sometimes a tricky situation may occur, whereby, all of our clients are able to access websites via our proxy server, but when we try to access websites on our server running Squid using our own proxy server, we may be denied access. This generally happens because while configuring Squid, we allowed all our networks using ACLs, but forgot to allow our Squid server's IP address. We can tackle this issue by extending the `localhost` ACL provided by Squid to include other IP addresses assigned to our proxy server. Please don't forget to reload or restart the Squid proxy server daemon after modifying the ACL.

Connection refused when reaching a sibling proxy server

While adding a sibling using the cache_peer directive, if we happen to enter a wrong HTTP port and a correct ICP port for the sibling, the ICP communication will work fine and our cache will believe that the configuration is correct. However, this will result in the connection being refused because of the wrong HTTP port. This may happen even if our configuration is correct and our sibling has changed their HTTP port. Double-checking the HTTP port will fix this solution.

Debugging problems

Mostly, we encounter problems that are well-known and are a result of configuration glitches or operating system limitations. So, those problems can be fixed easily by tweaking configuration files. However, sometimes we may face problems that cannot be solved directly or we may not even be able to identify them by simply looking at the log files.

By default, Squid only logs the essential information to cache.log. To inspect or debug problems, we need to increase the verbosity of the logs so that Squid can tell us more about the actions it's taking, which may help us find the source of the problem. We can extract information from Squid about its actions at our convenience by using the debug_options directive in the Squid configuration file.

Let's have a look at the format of the debug_options directive:

```
debug_options rotate=N section,verbosity [section,verbosity]...
```

The parameter rotate (rotate=N) specifies the number of cache.log files that will be maintained when Squid logs are rotated. The default value of N is 1. The rotate option helps in preventing disk space from being wasted due to excessive log messages when the verbosity level is high.

The parameter section is an integer identifying a particular component of Squid. It can have a special value, ALL, which represents all components of Squid. The verbosity parameter is also an integer representing the verbosity level for each section. Let's have a look at the meaning of different verbosity levels:

Verbosity level	Description
0	Only critical or fatal messages will be logged.
1	Warnings and important problems will be logged.
2	At verbosity level 2, the minor problems, recovery, and regular high-level actions will be logged.
3-5	Almost everything useful is covered by verbosity level 5.
6-9	Above verbosity level 5, it is extremely verbose. Individual events, signals, and so on are described in detail.

The following is the default configuration:

```
debug_options rotate=1 ALL,1
```

The preceding configuration line sets the verbosity level for all sections of Squid to 1, which means that Squid will try to log the minimum amount of information possible.

The section number can be determined by looking at the source of the file. In most source files, we can locate a commented line, as shown in the following example, which is from `access_log.cc`:

```
/*
...
 * DEBUG: section 46    Access Log
...
*/
```

The previous comment tells us that the section number for the Access Log is 46. A list of section numbers and corresponding Squid components can be found at `doc/debug-sections.txt` in Squid's source code. The following table represents some of the important section numbers for Squid version 3.1.10:

Section number	Squid components
0	Announcement Server, Client Database, Debug Routines, DNS Resolver Daemon, UFS Store Dump Tool
1	Main Loop, Startup
2	Unlink Daemon
3	Configuration File Parsing, Configuration Settings
4	Error Generation
6	Disk I/O Routines
9	File Transfer Protocol (FTP)
11	Hypertext Transfer Protocol (HTTP)
12	Internet Cache Protocol (ICP)
14	IP Cache, IP Storage, and Handling
15	Neighbor Routines
16	Cache Manager Objects
17	Request Forwarding
18	Cache Manager Statistics

Section number	Squid components
20	Storage Manager, Storage Manager Heap-based replacement, Storage Manager Logging Functions, Storage Manager MD5 Cache Keys, Storage Manager Swapfile Metadata, Storage Manager Swapfile Unpacker, Storage Manager Swapin Functions, Storage Manager Swapout Functions, Store Rebuild Routines, Swap Dir base object
23	URL Parsing, URL Scheme parsing
28	Access Control
29	Authenticator, Negotiate Authenticator, NTLM Authenticator
31	Hypertext Caching Protocol
32	Asynchronous Disk I/O
34	Dnsserver interface
35	FQDN Cache
44	Peer Selection Algorithm
46	Access Log
50	Log file handling
51	Filedescriptor Functions
55	HTTP Header
56	HTTP Message Body
57	HTTP Status-line
58	HTTP Reply (Response)
61	Redirector
64	HTTP Range Header
65	HTTP Cache Control Header
66	HTTP Header Tools
67	String
68	HTTP Content-Range Header
70	Cache Digest
71	Store Digest Manager
72	Peer Digest Routines
73	HTTP Request
74	HTTP Message
76	Internal Squid Object handling
78	DNS lookups, DNS lookups; interacts with lib/rfc1035.c

Section number	Squid components
79	Disk IO Routines, Squid-side DISKD I/O functions, Squid-side Disk I/O functions, Storage Manager COSS Interface, Storage Manager UFS Interface
84	Helper process maintenance
89	NAT / IP Interception
90	HTTP Cache Control Header, Storage Manager Client-Side Interface
92	Storage File System

Time for action – debugging HTTP requests

So, let's say that we need to debug a problem with HTTP, then we can set a higher verbosity level for section number 11, as shown in the following example:

```
debug_options ALL,1 11,5
```

We need to reconfigure or restart the Squid server after modifying the Squid configuration file. Now, if we try to browse www.example.com using our proxy server, then we'll notice an output similar to the following, in our cache.log file. Please note that we have removed the timestamp from the following log messages for a clearer view:

```
httpStart: "GET http://www.example.com/"
http.cc(86) HttpStateData: HttpStateData 0x8fc4318 created
httpSendRequest: FD 14, request 0x8f73678, this 0x8fc4318.
The AsyncCall HttpStateData::httpTimeout constructed, this=0x8daead0
[call315]
The AsyncCall HttpStateData::readReply constructed, this=0x8daf0c8
[call316]
The AsyncCall HttpStateData::SendComplete constructed, this=0x8daf120
[call317]
httpBuildRequestHeader: Host: example.com
httpBuildRequestHeader: User-Agent: Mozilla/5.0 (X11; U; Linux i686;
en-US; rv:1.9.2.3) Gecko/20100403 Fedora/3.6.3-4.fc13 Firefox/3.6.3
GTB7.1
httpBuildRequestHeader: Accept: text/html,application/
xhtml+xml,application/xml;q=0.9,*/*;q=0.8
httpBuildRequestHeader: Accept-Language: en-us,en;q=0.5
httpBuildRequestHeader: Accept-Encoding: gzip,deflate
httpBuildRequestHeader: Accept-Charset: ISO-8859-1,utf-8;q=0.7,*;q=0.7
httpBuildRequestHeader: Keep-Alive: 115
httpBuildRequestHeader: Proxy-Connection: keep-alive
```

```
httpBuildRequestHeader: If-Modified-Since: Fri, 30 Jul 2010 15:30:18
GMT
httpBuildRequestHeader: If-None-Match: "573c1-254-48c9c87349680"
comm.cc(166) will call HttpStateData::SendComplete(FD 14,
data=0x8fc4318) [call317]
entering HttpStateData::SendComplete(FD 14, data=0x8fc4318)
AsyncCall.cc(32) make: make call HttpStateData::SendComplete [call317]
...
```

As shown in the previous example, Squid will try to log as much information as possible. We can clearly see how the HTTP request is being built with appropriate HTTP headers. To debug problems with other components, we can set their verbosity level to a higher value and then inspect the cache.log file for possible problems.

What just happened?

We learned to use the debug_options directive to generate more debugging output for HTTP requests in the cache.log file. Similarly, we can debug other the components of Squid.

Now, let's learn a way to debug our access controls using the debug_options directive and cache.log.

Time for action – debugging access control

Normally, it's easy to construct ACLs using various ACL types and they will work as expected. However, as our configuration gets bigger, ACLs may get confusing and it'll be hard to point out the exact culprit ACL causing problems such as, access denied messages or allowing access to a denied object. To debug our ACLs in such a situation, we can take advantage of the debug_options directive so that we can see the step-by-step processing of ACLs by Squid. We'll learn to debug our example configuration.

Consider the following access control lines in our configuration file:

```
acl example dstdomain .example.com
acl png urlpath_regex -i \.png$

http_access deny png example
http_access allow localhost
http_access allow localnet
http_access deny all
```

If we consult the table of section numbers for the Squid components, the section number for access control is 28. So, we will add the following line to our configuration file:

```
debug_options ALL,1 28,3
```

The previous configuration line will set the verbosity level for the access control section to 3 and 1 for all other sections. Once we have added the previous line, we can reload or restart our Squid proxy server daemon.

Now, open a browser and try to access the URL `http://www.example.com/default.png`. We'll get an access-denied page. Now, if we look at our `cache.log` file, we can find a few lines similar to the following:

```
...
1.  ACLChecklist::preCheck: 0x8fa3220 checking 'http_access deny png
    example'
2.  ACLList::matches: checking png
3.  ACL::checklistMatches: checking 'png'
4.  aclRegexData::match: checking '/default.png'
5.  aclRegexData::match: looking for '\.png$'
6.  aclRegexData::match: match '\.png$' found in '/default.png'
7.  ACL::ChecklistMatches: result for 'png' is 1
8.  ACLList::matches: checking example
9.  ACL::checklistMatches: checking 'example'
10. aclMatchDomainList: checking 'www.example.com'
11. aclMatchDomainList: 'www.example.com' found
12. ACL::ChecklistMatches: result for 'example' is 1
13. aclmatchAclList: 0x8fa3220 returning true (AND list satisfied)
...
```

 Please note that timestamps have been removed from log messages for easier viewing and the messages have been numbered for explanation purpose only.

Now, let's try to understand what the different log messages listed previously mean. In the first line, Squid says that it's going to process the current request against the access rule `http_access deny png example`. In the second line, Squid picks up the first ACL used in the rule, png, for further processing. In the fourth line, Squid says that the ACL png is being checked against `/default.png`, which is the URL path in the URL we have requested.

In the sixth line, Squid logs that it has found the match for ACL png in the URL path for the current request. The seventh line declares the result for the ACL png, which is 1, meaning that the ACL was matched successfully. As a definite result for the access rule can't be determined yet, Squid will proceed with processing the rule further.

The eighth and ninth line says that the `example` ACL will be processed now. The tenth line says that Squid will be matching the ACL `example` against `www.example.com`, which is the destination domain in our request. The eleventh line says that the match is found. The thirteenth line says that it's returning true and that the AND list (AND operation on `png` and `example` ACLs) was satisfied. The current access rule `http_access deny png example` has been matched and access will be denied to this URL.

So, as we saw, we can configure Squid to log messages and then go on debugging our ACLs.

What just happened?

We just learned how to debug access controls by configuring Squid to log more information while processing individual access rules.

Have a go Hero – debugging HTTP responses

Try to debug HTTP responses from various servers using the `debug_options` directive.

Getting help online and reporting bugs

If we are really stuck with a Squid error and are not able to solve it ourselves, then we should consider posting the error or problem to the Squid users' mailing list. Information on the different mailing lists related to Squid is available at `http://www.squid-cache.org/Support/mailing-lists.html`. We should also consider subscribing to the Squid announce list using, from which we'll be able to get critical security and release announcements regularly. We can even participate in Squid development and can learn what Squid developers are up to by subscribing to the Squid developers mailing list.

Another good source of online information about Squid is the Squid wiki itself, which can be reached at `http://wiki.squid-cache.org/`. The Squid wiki contains a lot of FAQs and configuration examples for various operating systems. The Squid wiki is a community effort, and if outdated examples or configuration are found, then we can report them to Bugzilla under website bugs. Alternatively, we can get an account and help in improving the articles on wiki.

Finally, if we have really hit a bug in Squid itself, then we can file a detailed bug report at `http://bugs.squid-cache.org/`. Before filing a new bug, we must check if a similar bug exists. If a similar bug exists, we should append the bug report to the existing bug. We need to create a Bugzilla account before we can file a bug. Also, we should mention the following information while filing a bug report so that the developers can have enough information at hand while they try to get to the source of the bug:

- The version and release number of our Squid installation.
- The operating system name and version.

◆ What we were trying to do when the bug occurred?

◆ Is there a way to reproduce this bug? If yes, mention all the steps.

◆ Any trace backs or core dumps. Please check `http://wiki.squid-cache.org/SquidFaq/BugReporting` for getting trace backs or core dumps.

◆ Any other related system specific information that may help developers.

After filing a bug, we should regularly check the bug page for updates and should provide any additional information requested by the developers.

Pop quiz

1. What will be your first step when you encounter a problem with Squid?

   a. Send a personal message to a Squid developer about it

   b. Report a bug in Squid Bugzilla

   c. Check `cache.log` file for warnings or errors

   d. Restart Squid server

2. What is wrong with the following configuration line?

   ```
   debug_options 3,5 9,4 28,4 ALL,1
   ```

   a. Its the wrong syntax

   b. We can't use multiple section, verbosity level pairs

   c. `ALL` is not an integer and will result in a configuration error

   d. Although syntactically correct, this configuration line has semantic errors. The verbosity levels or all the sections will be set to 1 because `ALL, 1` is mentioned last and will overwrite the previous verbosity levels.

3. Generally, we should keep a low verbosity level in production mode. Why?

   a. Squid will not write to the access log when the verbosity level is set high.

   b. Squid will flood the `cache.log` file, resulting in unnecessary consumption of disk space when the verbosity level is high.

   c. Squid doesn't support a high verbosity level when deployed in production mode.

   d. Verbose logs can protect clients' private information.

Summary

We learned about some of the common problems faced by Squid users and how we can solve them quickly by modifying various directives in the Squid configuration file. We also learned about debugging various components of Squid via `cache.log`.

Specifically, we covered:

- Some commonly known problems and their solutions
- Debugging specific components of Squid via the `cache.log` file
- Using online resources to get help to solve issues with Squid
- Reporting bugs to Squid developers

We learned the various ways to track problems with Squid and steps to strategically debug and solve the issues. If we get stuck with a problem, we can always get in touch with fellow Squid users through the Squid users mailing list.

Pop Quiz Answers

Chapter 1, Getting Started with Squid

Question	Answer
1	c. Because all other web documents are static in nature and will not change over time.
2	b. Because the I/O option will only affect performance when caching on hard disks is enabled.
3	b. As better removal policy will utilize the available space more efficiently, whether the space is in RAM or hard disk.

Chapter 2, Configuring Squid

Question	Answer
1	d
2	c
3	a. No, because `192.0.2.21` will match against ACL `blocked_clients` and will be denied access. Squid stops looking for access rules after the first match.
4	b. The directive `cache_mem` specifies the space that can be used by Squid to cache the web documents in main memory. The actual memory occupied by Squid will be more than that specified using `cache_mem`.
5	d

Chapter 3, Running Squid

Question	Answer
1	b
2	b
3	b. While in `debug` mode, Squid produces a lot of output which may fill disks very quickly. But we can still use Squid in `debug` mode sometimes as it may be necessary to use it to debug critical problems.

Chapter 4, Getting Started with Squid's Powerful ACLs and Access Rules

Question	Answer
1	d
2	a
3	a. The second access rule will never be matched as a request can come either from `10.1.33.9` or `10.1.33.182` and all the three conditions will never be matched at the same time.
4	d. Because the last rule denies access to all replies which will not allow Squid to send any received data to clients and they will not be able to browse.

Chapter 5, Understanding Log Files and Log Formats

Question	Answer
1	b. Squid. It is the default log format.
2	b
3	a

Chapter 6, Managing Squid and Monitoring Traffic

Question	Answer
1	d
2	a
3	c

Chapter 7, Protecting your Squid with Authentication

Question	Answer
1	d. Username and password are transmitted after encoding the combination in `base64`. But they can be easily decoded back to plaintext.
2	c. Because string comparisons in most databases are case insensitive which will allow usernames john, John, jOhN, and so on provided correct password is entered. This will prevent us from detecting them as one user in case we have case-sensitive usernames which in turn will affect `max_user_ip` ACL lists.
3	c

Chapter 8, Building a Hierarchy of Squid Caches

Question	Answer
1	a. `p1.example.com`. When the default option is used with more than one peer, only the first one is considered irrespective of the other options specified.
2	c. Two possible ways: Using `cache_peer_domain` cache_peer sibling.example.com sibling 3128 0 no-query no-digest cache_peer_domain sibling.example.com !.local.example.com Using `cache_peer_access` cache_peer sibling.example.com sibling 3128 0 no-query no-digest acl local_example dstdomain .local.example.com cache_peer_access sibling.example.com deny local_example cache_peer_access sibling.example.com allow all

Chapter 9, Squid in Reverse Proxy Mode

Question	Answer
1	c
2	b

Chapter 10, Squid in Intercept Mode

Question	Answer
1	a. HTTP only.
2	c. Host
3	b

Chapter 11: Writing URL Redirectors and Rewriters

Question	Answer
1	c
2	d
3	d. Squid will process the request normally as the domain in the URL will not be matched by the ACL list `rewrite_domain`.

Chapter 12: Troubleshooting Squid

Question	Answer
1	c
2	d
3	b

Index

in intercept or transparent mode 195
loops, challenging 194
whitelisting selected websites 193

B

backend web servers
  adding, to Squid 229
backend web servers, adding
  cache peer options 229
basic_db_auth helper 176
basic_fake_auth helper 184
basic_ldap_auth helper 179
basic_pam_auth helper 180
basic_pam_auth Squid helper 180
basic_radius_auth helper 184
basic_smb_auth helper 179
basic authentication, Squid
  about 174
  database authentication 176
  database authentication, configuring 177, 178
  exploring 174-176
  fake basic authentication 184
  getpwnam authentication 182
  LDAP authentication 179
  MSNT authentication 180
  MSNT authentication, configuring 180
  MSNT multi domain authentication 181
  NCSA authentication 178
  NCSA authentication, configuring 178
  NIS authentication 179
  PAM Authentication 180
  POP3 authentication 183
  RADIUS authentication 183
  SASL authentication 182
  SMB authentication 179
Bazaar
  about 12
  URL 12
Bloom Filter
  about 216
  URL 216
broken_posts directive 70
browser, ACL types 111
browser reloads, ignoring
  ignore-cc option, used 233
  ignore-reload option, used 233

reload-into-ims, used 233
bug report
  about 284
  URL 284
Bugzilla account 284

C

cache_dir directive 52, 274
cache_dns_program directive 63
cache_effective_user directive 35, 68, 105, 272
cache_mem 276
cache_object URL scheme 102
cache_peer_access directive 210
cache_peer_access rule 116
cache_peer_domain directive 209
cache_peer directive 44, 116, 201, 278
cache_replacement_policy directive 55
cache_swap_high directive 54
cache_swap_low directive 54
cache client list 162
cache digest configuration
  about 217
  digest_bits_per_entry directive 217
  digest_rebuild_chunk_percentage directive 217
  digest_rebuild_period directive 217
  digest_rewrite_period directive 218
  digest_swapout_chunk directive 217
  digest generation directive 217
cache digests
  about 216
  enabling 217
cache directories
  adding 79
  creating 78
cache directory permissions
  fixing 273
cached objects, in hard disks
  about 49
  cache directory, adding 52
  cache directory, creating 51
  cache directory, selecting 53
  cache size, declaring 51
  object replacement limits, setting 54
  read-only cache 52
  size limits 53
  storage space, specifying 49

format codes, access log 140, 141
FQDN cache statistics 158, 159
FreeBSD
    Squid installation 30
fstat command 275

G

GDSF 54
general runtime information 156
Gentoo
    Squid installation 30
GET method 101
getpwnam() 182
getpwnam authentication 182
getpwnam authentication helper 182
GRE (Generic Routing Encapsulation) tunnel 245
Greedy dual size frequency policy. *See* GDSF
        policy

H

hard disks, for cached objects
    cache directory, adding 52
    cache directory, creating 51
    cache directory, selecting 51, 53
    cache object size limits 53
    cache size, declaring 51
    object replacement limits, setting 54
    storage space, specifying 49
    storage types 50
    sub directories, configuring 52
header_replace directive 61
helper-mux program 192
helper concurrency 192
hierarchical caching
    about 198
    benefits 199
    example 199
    forwarding loop, avoiding 200
    issues 199, 200
    issues, example scenario 200
hierarchy_stoplist directive 69, 213
Host HTTP header
    rewriting 265
hosts_file directive 64
hosts file
    setting 64

HTCP
    about 19, 114 218
    advantages, over ICP protocol 218
    reference link 218
htcp_access directive 203
htcp_clr_access directive 43
htcp_clr_access rule 115
htcp_port directive 203
HTCP access 43
HTCP CLR access 43
HTCP CLR requests 115
HTCP options, cache hierarchy
    about 203
    htcp 203
    htcp=forward-clr 203
    htcp=no-clr 203
    htcp=no-purge-clr 203
    htcp=oldsquid 203
    htcp=only-clr 203
http_access directive 38
http_port directive 233, 275
HTTP_PORT parameter 202
http_reply_access directive 42, 110
http_reply_acess rules 114
HTTP access control
    about 40
    with ACLs 41
HTTP authentication, Squid 174
httpd_accel_surrogate_id 231
httpd_accel_surrogate_remote 231
HTTP Digest authentication
    about 184
    auth_param parameters 184
    check_nonce_count parameter 185
    configuring 185
    eDirectory authentication 187
    file authentication 186
    LDAP authentication 186
    nonce_garbage_interval parameter 185
    nonce_max_count parameter 185
    nonce_max_duration parameter 185
    nonce_strictness parameter 185
    parameters 185
    post_workaround parameter 185
HTTP headers
    about 61
    contents, replacing 62

M

MAC (Media Access Control address) 96
mac_acl, ACL types 96
mailing lists
  URL 284
max_user_ip, ACL types 109
maxconn, ACL types 108
maximum_object_size directive 53
memory_cache_mode directive 49
memory_pools directive 277
memory_replacement_policy directive 55
memory cache mode
  about 49
  always 49
  disk 49
  network 49
memory utilization
  about 163
Microsoft NTLM authentication
  about 187
  fake NTLM authentication 188
  Samba's NTLM authentication 188
minimum_object_size directive 53
miss_access directive 43
miss_access rule 115
Miss access 43
MSNT authentication
  about 180
  configuring 180, 181
MSNT multi domain authentication 181
multiple authentication schemes
  implementing 190
myip, ACL types 95
myportname, ACL types 100

N

NCSA authentication
  about 178
  configuring 178
negative_dns_ttl directive 65
negative_ttl directive 61
negotiate_kerberos_auth authentication helper
    190
Negotiate authentication
  about 189
  configuring 189

neighbor proxy servers
  requesting 116
NetBSD
  Squid installation 30
Network Address Translation (NAT) 247
network devices
  configuring, for diverting HTTP requests 245
never_direct access list rule 117
never_direct directive 69, 214
new syntax, --enable-auth configuration option
    21
NIS authentication 179
non-concurrent helpers
  making concurrent 192, 193
nonce_garbage_interval parameter 185
nonce_max_count parameter 185
nonce_max_duration parameter 185
nonce_strictness parameter 185
none module, access log 139
nonhierarchical_direct directive 215
NTLM (NT LAN Manager)
  about 187
  reference link 187
ntlm_auth program 188
ntlm_fake_auth authentication helper 188
NTLM authentication. *See* Microsoft NTLM
    authentication

O

old syntax, --enable-auth configuration option
    21
OpenBSD 247
  Squid installation 30
OpenSSL
  about 226
  URL 226
operating system
  configuring, for diverting HTTP requests 246
  IP forwarding, enabling 246
  packets, redirecting to Squid 247
options, HTTPS options 227
our_network ACL 97
output
  debugging, in console 80, 81
  debugging, in terminal 81, 82

Thank you for buying
Squid Proxy Server 3.1 Beginner's Guide

About Packt Publishing

Packt, pronounced 'packed', published its first book "*Mastering phpMyAdmin for Effective MySQL Management*" in April 2004 and subsequently continued to specialize in publishing highly focused books on specific technologies and solutions.

Our books and publications share the experiences of your fellow IT professionals in adapting and customizing today's systems, applications, and frameworks. Our solution based books give you the knowledge and power to customize the software and technologies you're using to get the job done. Packt books are more specific and less general than the IT books you have seen in the past. Our unique business model allows us to bring you more focused information, giving you more of what you need to know, and less of what you don't.

Packt is a modern, yet unique publishing company, which focuses on producing quality, cutting-edge books for communities of developers, administrators, and newbies alike. For more information, please visit our website: www.packtpub.com.

About Packt Open Source

In 2010, Packt launched two new brands, Packt Open Source and Packt Enterprise, in order to continue its focus on specialization. This book is part of the Packt Open Source brand, home to books published on software built around Open Source licences, and offering information to anybody from advanced developers to budding web designers. The Open Source brand also runs Packt's Open Source Royalty Scheme, by which Packt gives a royalty to each Open Source project about whose software a book is sold.

Writing for Packt

We welcome all inquiries from people who are interested in authoring. Book proposals should be sent to author@packtpub.com. If your book idea is still at an early stage and you would like to discuss it first before writing a formal book proposal, contact us; one of our commissioning editors will get in touch with you.

We're not just looking for published authors; if you have strong technical skills but no writing experience, our experienced editors can help you develop a writing career, or simply get some additional reward for your expertise.

Nginx HTTP Server

ISBN: 978-1-849510-86-8   Paperback: 348 pages

Adopt Nginx for your web applications to make the most of your infrastructure and serve pages faster than ever

1. Get started with Nginx to serve websites faster and safer

2. Learn to configure your servers and virtual hosts efficiently

3. Set up Nginx to work with PHP and other applications via FastCGI

4. Explore possible interactions between Nginx and Apache to get the best of both worlds

OpenVPN: Building and Integrating Virtual Private Networks

ISBN: 978-1-904811-85-5   Paperback: 272 pages

Learn how to build secure VPNs using this powerful Open Source application

1. Learn how to install, configure, and create tunnels with OpenVPN on Linux, Windows, and MacOSX

2. Use OpenVPN with DHCP, routers, firewall, and HTTP proxy servers

3. Advanced management of security certificates

Please check **www.PacktPub.com** for information on our titles

Cacti 0.8 Network Monitoring

ISBN: 978-1-847195-96-8   Paperback: 132 pages

Monitor your network with ease!

1. Install and setup Cacti to monitor your network and assign permissions to this setup in no time at all

2. Create, edit, test, and host a graph template to customize your output graph

3. Create new data input methods, SNMP, and Script XML data query

4. Full of screenshots and step-by-step instructions to monitor your network with Cacti

Tcl 8.5 Network Programming

ISBN: 978-1-849510-96-7   Paperback: 588 pages

Build network-aware applications using Tcl, a powerful dynamic programming language

1. Develop network-aware applications with Tcl

2. Implement the most important network protocols in Tcl

3. Packed with hands-on-examples, case studies, and clear explanations for better understanding

Please check **www.PacktPub.com** for information on our titles

www.ingramcontent.com/pod-product-compliance
Lightning Source LLC
Chambersburg PA
CBHW080352060326
40689CB00019B/3978